Weeds and the Carolingians

Why did weeds matter in the Carolingian empire? What was their special significance for writers in eighth- and ninth-century Europe and how was this connected with the growth of real weeds? In early medieval Europe, unwanted plants that persistently appeared among crops created extra work, reduced productivity, and challenged theologians who believed God had made all vegetation good. For the first time, in this book weeds emerge as protagonists in early medieval European history, driving human farming strategies and coloring people's imagination. Early medieval Europeans' effort to create agroecosystems that satisfied their needs and cosmologies that confirmed Christian accounts of vegetable creation both had to come to terms with unruly plants. Using diverse kinds of texts, fresh archaeobotanical data, and even mosaics, this interdisciplinary study reveals how early medieval Europeans interacted with their environments.

Paolo Squatriti is Professor of History at the University of Michigan. His previous publications include *Water and Society in Early Medieval Italy* (Cambridge, 1998) and *Landscape and Change in Early Medieval Italy* (Cambridge, 2013).

T0370735

Weeds and the Carolingians

Empire, Culture, and Nature in Frankish Europe, AD *750–900*

Paolo Squatriti

University of Michigan, Ann Arbor

CAMBRIDGE
UNIVERSITY PRESS

CAMBRIDGE
UNIVERSITY PRESS

Shaftesbury Road, Cambridge CB2 8EA, United Kingdom

One Liberty Plaza, 20th Floor, New York, NY 10006, USA

477 Williamstown Road, Port Melbourne, VIC 3207, Australia

314–321, 3rd Floor, Plot 3, Splendor Forum, Jasola District Centre, New Delhi – 110025, India

103 Penang Road, #05–06/07, Visioncrest Commercial, Singapore 238467

Cambridge University Press is part of Cambridge University Press & Assessment, a department of the University of Cambridge.

We share the University's mission to contribute to society through the pursuit of education, learning and research at the highest international levels of excellence.

www.cambridge.org
Information on this title: www.cambridge.org/9781009069342

DOI: 10.1017/9781009072328

First published 2022
First paperback edition 2024

A catalogue record for this publication is available from the British Library

ISBN   978-1-316-51286-9   Hardback
ISBN   978-1-009-06934-2   Paperback

Esse autem omnia quae fecit deus bona valde: mala vero non esse naturalia.

Augustine, *De Genesi ad Litteram Liber Imperfectus* 1, ed. J. Zycha (Vienna, 1893), 460.

Contents

Figures

Preface

It took far longer than expected to write this book: weeds turned out to be a tangled subject. Consequently, my attempts to impose some order on it came to rely on the help of many friends and colleagues, on attentive audiences at academic presentations, as well as on the support of several institutions. My research was made possible by an American Council of Learned Societies fellowship, and a John Simon Guggenheim Memorial Foundation fellowship: I am deeply appreciative of both. I also owe a great deal to my employer, the University of Michigan, which allowed me time off to research the history of weeds in the first millennium AD, and to the Office of the Vice President for Research for supporting the publication of color images. Cathy Pense Rayos and Birgit Bucher helped me way beyond the call of duty in securing images, too. Thanks are due to groups of listeners at the University of Illinois, at Princeton University, at the University of Colorado, at Cal Tech, and at Yale University, who both egged me on and pointed out weaknesses in earlier versions of my weed studies.

For their willingness to read half-germinated drafts of chapters, for their saintly patience, and for suggesting numerous improvements, I must single out Alison Cornish, Deborah Deliyannis, Rich Hoffmann, Megan Holmes, Peggy McCracken, Laura Motta, Ellen Muehlberger, Tom Noble, and Marijke van der Veen. Vincenzo Binetti read a version of one chapter and encouraged me to iron out some of its wrinkles. My Michigan History colleagues Sue Juster, Val Kivelson, and Helmut Puff deserve a separate thank you for gamely including my writings in our reading circle, and for their helpful critiques. Thanks also to Noah Blan and David Patterson for teaching me much about Carolingian history. Cambridge University Press's three anonymous referees plowed through (and harrowed) the book with both acuity and kindness, proposing several ways to make it better. I am also indebted to Liz Friend Smith for overcoming her initial skepticism and loyally supporting the project as it evolved over several years. Finally, Hans Hummer was exceptionally generous with his time and wisdom, and swiftly read the entire manuscript at a critical juncture, producing a rich harvest of observations on how to turn it into a more coherent text.

I dedicate this book to someone who had nothing to do directly with its production, beyond listening occasionally to my ruminations on weeds. Yet long ago Jack Ullman showed me the great interest in unexpected histories, and the great beauty of historical landscapes. He also introduced me to early medieval Europe's past. More than forty years on, a book that examines some of the complexities of first-millennium agroecosystems is also a tribute to his infectious passion for comminglings of environment and history.

Abbreviations

CISAM   Centro italiano di studi sull'alto medioevo
MGH   Monumenta Germaniae Historica
PL   J. Migne, ed., *Patrologiae Cursus Completus. Series Latina*

Introduction

After contemplating the past few seasons of devastation in his realm, in 864 the west Frankish king Charles the Bald issued a capitulary at Pîtres. This piece of legislation is remarkable for its repentant tone. In it Charles recognized failings of both the king and the community over which he ruled as the root cause of the recent troubles. Curiously, he expressed the failings in botanical terms. While he ordered several military and infrastructural innovations to counter the Vikings, Charles also noted that success depended on the prior eradication of "the thorns of vices, the stinging nettles of sins, and the hemlock of vanities." Such choice of metaphors was by then customary in secular and ecclesiastical official documents. It reveals an ongoing engagement with undesirable plants and with their proper management in literate Carolingian culture.[1]

This study surveys both the cultural theme of weeds in eighth- and ninth-century texts, and the growth of real weeds in the territories ruled by the Franks, in order to illuminate these plants' surprisingly large role in the "Carolingian project."[2] It shows that weeds stimulated thought and action more than most other components of creation. Weeds mattered so much to Carolingian writers for several reasons, beginning with the fact that it was so hard to delimit them. As simultaneously natural *and* cultural phenomena, they fit awkwardly into accepted understandings of the universe, and of that corner of it called the Carolingian empire. Weeds entwined human cultural norms and expectations so tightly with vegetable biological patterns that they challenged orderly taxonomies of the natural world and the hierarchies that Genesis had laid out for nature.

---

[1] "Capitula Pistensis" 1, ed. A. Boretius and V. Krause, *MGH Legum Sectio II* 2.2 (Hanover, 1893), 304: "spinas vitiorum et urticas peccatorum et cicutas vanitatis." Voluntary public professions of contrition enhanced ninth-century rulers' authority: M. de Jong, *The Penitential State* (Cambridge, 2009), 260–70. Other legal weed metaphors: "Concilium Cabillonense" 2, ed. A Werminghoff, *MGH Legum sectio III* 2.1 (Hanover, 1906), 274; "Concilium Aquisgranense" 98, in ibid., 377.
[2] M. Costambeys et al., *The Carolingian World* (Cambridge, 2011), 430.

Carolingian grappling with and adaptation to weeds thus reflected these bad plants' fundamental ambiguity, or slipperiness.

Intellectually uncontrollable, weeds were also physically irrepressible, and so occupied a larger terrain than other organisms in God's creation. Unlike other negative environmental phenomena, such as ravening wolves, or landslides, or hailstorms, weeds were omnipresent. Wherever people went, they found weeds. Their "in-your-faceness" rendered them different from other God-ordained disasters. This insolence, and humans' grudging intimacy with them, meant weeds had far greater economic impact than sporadic natural hazards. Particularly in a Christian culture aware that weeds must be an instrument of divine communication, and probably chastisement, they attracted attention.[3]

Quietly persistent, ubiquitous, and demanding untold back-breaking effort to repress, weeds' liminal status between spontaneous creature and product of human activities like sin and agriculture lent them importance in the Carolingian imaginary. As a new imperial order arose in the eighth and ninth centuries, weeds' real sprouting in Frankish fields and gardens made them a matter of state, and goes some way toward explaining why Charles at Pîtres could think of no better expression of his anxieties about the disarray into which the state had fallen than to evoke weeds and weeding. Realms like his existed to create harmony, to ensure that human communities observed their roles and performed their duties in the world, and to enforce divine mandates so heavenly and earthly spheres were congruent. The endurance of plants no one liked, that hampered the attainment of legitimate human goals, and that even poisoned people, undermined rulers like Charles, who expected to maintain the kind of order that checked chaos and won divine favor, enhancing everyone's chances of salvation.

For about a century and a half (750–900), rulers, ecclesiastics, and exegetes in what this book considers Carolingian Europe doggedly tackled the problems raised by weeds. They did so with a characteristic zeal that justifies treating as a unit the texts and other cultural products generated in disparate parts of the empire Charlemagne assembled. The Carolingian state did not of course enforce cultural homogeneity from the North Sea to the Ionian one. On the contrary, despite considerable coherence in weed assessment in the period when members of the Carolingian dynasty held sway in much of what would later become France, Germany, Italy, and northern Iberia, multiple vegetable hierarchies prevailed throughout the empire. But whether they sat in Aachen, or

---

[3] On early medieval constructions of natural shocks, hazards, and disasters, see T. Wozniak, *Naturereignisse im frühen Mittelalter* (Berlin, 2020).

Innsbruck, or Rome, literate people participated in a "discourse community" that the Carolingian hegemony supported.[4] This community shared optimistic assumptions about the world and human activity in it that deeply tinged Carolingian-era texts and artifacts, including those related to botanical affairs.

This specifically Carolingian dedication to figuring out what weeds were doing on earth makes possible a culturally inflected environmental history of marginal plants in a specific place and time. For the exceptional literacy of the Carolingian elite, and the good survival rate of their writings, offers access to the European vegetable imaginary in ways that are unparalleled for the rest of the first millennium AD. It also affords glimpses into what weeds were up to on the ground, not just on parchment pages, since, however idealized, the literary weeds were linked to the real ones. And, as actual weeds are now knowable through archaeobotany, this study combines archaeological and textual insights to uncover the fulness of weed discourse in Carolingian Europe, while probing the relation of that discourse (what we might call Carolingian weedology) to agricultural practices in a period when these underwent significant change. Whether or not cultivators confronted the same challenges in a territory as vast as Carolingian Europe's, from the heartlands of Neustria and Austrasia to the fringes of Provence and Tuscany they all managed insidious undesirable plants. In this sense, weeding worries united the Carolingian polity.

But since Carolingian written sources are so unusually abundant and various (of course by early medieval standards), it is the written word that receives most attention in what follows. For this reason, the Carolingian vocabulary pertaining to weeds is of special importance. It requires some preliminary consideration.

Early Medieval Words for Weeds

To deal effectively with weeds people need tools. Yet more than the weed-hooks, sickles, hoes, diggers, forks, clippers, tweezers, and, nowadays, sprayers, the most important tools for coping with weeds have always been lexical. For from the very moment when they begin to define weeds, humans require a vocabulary to confine and control them. Hence it is thought-provoking to realize that, unlike modern English – beneficiary as we shall see of Old English inventiveness – many other modern European

---

[4] R. Kramer, *Rethinking Authority in the Carolingian Empire* (Amsterdam, 2019) shows how in eighth- to ninth-century Francia, under loose court supervision, a multivocal culture of negotiation was based on a common "mindset" that aspired to improve the world.

languages lack a special term for undesirable plants. This poverty derives from Latin, which also had no word for weed, a condition that proud German agronomists of the nineteenth century ascribed to the ancient Mediterranean tongues being more archaic and rustic than the younger, more modern, and vigorous Germanic ones.[5]

Most of the vocabulary we know about that early medieval Europeans used to identify and discuss bad plants derives from texts, and hence is Latin, though a few inflections of vernacular Germanic and Romance languages entered into the toolkit of those whose ruminations on weeds survive. But for modern people the interest of the words Carolingian people used for weeds lies less in the linguistic pedigrees, the etymologies, they carry, than in the surprising differences between (at least Anglophone) modern amd early medieval ways of talking about weeds. The lack of an abstract word encompassing all bad plants signals something of the elasticity with which the Carolingians approached the categorization of vegetation. Perhaps it reveals their sense that all plants were equally weedy and equally domestic; to them, it just depended on the situation.

In Latin, "herba" sufficed for all small forms of vegetation, whether economically useful or toxic (it contrasted with shrubs and trees, whose size and tougher external structure set them apart).[6] "Herba" could be inflected in various ways to signal human evaluations, becoming "noxious herb" or "useless herb" when people perceived a plant as uncooperative or contrary to their interests; though his beloved *Aeneid* (2.471) did refer to "bad grasses," Augustine was the first Latin writer (that I am aware of) to propose the more general grouping "bad herbs," a formulation with a rosy future in the Romance languages but not overly popular in early medieval texts, particularly those of Carolingian date.[7] Likewise, Latin allowed "healthful herbs," "good herbs," and even "celestial herbs" when the plants in question seemed to advance human well-being.[8] Notker "the Stammerer", writing toward the end of the Carolingian epoch, described the extraction of "nettles and noxious plants" from a garden setting, and

---

[5] J. Ratzenburg, *Die Standortsgewächse und Unkräuter Deutschlands* (Berlin, 1859), xxx. See also N. Clayton, "Weeds, People and Contested Places," *Environment and History* 9 (2003), 302–6.

[6] J. André, *Lexique des termes de botanique en Latin* (Paris, 1950), 160; J. Trumper and M. Vigolo, "Il perché della 'malerbologia'," in *Malerbologia*, ed. P. Catizone and G. Zanin (Bologna, 2001), 11–12.

[7] Augustine, *Sermons pour la Pâque*, ed. S. Poque (Paris, 2003), 288: "herba mala." The Old High German glossaries did contemplate "herba bona," but it was a specific plant (fennel): "Das Pflanzenreich," in *Die althochdeutsche Glossen* 3, ed. E. Steinmeyer and E. Sievers (Berlin, 1895), 558. See also Trumper and Vigolo, "Il perché," 13 on the toxicity of Virgil's "mala gramina."

[8] E.g. Sedulius Scottus, "Carmina" 14, ed. L. Traube, *MGH Poetae* 3 (Berlin, 1886), 161.

contrasted these "useless" plants to the "necessary" ones that would "grow more freely" once the garden was properly weeded with a special forked tool.[9] But, however many qualifiers people added to them, plants' essential neutrality remained fixed. There were few and situational differences among them, and in consequence modern speakers of French, Italian, Spanish, and even German, do not use specialized vocabulary to distinguish plants they don't like, but inflect the neutral word for plant to signal their displeasure. Hence *mauvaise herbe, erbaccia, mala hierba, Unkraut*, and so on, terms in circulation since the high and late Middle Ages.[10]

In Carolingian literate culture, "herb" was a flexible term. Isidore of Seville, the erudite bishop who supplied early medieval Europe, and also Carolingian scholars like Hrabanus Maurus, with its most widely consulted encyclopedia, had left economic and moral evaluations open when he offered an etymology of the Latin "herba" that connected it to the word for field ("arvum") by means of plants' rootedness in the earth.[11] Closely following his lead, Carolingian lexicographers proclaimed "the name of herbs is thought to be inflected from the word for land, because herbs are fixed to the soil by their roots."[12] By implication, good and bad plants were all basically "herbs" waiting patiently for a human opinion.

Virgil had muddled things a little for early medieval Latin readers when he used "herba" without qualifiers to mean weeds in his *Georgics* (1.69). It was an idiosyncrasy few other Roman authorities adopted. Thus, Pliny the Elder generally explained the nature of those "herbs" he treated in his massive *Natural History*, though he did very occasionally use an unqualified "herbis" to mean weeds.[13] Similarly, the fourth-century agronomical writer Palladius, whose manuals demonstrably circulated in Carolingian libraries, could deploy plain "herbs" as weeds, and call weedy places "herbosis locis," but tended to prefer "noxious herbs" when speaking of weeds.[14] But as the

---

[9] Notker, *Gesta Karoli Magni* 2.12, ed. H. Haefele, *MGH Scriptores Rerum Germanicarum* n.s. 12 (Berlin, 1959), 73, with "urticas et noxia" and "inutilia recrementa" contrasted to "usui proficua" and "holera necessaria."

[10] Low German does use "wêd": *Oxford English Dictionary* 20 (Oxford, 1989), 76. See also Trumper and Vigolo, "Il perché," 13–16.

[11] Isidore of Seville, *Etymologiae* 17.6.1.

[12] *Liber Glossarum Digital*, ed. A. Grondeux and F. Cinato (Paris, 2016) (http://liber-glossarum.huma-num.fr): "herbarum nomen ab arvis inflexum creditur, eo quod terris fixis radicibus adherent"; Hrabanus Maurus, *De Universo* 19.5, ed. J. Migne, *PL* 111 (Paris, 1864), 508.

[13] Pliny, *Naturalis Historia* 18.16 (44), ed. C. Mayhoff (Stuttgart, 1967), 182–3 uses "internascentes herbas," "reliquae herbae," "ceteris herbis," and once just "herbis," to mean weeds (but in a passage about weeding lucerne fields that justifies this usage).

[14] Palladius, *Opus Agriculturae* 2.9 considers "herbosis locis" weedy and "herbas" weeds, though in 2.10 he qualifies "noxious herbs."

Georgics were much consulted, and Rome's pre-eminent poet came to be seen as a supreme linguistic and botanical authority in the course of the first millennium, Virgil influenced some with his blithe and unspecified "plants" to signify weeds.

Among them was Walafrid Strabo when he composed what is probably the Carolingian period's most celebrated botanical text, the poem *Hortulus*.[15] Strabo used the term "herbs" mostly in the technical sense of aromatic and medicinal plants (for instance of the rose, "winner of all herbs in strength and perfume"), yet was not averse to using the word without qualifiers for weeds awakened early by warm breezes after winter left his garden.[16] Still, however charming Carolingian readers found Strabo's horticultural poem and its Virgilian echoes, on the whole post-classical Latin eschewed unqualified herbology, and most Carolingian writers did not follow the Mantuan poet in this regard. They added qualifiers when they referred to bad plants.

Carolingian ambivalence toward "herbs," and the Frankish recognition that plants could lean in several epistemological directions, did not translate precisely in all early medieval cultures. The *Oxford English Dictionary* suggests that the first occurrence of the Old English "weod," the ancestor of modern English weed, appears in the Alfredian translation of Boethius' *Consolation of Philosophy*, a work people at the court of Wessex at the turn of the tenth century found relevant because it advocated a certain indifference to the vicissitudes of this world.[17] In *The Consolation*'s third book, Philosophy launches her first song with an account of the plants that get in the way of anyone who wants to grow grains: they are "frutex," "rubus," and "filix."[18] As most shrubs, brambles, and ferns do not grow much in heavily manipulated soils (arable or garden), because they are perennials, and also because they tend not to enjoy the full sun conditions of open areas, the Anglo-Saxon translator, who retained these species, also intelligently conveyed Boethius' sense with the addition of the general and abstract term "weeds" and an allusion to their infestation of grain fields.[19] The anonymous English writer was not the only early medieval reader of

[15] J. Gaulin, "Tradition et pratiques de la littérature agronomique pendant le haut Moyen Âge," *Settimane del CISAM* 37 (Spoleto, 1990), 109–16, 128–9.

[16] Walafrid Strabo, "Carmina" 4, ed. E. Dümmler, *MGH Poetae* 2 (Berlin, 1884), l. 27, p. 336 (weeds' awakening), l. 305, p. 346 (pennyroyal is "hac herba"), l. 400, p. 348 (rose, considered one of the herbs).

[17] *The Old English Boethius*, Meter 12, ed. S. Irvine and M. Godden (Cambridge, MA, 2012), 132 uses "wiod." The etymology of "weod" is unknown: F. Holthausen, *Altenglisches etymologisches Worterbuch* (Heidelberg, 1963), 389.

[18] Boethius, *Philosophiae Consolationis* 3.1, ed. L. Bieler (Turnhout, 1957), 37. See André, *Lexique*, 138, 142, 275 on these plants.

[19] Manipulated soils and annual weeds: E. Salisbury, *Weeds and Aliens* (London, 1961), 313; R. Zimdahl, *Fundamentals of Weed Science* (Amsterdam, 2013), 264–7.

the *Consolation of Philosophy* to find Boethius' botany confusing: a Carolingian-era commentator on Boethius' work, likely Eriugena, also tried to clarify the text with the helpful addition of "other kinds of harmful herbs" after the botanically and agronomically improbable list of shrubs, brambles, and ferns.[20]

The Anglo-Saxon translator obviously did not invent the weed word, nor the abstract category it represents, the opposite of "wyrt," probably the Old English word that comes closest to the Latin word signifying plant, "herba."[21] For "weodhoc," a weeding tool, appears in a glossary of AD 725, and implies a previous history of familiarity with the idea, and the category of plants, as well as with long-handled hooks designed to ease the removal of unwanted plants from the soil.[22] Moreover, around the same time as the glossary was assembled, when the Venerable Bede was composing *De Temporibus Ratione* to refute Irish methods of calculating the exact Sunday for celebrating Easter, he used "weod" too.[23] He further alluded to the word's antiquity by telling his readers that "the ancient English people" applied the word to the month of August (as discussed in Chapter 3). It appears that early on in their history, speakers of English developed a concept of immutable, almost genetic weediness and a word to express it, and both entered their texts during the Dark Ages.[24]

Since Britain is observably no weedier than the next place, it is unclear why the Anglo-Saxons embraced the notion of a general category of plants that were inherently bad. Lawrence King, a leading weed scientist who bravely delved into the matter, suggested that a semantic slippage had given rise to the word and concept: since woad (*Isatis tinctoria*) grew rampant across English landscapes, early medieval people had come to associate that plant, called "wad" but pronounced rather like "weod," with obnoxious vegetation, whence the term came to cover all plants the English disliked.[25] But aside from the fact that the earliest record of the old word for woad in English is five centuries later than that for weed, King's ingenious explanation for the odd emergence of "weed" in eighth-century texts is purely etymological and does not make sense of the

---

[20] *Saeculi Noni Auctoris in Boetii Consolationem Philosophiae Commentarius*, ed. E. Taite Silk (Rome, 1935), 116: "alia quaeque nociva [herba]."

[21] J. Roberts et al., *A Thesaurus of Old English* 2 (London, 2005), 1547. See also Trumper and Vigolo, "Il perché," 15.

[22] *Oxford English Dictionary* 20, 79.

[23] Bede, *De Temporibus Ratione*, ed. C. Jones (Turnhout, 1977), 331–2.

[24] Old Irish, another language whose interaction with Latin generated lexico-botanical frictions, did not have an equivalent term, though vernacular Irish laws worried about infesting plants and clearing fields of them: F. Kelly, *Early Irish Farming* (Dublin, 2000), 233–5, 396, 452.

[25] L. King, *Weeds of the World* (New York, 1966), 3–6. King recognized the limitations of the woad etymology.

Anglo-Saxon word's intellectual history. For woad grows vigorously in
many other parts of northwestern Europe where there is no evidence of
a word for or general idea of weed; and in any case, as King himself
recognized, woad requires two seasons to reach maturity and reproduce
itself, so is highly dependent on human care and very seldom becomes an
infesting nuisance.[26] Why the English, as opposed to the Burgundians or
the Visigoths or the Vandals, should develop and deploy the semantic
tools for sorting vegetation encapsulated in the word "weed" does not, in
sum, seem to be related to the presence of *Isatis tinctoria*, a plant premodern Europeans had long relied on and cultivated to dye cloth and skin
blue.

Rather, the Old English word "weed" may reflect a pre-Christian
botanical sensitivity, a notion of plant life detached from scriptural esti-
mations of right and wrong. Since late antiquity, when the Church
Fathers had popularized "bad herbs," Christians had found it expedient,
even necessary, to moralize plants and divide them into good and bad
kinds. When a Carolingian author like Walafrid Strabo wrote of "bad
herbs," he followed earlier Christian authorities who had invented the
category, even while mostly clinging to the less sweeping, adjectival constructions popularized in classical Latin.[27] The Anglo-Saxon lexicon,
with its ample but morally non-committal category of plants called
weeds, deviated significantly from the Latin one that dominated textual
production during the early Middle Ages. Perhaps if more vernaculars
had left written traces of themselves before the first millennium ran out,
Old English would look less anomalous in its approach to systematizing
the vegetable universe, and Carolingian writers, most of them familiar
with a Germanic language, might have dipped into a lexicon less laden
with Christianized botanical evaluation.[28]

But as it stands, the linguistic evidence suggests that the vast majority of
early medieval Europeans thought plants were inherently equal, that is, all
were "herbs"; it was up to people to add adjectives according to their
estimation of them. As explained more fully in Chapter 3, this more
situational approach to plants' qualities reflects a Christian understanding of the universe, in which God made "green herb such as may seed" on
the third day of His creation effort, as spelled out in Genesis 1.11–12, and
when He also determined that this herb was good.[29] This induced

---

[26] The modern European languages all use a similar word for woad (guède, Waid, wede,
guado, etc.), but few adopted "weed": see Clayton, "Weeds," 304. Woad as dicyclic:
King, *Weeds*, 5.
[27] Strabo, "Glossa Ordinaria," ed. J. Migne, *PL* 114 (Paris, 1879), 353.
[28] Clayton, "Weeds," 308; Trumper and Vigolo, "Il perché," 13–14.
[29] The Vulgate divides vegetation into "herbam virentem" and "lignum pomiferum."

attentive early medieval readers of Genesis to hesitate before identifying some slice of the herbal world as inherently bad. It always depended. Earthly vegetation was ambiguous, and the vocabulary early medieval Christians applied to it faithfully mirrored this botanical ambiguity. Some herbs might behave like weeds in some contexts, but to adopt a blanket label for the designated bad species went too far. Early medieval Christian observers approached the vegetable world flexibly, and knew that what seemed a noxious herb now might at another time look altogether different. In the Dark Ages, at least away from the British Isles, total weeds did not exist, so no word for them was needed.

A solitary exception to this early medieval continental indifference to more abstract concepts of weediness is the monk of St. Gall and biographer of Charlemagne Notker (+912), whom we encountered earlier applying qualifiers to the general word "herbs." In the just-so story he wrote in the 880s about Charlemagne consulting his exiled eldest son, Pippin (a story suspiciously reminiscent of Livy's account of Tarquin the Proud's suggestion for dealing with dissent at Gabii, duly modified by monastic memory), Notker described the weeds being removed from the monastic garden at Prüm as useless refuse ("inutilia recrementa").[30] Notker's generalization reveals that on occasion Carolingian writers did feel the need for a broad and capacious term covering the idea of unwanted "trash" plants. But Notker's usage of the term is unusual in early medieval Latin. On the very rare occasions when the word "refuse" appears in first-millennium literature it is applied to the non-comestible parts of grain, the chaff from grain processing before its consumption.[31] For the rest, postclassical writers in Latin, including Notker, preferred to label small plants good or bad according to the particular relationship people developed with each one. They did not lump them together as vile weeds.

For the Franks, whose literacy was Latin and orthodox Christianity ancient, small plants were all herbs. In their laws, the very same word, "herba," covered both the pasture that a mounted warrior was entitled to on his way to war and the toxic plants whose potency the wicked used in order to kill other people or steal their fertility.[32] Certainly Carolingian

---

[30] See note 9 above. Livy, *Ab Urbe Condita* 1.54; M. Innes, "Memory, Orality and Literacy in Early Medieval Society," *Past and Present* 158 (1998), 17–18.

[31] Pliny, *Naturalis Historia* 18.16 (41), 181; Prudentius, "Apotheosis," Praef. 54, in Prudentius, *Aurelii Prudentii Clementis Carmina*, ed. M. Cunningham (Turnhout, 1966), 76.

[32] Pasture herbs and toxic herbs: *Lex Salica* 9, 25.1, 25.3, ed. K. Eckhardt, *MGH Leges Nationum Germanicarum* 4.2 (Hanover, 1969), 66 ("Additamenta ad Capitularia Regum Franciae Orientalis" 50, ed. A. Boretius and V. Krause, *MGH Capitularia Regum Francorum* 2(Hanover, 1897), 241, proscribed similar homicidal "herbs" in AD 895).

literati knew that some vegetation was undesirable: following Bede, they compared the doubts of the Apostles before the resurrected Jesus to "bad herbs" that grew up from below ground without having been seeded from above. Carolingian authors also discussed "noxious herbs" that could poison people when mixed up with more beneficent plants. But they remained anchored to the idea that plants were not in and of themselves harmful or helpful to humans, and everything hinged on what purposes people put them to and on the relationships humans and vegetation established. Carolingian Latin vocabulary therefore perpetuated Roman understandings of the vegetable kingdom and accepted the Christian view of a fundamentally beneficent creation within which botanical misfits were such primarily in the eye of the (sinful) beholder. This confirms the Carolingians needed no special word for weeds.[33]

Instead they deployed a vast number of names for the *individual* plants they disliked. No doubt because for them no blanket term could satisfactorily capture the infinite variety of plants that were a nuisance, or the particular situations in which this became true, Carolingian writers preferred to call each type of weed by its own name. Individualizing them made clearer just how each plant was bad. Thus, a literature that is utterly silent about the category weeds, and lacked a word for them, teems with stinging nettles, prickly thistles, brambles, darnel, wild oats, and caltrop.[34] Most of the offending plants were known to be bad from their appearance in the scriptures, the botany of which did not match Carolingian Europe's perfectly but nevertheless was a great inspiration for any who wondered about what attitude to take toward any given plant. A few species whose representation in Carolingian texts is consistently negative instead had a bad reputation in earlier Latin literature. Overall, while they certainly knew which kinds of plants were undesirable, the Carolingians did not add much to the Latin repertory or vocabulary. They were satisfied with the botanical baggage inherited from the ancient and late antique Mediterranean.

Carolingian efforts to raise the levels of Christianity within the empire hinged on improving clerical access to the scriptures, the Latin text of

---

[33] Bad herbs: Bede, "In Lucae Evangelium Expositio," ed. D. Hurst, *Bedae Venerabilis Opera* 2.3 (Turnhout, 1960), 418: "sicut herba mala"; Smaragdus of St.-Mihiel, "Collectiones in Epistolas et Evangelia," ed. J. Migne, *PL* 102 (Paris, 1865), 237; Hrabanus Maurus, "Homeliae" 8, ed. J. Migne, *PL* 110 (Paris, 1864), 148; Hrabanus, "Glossa Ordinaria, Evangelium Secundum Lucam" 24.37–8, ed. J. Migne, *PL* 114 (Paris, 1879), 353.

[34] This "speciesism" reflects a sensibility to natural variety quite unlike the more anthropocentric conception behind the idea of weeds. J. Kreiner, *Legions of Pigs in the Early Medieval West* (New Haven, 2020), 30–4 aptly discusses postclassical theories of (animal) speciation, and unease about generalizations like genus and species that failed to account for individual characteristics.

which scholars purified and standardized. Good Latin was henceforth a keystone in Charlemagne's *renovatio*. But since by the late eighth century Latin was not the mother tongue of anyone in the Carolingian empire, another aspect of the Carolingian investment in Christian learning was the creation of good dictionaries wherein unfamiliar Latin words could be looked up by the increasingly literate clergy. The compilation of such word lists and encyclopedias was essential to the imperial project of improving comprehension of Christian truths among both the clergy and their lay audiences, to whom priests disseminated their knowledge in the vernacular.

The great lexical monument to this late eighth-century attempt to render Latin vocabulary more user-friendly is the massive *Liber Glossarum*.[35] This encyclopedia synthesized huge amounts of learning, much of it of Iberian origin, for the benefit of Carolingian readers. In it one learned that thistle ("cardus") was "a type of prickly plant whose nature is biting and almost austere" and that caltrop was "a type of bush, a prickly plant which is the same as zura, a prickly plant they also call tugzira. It is a prickly plant with one thorn upright and one lying flat; a most bitter and spiny plant."[36] Both of these weeds figured prominently in the Bible, and the *Liber Glossarum*'s integration may have helped some Carolingian students of the scriptures to envision the bad plants of the Holy Land in more down-to-earth and vernacular terms. The *Liber* could also guide readers baffled by these plants' appearance in classical literature (in Virgil's fourth *Eclogue*, for instance). But if the glossators also supplied some linguistic data drawn from classical sources (Pliny had claimed the Berber translation for caltrop was "zura"), their intention was not to open up ancient botany to early medieval readers. Along with the information about the nature and appearance of the plants, the *Liber*'s authors made no room for ancient wisdom on these plants' efficacy against scorpions or coughs, or utility in wool-processing.[37] This suggests that more than aiding readers to recognize the botanical criminals, the function of this material was to show them that the botanical world was known, classified, and ultimately under control. Comforted by the correspondence between the difficult, technical Latin term and a plant they could envision, even label in several languages, no doubt any who

---

[35] *Liber Glossarum Digital* (http://liber-glossarum.huma-num.fr).

[36] Ibid.: "cardus Yppocratis genus herbae spinosae huius natura mordax et subaustera est"; "paliurus genus fructeti est. haerba spinose, hoc est zura. spina quam tugzira dicunt. herba spinosa altero adunco, altero mucrone erecto. herba sperrima et spinosa," a definition that relies on Isidore's *Etymologies* and Pliny's *Natural History*.

[37] Pliny, *Naturalis Historia* 24.71 (115), 92 (scorpions and coughs); Isidore, *Etymologiae* 17.9.56 (wool).

consulted the *Liber Glossarum* left this hefty tome reassured that they now understood what the words meant.

The specificity and precision in identifying bad plants visible in the *Liber Glossarum* underlines how Carolingian Europe needed no general weed concept, or word. Each plant had its own properties, and some of these were often negative. But weediness was evaluated on a case by case basis, each plant's qualities audited within the relationship it created with humans in a particular time and place. However ecologically astute they appear, in apprehending and respecting the stunning variety of botanical creation Carolingian literati remained anthropocentric, for, according to their understanding, all plants had been created on the third day for human use. Hence it was up to humans, even in their fallen condition, to evaluate which plants were good and which were not, and when and why. The vocabulary they developed to do so was attentive to the botanical identity of each plant and yet flexible enough to permit judgement. Even in the absence of any one word for weeds it was possible to accurately identify the kind of relation a plant established with people. The Carolingian vocabulary for weeds was both precise and supple, nicely adapted to botanical and theological reality.

Modern Words for Weeds

It may seem surprising for people living in an agrarian society, with more than nine-tenths of the population engaged in tending to plants, to neglect convenient blanket terms for obnoxious plants. Yet hesitation over what to call and how satisfactorily to define weeds is not restricted to the Carolingians and their Latin texts. For if early medieval commentators avoided abstract definition of all bad plants (though they could definitely tell a weed from a plant when they saw one), modern discussions of weediness are equally uncertain. Contemporary agronomists or weed scientists are hardly unanimous about how to define weeds. In his 1975 classic *Crops and Man*, the American agronomist and plant geneticist Jack Harlan tabulated nineteen different authoritative opinions on what a weed is, plus a thick undergrowth of sub-definitions and distinctions. Clearly the famous "plant out of place" does not satisfy everyone.[38] Even the palaeobotanists who, as we shall see in Chapter 2, furnish so much valuable information about which weeds actually grew in Frankish fields, are often unsure whether a given ninth-century seed came from

---

[38] J. Harlan, *Crops and Man* (Madison, 1992), 85–7, table 4.1. See also M. van der Veen, "The Materiality of Plants," *World Archaeology* 46 (2014), 801.

a cultivated or uncultivated plant or, in other words, whether past people considered it a weed or a crop.[39]

Like Harlan's nineteen, other contemporary determinations of what makes a plant a weed use either biological characteristics or economic criteria to attain some certainty. Among the most popular botanical features used to pinpoint weediness are the ability to thrive in very diverse environmental conditions, exceptionally efficient reproductive strategies that lead to rapid propagation of the species, early germination of seeds and fast growth of seedlings, and the production of growth inhibitors for other species that give the plant that produces them advantages in the field. Though weekend gardeners who do not grow commercial crops, just ornamentals, might object, where economic criteria are applied to identifying weeds, whether the plant in question causes measurable financial losses to people is the decisive consideration.[40] Some, including Harlan himself, blend the two approaches in order to obtain a complete identikit of offensive plants, at once adaptable, fast-growing and -spreading, *and* costing people lots of money in additional inputs and lost crops.

In the past three decades, as environmentalists have become interested in "invasive species," perhaps reflecting the worries of supposedly homogeneous western societies confronting the influx of immigration from the poorer parts of the world, they too have taken an interest in weeds and what makes them weedy.[41] Therefore, a plant's ability to reduce "biodiversity," one of the very few absolute goods left in postmodern culture, has also become part of current weed definitions.[42] Ecologists stress that botanical features of weeds interact with the "disturbances" that humans, especially, cause in ecosystems, to increase the plants' populations, further destabilizing the ecosystems.[43] Agriculture was, of course, the main human "disturbance" to premodern ecosystems, and today remains

---

[39] E.g. V. Zech-Matterne et al., "Should *Bromus secalinus* (Rye Brome) Be Considered a Crop?" *Vegetation History and Archaeobotany* (2021), DOI 10.1007/s00334-021–00830-5.

[40] L. Ziska and J. Dukes, *Weed Biology and Climate Change* (Ames, IA, 2011), 1–3; S. Radosevich et al., *Ecology of Weeds and Invasive Plants* (Hoboken NJ, 2007), 6–15; Zimdahl, *Fundamentals*, 17–23; J. Holt, "Weeds," in *Encyclopedia of Biological Invasions*, ed. D. Simberloff and M. Remánek (Berkeley, 2011), 692–3; G. Manin et al., "Definizione e classificazione," in *Malerbologia*, ed. Catizone and Zanin, 23–4.

[41] P. Coates, *American Perceptions of Immigrant and Invasive Species* (Berkeley, 2007), 7–26.

[42] Biodiversity: Ziska and Dukes, *Weed Biology*, ix, 12; D. Simberloff, *Invasive Species* (Oxford, 2013), 11–15, 198–9; E. Weber, *Invasive Plant Species of the World* (Wallingford, 2017), vii. Biodiversity has its critics: F. Pearce, *The New Wild* (London, 2015), 152–3, 235–6.

[43] For a critique of equilibrium thinking in ecology that makes any change a "disturbance," D. Botkin, *The Moon in the Nautilus Shell* (Oxford, 2012).

a formidable source of instability and of weed creation, but road-building, logging, commerce, a host of other activities, and especially warfare, will do nicely as well: all furnish opportunities for weeds to spread and to prevail, bringing attendant reductions of other species in the wake of their success.[44] And as Chapter 1 spells out, empire-building, too, is one of the very best incubators for weeds.

Thus, twenty-first-century understandings of what a weed is have expanded to include those species whose opportunism enables them to outcompete slower plants and displace them, in the process sometimes reducing the number of "native" plants in a given place and giving rise to fears of a coming "Homogeocene," a time period even more dismal than the Anthropocene fashioned by modern industry, when the same handful of species of cosmopolitan plants, most of them weeds, will be found everywhere.[45] Perhaps ironically, this was something that Aldo Leopold, the German-American ecocritic *avant la lettre*, feared already in the 1940s.[46]

Postmodern conditions have rendered clear-cut boundaries between good and bad plants still more difficult to discern than they used to be. As contemporary agronomists begin to doubt it is even possible to completely extirpate undesirable plants, and farmers settle for "invasive plant management" as opposed to the complete extirpation that was earlier weed science's goal, a standard crop like wheat has come to be understood as a complex of plants, including those that inevitably compete with the wheat in the field, namely weeds.[47] Following an insight of the celebrated Soviet botanist Nikolai Vavilov, an early theorist of the fecund relationships among related species of wild and cultivated cereal plants, recently agronomists have proposed that the distinction between crop and weed is best represented by a spectrum, or "continuum of physiological states of plants used by humans," from wild to genetically

---

[44] Procopius (*Wars* 6.3.1–9) claimed Rome was an especially weedy place, but may simply have noted a side effect of the many sieges of 535–54.

[45] The "Homogeocene" is a not-so-veiled attack on globalized economies: Simberloff, *Invasive Species*, 262–8; Ziska and Dukes, *Weed Biology*, 201. Spirited critiques of such views: Pearce, *The New Wild*, 1–4, 152–3; M. Davis et al., "Don't Judge Species on their Origins," *Nature* 474 (June 9, 2011), 153–4.

[46] Aldo Leopold, *A Sand County Almanac* (New York, 1949), 217.

[47] "Management" as coexistence: L. Head, "Living in a Weedy Future,"*in Rethinking Invasion Ecologies from the Environmental Humanities*, ed. J. Frawley and I. McCalman (Abingdon, 2014), 88. Early weed science: L. King, "Some Early Forms of the Weed Concept," *Nature* 179 (June 29, 1957), 1366, with reference to Giovanni Lapi's 1767 *Discorso sull'esterminio del loglio e di altre piante nocive*. Crops as a complex of species: Harlan, *Crops and Man*, 92–3; see also L. Head, *Ingrained* (Farnham, 2012), 37. Darwin too doubted species were so distinct: H. Ritvo, *The Platypus and the Mermaid, and Other Figments of the Classifying Imagination* (Cambridge, MA, 1997), 85–6.

modified.[48] Actually, this idea is old, and the Roman encyclopedist Pliny the Elder, in the first century AD, recognized that some organisms were neither wild nor domesticated, but liminal, in-between; his proposition enjoyed a limited early medieval reception, too.[49] According to this way of defining weeds, which is more botanical than economic, not much separates the weed from the crop, and genetically the two might be very intimately related.

In this vein, some weed scientists think weediness is a function of the relationship a plant creates with people, anywhere from symbiotic to parasitic.[50] This attractive definition of weeds, one Carolingian thinkers might have appreciated, departs from the botanical and genetic "continuum" of the spectrum theorists to emphasize the kind of interactions that arise between people and any given plant. Certain plants fit so perfectly into the lives of people that the two species establish a comfortably harmonious relationship, while other plants, just as proficient at benefiting from human activities and the humanized ecosystem, do so without offering discernible benefits to people: the lack of reciprocity in the relation with humans is what condemns some plants to weediness. Of course, any definition of weeds that derives from a relationship is dynamic and hence is fragile, liable to change. A plant's relation with people can evolve, altering the plant's status. In Latin literature, Pliny recognized this when he described barley as a pest, a weed of wheat fields, except in Germany where farmers had given up on controlling it in their fields, had accepted it as a crop, and begun to eat a gruel made from a plant their ancestors deemed weedy.[51] On an even quicker schedule than evolution and adaptation, plants also switch from tolerable to pest with the season, as human land use changes.

Divided into "archaeophytes" (as plants thought to have been introduced into a landscape before AD 1500 are known), "neophytes" (introduced later than AD 1500), and "apophytes" (introduced in very remote times; *grosso modo* the meaning is the same as "naturalized"), or categorized as "ruderal" (living in places humans create but do not use, like roadsides),

---

[48] Vavilov's "secondary domesticates" underlie the "intensity of dislike" model for classifying plants in Harlan, *Crops and Man*, 89. Continuum: A. Chevalier et al., "Factors and Issues in Plant Choice," in *Plants and People: Choices and Diversity through Time*, ed. A. Chevalier et al. (Oxford, 2014), 7.

[49] Pliny, *Naturalis Historia* 8.56 (82), ed. Mayhoff, 155. On this idea's early medieval afterlife: F. Guizard-Duchamp, *Les terres du sauvage dans le monde franc (IVe–IX siècle)* (Rennes, 2009), 39–40.

[50] D. Rindos, *The Origins of Agriculture* (Orlando, FL, 1984), 123; J. Frawley and I. McCalman, "Invasion Ecologies: The Nature/Culture Challenge," in *Rethinking Invasion Ecologies*, ed. Frawley and McCalman, 4–5.

[51] *Natural History* 18.17 (44), ed. Mayhoff, 183. See J. Devroey, "La céréaliculture dans le monde franque," in *Settimane del CISAM* 37 (Spoleto, 1990), 232.

"obligate" (living in crop fields; also sometimes called "agrestal"), or "facultative" (able to survive without agriculture but also agile enough to insert themselves into agroecosystems), weeds remain as difficult to grasp in theory as they are in practice.[52] Even equipped with precise scientific vocabulary, modern specialists in agronomy and weed science cannot agree on how to define weeds once and for all.

Perhaps then Carolingian unwillingness to make general pronouncements about weeds and how to define them, and the related recognition of the contingencies in botanical classification, derived from a quite astute assessment of the plant kingdom, shaped by Christian theology. Like Charles at Pîtres, Carolingian commentators stressed each species' particularities (prickliness, toxicity, etc.), or each specific kind of bad plant's relationship to humans. In recognizing that a weed is a situational construct, they agreed with such brilliant thinkers on weeds as Aldo Leopold.[53] From his Wisconsin vantage point, Leopold observed that actually it is the particular situation of the observer that determines whether a plant ends up labeled weed or crop, for "good and bad are attributes of numbers, not of species": when the situation is agricultural, as it often was in the early 1900s Midwest, many plants that had hitherto been decorative or ecologically useful, end up on the wrong end of human constructions and become enemies to extirpate, or weeds. We shall see in Chapter 3 that Leopold's musings unwittingly echoed Augustinian and Carolingian weed theology, and indeed so do those modern weed scientists who evaluate plants' fluctuating relationships with people to establish which are weeds.

The Matter with Weeds

Though eighth- and ninth-century people in Frankish Europe seem to have lacked a word like weed and to have eschewed the idea that specific plant species were inherently noxious and irredeemable, and though the Carolingians who left written traces behind did not tidily classify certain bad plants as early colonizers of clearances, infesters of the cabbage patch, or specialists in spring-sown grains, they agreed with modern agronomists on one thing: weeds matter deeply. Carolingian-era writers emphasized the cultural relevance of bad "herbs," but also recognized that such relevance derived from weeds' economic impact. This study highlights weeds' double significance as agricultural pests and cultural artifacts. To

---

[52] Such terms are discussed by Radosevich et al., *Ecology of Weeds*, 5–20; R. Mabey, *Weeds* (London, 2012), 268–9; I. Godinho, "Les definitions d'adventice et de mauvaise herbe," *Weed Research* 24 (1984), 121–5.

[53] A. Leopold, "What Is a Weed?" in his *River of the Mother of God and Other Essays* (Madison, 1992), 306–9 (quote on p. 309).

do so, it attempts to conjugate environmental with early medieval, specifically Carolingian, history in a way that broadens both disciplines.

Admittedly, how weeds mattered to Carolingian cultivators differs from how they matter to modern commercial farmers or weed scientists. For today weeds are accused of depleting soils of nutrients that crops could use, of robbing crops of needed sunlight, of manufacturing and circulating chemicals that stymie crop growth, of altering hydrology in ways detrimental to other (cultivated) plants, of accelerating topsoil erosion, of harboring pests (insects, fungi, viruses) and facilitating their dissemination among crops, and of building inflammable biomass dangerous for desirable species. And nowadays the economic repercussions of these ecological facts matter most. Overall, weeds are estimated to reduce conventionally grown US harvests of wheat and rice (the world's two most commonly cultivated cereals) by some 10 percent, and harvests untreated with herbicides by up to 35 percent, far more than what insect or fungal pests achieve; in Italy wheat harvests without weed control (which today mainly means chemical weed control) would be 20–30 percent lower than they are. The attempt to restrict weeds' vigorous competition in modern agroecosystems costs farmers a sizable portion of their income, and adds a burden in labor. In Britain, the post-1945 leap into subsidized wheat farming vastly reduced populations of field weeds and vastly increased the costs of weed control, in the process creating monocropped "ecological deserts" inhospitable to all wildlife. A similar reduction of crops' competitors in French fields since World War II, achieved by liberal use of "chemical controls," was also associated with more homogeneous cultivations and with higher costs in inputs and labor.[54]

In the 1800s, when modern farming resembled premodern practice more because chemical fertilizers and herbicides were unknown, when rotations remained important, and when monocropping did not yet prevail (nor its vulnerabilities and added inputs), weeds still reduced wheat yields by 5–15 percent, depending on plowing methods, on how much laborious weeding and harrowing farmers lavished on their fields, and how much crop rotation they practiced.[55] In other terms, premodern crop

[54] US harvest losses: Ziska and Dukes, *Weed Biology*, 16; Italy: M. Sattin and F. Tei, "Malerbe componente dannosa degli agroecosistemi," in *Malerbologia*, ed. Catizone and Zanin, 175. Zimdahl, *Fundamentals*, 36 thinks farmers' losses to weeds incalculable; Simberloff, *Invasive Species*, 99 estimates weeds cost American farmers $27 billion per year in lost crops and weeding costs. Britain: "Farming after Brexit," *The Economist*, November 28, 2020, 52–3. France: R. Fourche, "Les nuisibles, symbole inamovible de l'utilitarianisme agricole?" in *Sale bêtes! Mauvaises herbes!*, ed. R. Luglie (Rennes, 2017), 297–9.
[55] Nineteenth century: A. Olmstead and P. Rhode, *Creating Abundance* (Cambridge, 2008), 55–7.

losses to weeds tended to be smaller than they are (potentially) on modern farms today. But as premodern yields and productivity were lower as well, agrarian societies were more vulnerable to shortfalls, and more acutely sensitive to even quite small losses.[56] Though many Carolingian farmers were not motivated by calculations of yield, but measured productivity in terms of labor inputs in relation to household needs, at a time of low yields even small crop losses rendered weed infestations relatively more damaging.[57]

We cannot quantify accurately the losses of Carolingian farmers to undesired plants, but their impact on the Franks' agrarian economy was not limited to their ability to shrink harvests. It is equally hard to estimate how much additional labor the women and men of the eighth and ninth centuries put into their gardens and fields in order to reduce the impact of the plants they saw as "out of place" there. But labor is a key difference in weed control on Carolingian farms and modern agribusinesses. For early medieval farmers, the labor weeds imposed, not only before and during, but also after the harvest, was significant. From the beginning of the productive process, weeds imposed burdens. Careful plowing and harrowing served to control weeds, among other things, and forced cultivators to spend more time and energy in their fields.[58] A still bigger demand was the weeding which took place in early spring when the crops had germinated.[59] In broadcast-sown grain fields, without orderly ranks of crops, hoeing, for example, had to be attentive so as to avoid wrecking the roots of grain plants. It could therefore take twenty people a full winter's day to hoe-weed a hectare of land sown with grain. Given that an early medieval household of five needed two and a half hectares sown with grain to feed itself, the investment in hoeing labor was large: assuming all hands were on deck, ten full days of work just to weed the family grainfield once. If the weeding was done by plucking, using bare hands, it likely took longer.[60] Nor had weeds finished exacting their laborious toll.

---

[56] J. Devroey, "La politique annonaire des carolingiens comme question économique, religieuse et morale," in *Settimane del CISAM* 63 (Spoleto, 2016), 303–6; studies of fourteenth-century English manorial records suggest a shortfall of 20 percent every six years (306). In his *La nature et le roi* (Paris, 2019), 287–337, Devroey considers vulnerability to fungi and insects, but not weeds.

[57] Yields: Devroey, "La politique annonaire," 303–5. Household production: J. Devroey, *Économie rurale et société dans l'Europe franque (VIe–IXe siècles)* (Paris, 2003), 117.

[58] P. Halstead, *Two Oxen Ahead* (Chichester, 2014), 44, 233–5.

[59] A good guide to medieval weeding work is D. Postles, "Cleaning the Medieval Arable," *Agricultural History Review* 37 (1989), 130–3.

[60] Labor speed: G. Comet, *Le paysan et son outil* (Rome, 1992), 168, using early modern data. Late 1900s Asturian weeding operations were more time-consuming than sowing or tillage, and equal to harvesting: Halstead, *Two Oxen*, 234–5. Family land needs: Devroey, *La nature*, 125.

During harvests, they slowed down operations, compelling people to choose between speed and the purity of what they gathered. Afterwards, the task of throwing threshed grain across the threshing floor with a shovel to separate the heavier from the lighter seeds (and thus weed seeds from crop seeds) required a strong and skilled worker. Further riddling, by sieve, was a burden big enough that nineteenth-century English farmers skimped on it.[61]

In the end, it was weeding crops that demanded the most. Whether in grain fields, vegetable gardens, or even where fodder was grown for domestic animals (e.g. oats), to keep the bad plants separate from the good ones took great human ingenuity and effort, and no doubt caused exhaustion, anxiety, and pain. This vast time-sensitive and back-breaking labor, in sum, was the crucial reason why weeds mattered so much in a premodern agrarian economy.

While we can only estimate how many days and hours Carolingian peasants spent gouging weeds from the dirt, and really only be certain that weeds mattered because of the vast and urgent toil they imposed on cultivators' bodies, we can reconstruct something of how and why certain plants came to be abhorred in Carolingian weed discourse. For weeds mattered in cultural terms, too, not just in economic ones, and therefore crept into Carolingian legislation, becoming endemic in other kinds of text too. Alfred Crosby sagely defined weeds as those plants that attract anthropomorphic metaphors most readily.[62] Yet weeds' textual prominence in Carolingian times is not only a sign of this irresistible feature of theirs. It also depends on their broader cultural importance, and one object of this study is to illustrate that importance by rescuing the noxious plants of early medieval history from neglect. For a balanced reconstruction of the Carolingian past should extend beyond state formation, ecclesiastical organization, *renovatio*, and North Sea trade, to encompass plants about which Carolingian writers evidently cared a good deal and that shaped the existences of postclassical cultivators. Weedless Carolingian histories overlook some of the protagonists of early medieval European environments.

The Carolingian history of weeds offers insight into the chasm that seems to have separated the vegetation of literate discourse from the weeds that harried landowners and peasants in the fields. As this book demonstrates, the "bad herbs" of the Christian imagination, the species listed as most unwelcome plants in Carolingian books, seldom were

---

[61] Salisbury, *Weeds and Aliens*, 118.
[62] A. Crosby, *Ecological Imperialism* (Cambridge, 1986), 150 noted how quick weed scientists are to call weeds aggressive or opportunistic.

exactly the same ones that archaeobotanists discern infesting eighth- to ninth-century barley fields, reducing wheat yields, robbing bean stalks of soil nutrients, and demanding so much work from rural people. Yet Carolingian authors' preference for biblical bad plants did not derive from cultural myopia, an unwillingness to observe what actually sprouted from the cultivated soils around them. The weeds that exercised the learned seemed qualitatively different from, and more dangerous than, the homey weeds in gardens or plowed fields because of the relations they established with people. Yet the learned had no aversion to observing the agroecosystems around them: familiarity with humble, common weeds made the Bible's bad plants more exciting and interesting. In fact, the differences between the weeds of discourse and those rooted in the soil are only apparent, and the human–weed dialectic described in Carolingian books nicely rendered agroecological reality. The abstraction of the Carolingian epoch's discursive botany served to make it broadly applicable in real economic, social, and political contexts.

Early medieval conceptions of creation innovated over the past by including among the gifts of God to humans "savage spaces," lightly humanized areas that ancient people thought worthless wasteland.[63] This rehabilitation lies behind the willingness in Carolingian culture to see complexity in the shifting relationship between people and weeds. Acknowledgment of noxious plants' ability to climb out of the negative evaluation to which people consigned them most of the time, and their offer of benefits to humans, is one of the hallmarks of Carolingian weed discourse, and helps in comprehending the Carolingian reluctance to adopt generalizing words and concepts like weed.[64] Recognition of what we shall call phytosocial mobility was an important characteristic of eighth- and ninth-century writings. Indeed, in Carolingian texts what set weeds apart from domesticated plants, evaluation of which was far more static and consistently positive, was this mobility. This powerful awareness of the value in all plant life, including that which people normally devalued, distinguished early medieval approaches to vegetation. In certain contexts, the foulest weed could reveal itself as a most useful component of an ecosystem, and offer unexpected benefits at least to those who considered it carefully. By moving up, even briefly, in the vegetable hierarchies, lowly, marginal plants proved the fundamental

---

[63] Guizard-Duchamp, *Les terres*, 36–7. See also P. Dendle, "Plants in the Early Medieval Cosmos," in *Health and Healing from the Medieval Garden*, ed. P. Dendle and A. Touwaide (Woodbridge, 2008), 52–4.

[64] Kreiner, *Legions of Pigs*, 34 observes that for postclassical thinkers, "although God had established a set of finite possibilities or *termini* for every species, those parameters did not confine any individual creature to a single trajectory."

goodness of God's creation, and by accepting weeds' potential, Carolingian writers located them within a cosmology that implied all nature was good. Hence Carolingian writers accepted weeds' agility. It was difficult but also necessary to understand that all plants were created equal, whatever misguided uses people tried to put them to.

Weeds are sensitive proxies of social and cultural priorities, and not just in Carolingian Europe. As Di Palma argued in her acute study of early modern conceptions of badlands, the kinds of ecology that people find abominable are just as revelatory of what they think is important as the landscapes they cherish.[65] For environmental historians, therefore, a historically grounded understanding of weeds complements and completes accounts of past woodlands, gardens, or agroecosystems. It enriches environmental historical reconstructions of the diverse and complex relations people have established with vegetation. The exceptional abundance of Carolingian writings allows an early glimpse into medieval Europe's elaboration of Christian environmental ideas. Just as Di Palma's wastelands began to evoke new emotive reactions in the 1700s, and became a problem that nations must solve, in the Carolingian epoch for the first time we may observe weeds eliciting disdain and acceptance, exclusion and inclusion, on the basis of Christian cosmological sensibilities.

That these sensibilities at times seem to have been out of touch with the harsher realities of Carolingian agroecosystem management only adds to the interest of the story. For the dialectic between economic and cultural adaptations to ecologies is one of the classic topics of environmental history, modern or premodern.[66] As the fairly swift adaptation of early medieval literate culture to the rise of chestnut cultivation suggests, postclassical readers and writers could respond to changes in the land with some alacrity: they understood phytosocial mobility.[67] After all, the eighth- and ninth-century intellectuals who read books and wrote treatises inhabited a fully organic economy in which everyone knew about the agricultural process that produced the clothes they wore, the food they ate, and the tools they used, and what could happen when this process faltered: shortages and shortfalls remained a painful possibility that touched everyone, including the fortunate few who almost always knew where their next meal was coming from.[68] In such a context, the

[65] V. Di Palma, *Wasteland: A History* (New Haven, 2014), 4–9.

[66] D. Worster, "Doing Environmental History," in his *The Ends of the Earth* (Cambridge, 1989), 289–308; J. Hughes, *Environmental Problems of the Greeks and Romans* (Baltimore, 2014), 1–6.

[67] P. Squatriti, *Landscape and Change in early Medieval Italy* (Cambridge, 2013), ch. 3.

[68] T. Newfield, "The Contours, Frequency, and Causation of Subsistence Crises in Carolingian Europe (750–950)," in *Crises alimentarias en la edad media*, ed. P. Benito i Monclús (Lleida, 2013), 117–72; Devroey, "La politique," 303–4, 336–9.

reduction of productivity and the increase in laboriousness occasioned by weeds mattered a great deal more than it does in the rich countries of Europe today. For this reason, the apparent abstraction of Carolingian weed discourse is poignant: it sheds light on a culture that subordinated the natural world to supernatural imperatives, but always remained alert to ecology and in particular to the biological processes of vegetable life.

This study seeks to establish a corridor between the territories of Carolingian and of environmental history. It is predicated on the belief that communication between the two academic fields of research will improve both. The careful attention to text that is one distinguishing feature of Carolingian studies can enrich understanding of how past people fit into their ecosystems. Discussion of landscape sensibility and landscape management in the relatively deep past of the first millennium AD can also give perspective to environmental histories that privilege the modern and industrial European past and perhaps idealize ecological relations before the Anthropocene. Meanwhile, the archaeological science that has become a preferred source for environmental histories in the past few decades, in this case particularly archaeobotany, vastly improves the database on which to build historical visions of Carolingian Europe. It also allows some independent checks on the Latin words whose authority in traditional Carolingian history has no rivals. In sum, improved traffic between the two academic fields this book addresses most directly generates insights and has the potential to introduce new perspectives for both. The study of bad plants is a chance to see things differently.

Outline

This study opens by proposing that Frankish hegemony between the North and Ionian seas during the eighth and ninth centuries was properly imperial. Carolingian power determined new political relations between a metropolis, the Frankish heartland bounded by the Rhine and Loire rivers, and its peripheries in western Europe, mostly subdued by 790. It enabled an elite (the "Reichsaristokratie") to own land in multiple regions. It also fostered deeper integration among its many regional economies, not least because such novel relations matched the interests of the new transregional landowners. But the small scale of the Carolingian empire, and its brevity (it lasted little longer than contemporary European integration efforts have), may have attenuated the phytosociological impact of imperial unification. By redirecting the traffic of humans and commodities to suit their purposes, and channeling energy flows in new ways, empires shape the populations and distribution of plants in space, both intentionally and by mistake. Yet, however transformative for early medieval European agriculture the Carolingian period may have been, it did not generate a Braudelian "civilizational plant" (such as wheat or grapes might have been for Rome) nor, in consequence, a discernible civilizational weed, an infesting competitor of the preferred cultivations of eighth- and ninth-century Europeans.

Chapter 2 uses archaeology to measure the distance between the learned discourse of weeds in Carolingian codices and the weeds that seem to have actually grown on the ground in the eighth and ninth centuries. Archaeobotany brings into focus some astonishingly fine-grained pictures of what grew in early medieval fields and gardens, and though, like all archaeology, it does not always emerge from exactly the places a historian might like to know about, it still represents a great opportunity to evaluate the verisimilitude of Carolingian texts and images. Though some obligate weeds of rye, oats, and wheat appear to have done well in Carolingian Europe, by and large the undesirable plants in agricultural contexts were not the same ones as in contemporary poems, laws, exegesis, chronicles, and letters. The wicked species identified in Carolingian Latin texts were different from what most people encountered on a daily basis in their fields and in their gardens as revealed by carbonized and waterlogged plant remains. In other words, the weeds of the peasant and of the monastic gardener were not the weeds of the literate.

Carolingian Europe's literate weedology had passed through the filter of late antique Christianity, and particularly the meditations of the Church Fathers and of Augustine. The lack of a word for weeds did not hamper a luxuriant discourse about "bad herbs" that identified most of these latter on the basis of their scriptural status. That status, as shown in Chapter 3, was darkly colored by Adam's exclusion from Eden and God's condemnation of his progeny to struggle against thorns and thistles in order to gain their sustenance. But, as the account of vegetable creation at the beginning of Genesis suggested that originally plants had been made good, Carolingian Christians followed late antique exegesis to the conclusion that human inadequacy mattered more than the intrinsic nature of any plant for its placement in botanical hierarchies. Human labor on the ground, that unfortunate necessity of postlapsarian living, caused certain plants to seem evil, though they might have another, totally different, moral profile if viewed ecologically.

Perhaps the most celebrated contemporary definition of weeds is the Mary Douglas-inflected "plants out of place."[69] Chapter 3 further

---

[69] B. Campkin, "Placing 'Matter Out of Place'," *Architectural Theory Review* 18 (2013), 46–9 reconstructs the genealogy of the aphorism "dirt is matter out of place" in Douglas' *Purity and Danger*.

suggests that, actually, for agrarian societies accustomed to plants bur-geoning all over the place, the problem with weeds lay in their choice of time, more than their choice of where to live. The Carolingian empire was more than ordinarily concerned with its routines and their correct timing, as demonstrated by Charlemagne's effort to reform and harmonize the calendrical observances of his subjects, and subsequent support for that effort. That certain plants might sprout of their own accord, not in obedience to a farmer's plan, was natural enough, but that they did this when the farmer expected crops to grow was an intolerable calendrical infringement. For the Carolingians weeds were "plants out of time," unable to respect the human economic schedule and therefore detrimen-tal to farming, which is based on carefully modulated rhythms.

Yet for all their attention to the times when weeds were thickest on the ground, Carolingian authors detached their rankings of the most perni-cious plants from agronomical considerations. Indeed, as observed in Chapter 4, to them the worst weeds were the same weeds that had most impressed the ancient Hebrews in Palestine, namely the ones enumerated in the scriptures. Thus, the vegetable characteristic that most alarmed Carolingian writers was thorniness, an asset to plants living in arid cli-mates populated by herders and their livestock, but a much less necessary defense against evaporation and animal browsers in temperate northwest-ern Europe. And though they likely had never seen the plant, Carolingian readers of the Gospel of Matthew knew darnel as the absolute nadir of weediness, because the Evangelist recorded Jesus' story that linked darnel to the devil's intention to harm good folks. Darnel traversed the Carolingian literary landscape as a vegetable pariah, consistently catalo-gued as the most wicked plant, particularly because it was thought diso-bedient to God's command that all vegetation be true to its seed. A unique ability to mutate during growth and transform its botanical nature, certified by ancient scientific botany, lent to darnel a note of treachery and further contributed to Carolingian people's low opinion of it.

Chapter 5 explores some of the aesthetic choices deriving from the conviction that postlapsarian vegetation differed from Edenic in several radical ways. The survival in Rome of several depictions of paradisiacal landscapes permits an analysis of how Carolingian-era patrons and artists, and presumably spectators, liked to think about perfection in plants. This ideal vegetable world by definition eluded the limitations of weediness, and thus enables a look at plant life through the rosiest-tinted of glasses.

As explained in a previous section of this introduction, the edgy, mutable nature of weeds deeply impressed Carolingian writers. The very same plants whose mistimed growth made them weeds might become acceptable, with just a little more patience or wisdom. Chapter 6 of this study highlights how plants deemed enemies of humanity in most circumstances could, in certain other circumstances, be rehabilitated. Some weeds were fine pasture for domestic animals. But it was their utility to human health, defined both biologically and spiritually, that mostly elevated them. Carolingian pharmacology was sophisticated in its acceptance and redeployment of ancient herbal lore, and in some cases scribes edited their ancient texts to better match northwestern European botanical possibilities, omitting those simples (plants able to cure disease unadulterated) that did not grow north of the Alps or were unknown outside the Mediterranean. But whatever their strategies, the medical writers knew that some spiny or notoriously toxic plants could produce physiological changes that were beneficial to afflicted people.

Furthermore, rather as in the nineteenth-century tales of Br'er Rabbit from the American South, early medieval ascetics saw an opportunity in prickly and thorny plants. Br'er Rabbit was liberated from the gummy trap set for him by his antagonist Br'er Fox when he persuaded his captor to roll him in the briar patch, known to all in the neighborhood as a painful place to pass through, but just rough enough to catch on the mass of sticky material that left the astute rabbit at the mercy of his predator, and allow him to skip off free.[70] The insight of the story derives from the recognition that the very same plants that are dangerous and harmful may on certain occasions serve very useful purposes. Carolingian-era ascetics would have recognized this insight. They practiced several forms of bodily mortification thanks precisely to the physical properties of plants generally considered awful. The plants thereby participated actively in the ascetical program of spiritual improvement. In doing so they confirmed that when people were excellent, the botanical universe worked in their favor, as God's approval of that universe on the third day suggested had been the original intention. Weeds were liminal, their virtuous or vicious nature deriving from the purposes of the people who manipulated them.

With the lone exception of the Romantic poets in the early 1800s, who idolized "wild" nature in all its forms, including the more unkempt ones, for millennia Europeans have consistently disliked weeds.[71] This makes the sovereign as gardener motif probed in Chapter 6 all the more interesting. Carolingian rulers, especially Charlemagne, Louis the Pious, and

---

[70] A. Espinosa, "A New Classification of the Fundamental Elements of the Tar-Baby Story on the Basis of Two Hundred and Sixty-Seven Versions," *Journal of American Folklore* 56 (1943), 31–7 shows this fox and rabbit tale in J. Harris, *Uncle Remus, His Songs and Sayings* (of 1881) was only one of many orally transmitted versions.

[71] Clayton, "Weeds," 309–10 has a useful (and short) list of the (western) people who have appreciated weeds.

Charles the Bald, presented themselves as ecologically responsible, or as uniquely positioned to assure to their realms and subjects favorable environments. They did so by behaving in the morally upright ways that obtained divine favor: in a certain sense their solicitude mimicked God's care for the world He created. They did so also by ensuring the smooth succession of the several phases of the agricultural cycle, and therefore they could be held accountable not just for poor weather that endangered harvests, but also for outbreaks of vegetable disorder that entangled farmers. That made the weed political, a perfect reflection both of the performance of a regime and of the status of the soul of its head, the kings and emperors of the Carolingian dynasty.

To conclude, the Epilogue considers the classification of things, including bad ones like weeds, as an ongoing effort in early medieval European culture. It proposes that the Carolingian way of sorting out plants was ecologically as well as theologically informed.

1   Weeds, Nature, and Empire

The salient characteristics of imperial phytosociology have drawn increasing attention from historians since the publication of Alfred Crosby's studies on the "Columbian Exchange" in the 1970s.[1] The subsequent growth of environmental history has made it possible to establish some general features of the kind of botanical communities and relations that empires create. It seems that empires tend to reduce the isolation of regional floras, and to cause, or accelerate, mixtures of plants, both on purpose and unwittingly. Furthermore, the economic exploitations empires sponsor have important effects on the conditions in which vegetation lives, or does not live.

A comparative imperial botany is a useful backdrop against which to set the weed history of the Carolingian empire. For the Carolingians' hegemony was an environmental fact as much as a political or cultural one. For more than a century, the Franks stimulated the agrarian economies of their heartland, and also of its peripheries, in the process increasing transregional movements and mixing together European plants. Therefore, after a foray into comparative imperial phytosociology, the second part of this chapter lays out how Carolingian economic integration and activity reformed growing conditions for plants, and particularly for weeds. A more complicated and more ecological account of the forces at work in the Carolingian sphere of influence enhances understanding of Europe's first postclassical empire. Plants, and specifically unwanted plants, were partners of the people who united much of Latin Christendom between the eighth and the ninth century.

Empires and Weeds

Weeds are opportunistic. Empires offer them one of their greatest opportunities for multiplication and propagation. The evidence for weeds' opportunistic dissemination is best for modern empires, of course, but

---

[1] A. Crosby, *The Columbian Exchange* (Westport, 1972) was not an immediate success.

it is hardly lacking for premodern ones, too. For, by their nature, empires tend to share the same cosmopolitan urges and policies, and seek to create similar transregional economic linkages.[2] These imperial linkages are in effect what weed scientists call "disturbance corridors," pathways along which weeds move from one place to another.[3] Exploiting these linkages, or corridors, the undesirable plants of one imperial region expand their range by trickling into others. Once they get there, free of pesky competitors from their native places, they increase their population, sometimes quite quickly. At least in the short term, their emigration is a triumph.

Some awareness of this botanical reality existed in ancient and early modern empires, but alarm over the spillage of spontaneous plants into new terrains, revealingly called by modern botanists "colonization" or "invasion," or lately "bioinvasion," really developed a fever pitch in the twentieth century. No doubt this heightened awareness depended on the scale and rapidity of the phenomenon in industrial and postindustrial times.[4] For the "globalized" economies of the twentieth and twenty-first centuries, with their vastly increased production and consumption patterns and attendant quickened circulation of goods and services (which really means people), have witnessed an "explosion" in the number of weeds common to different parts of the earth.[5] At the fountainhead of such explosive botany was the British empire, or so at least it seemed to some of its protagonists and to many later historians of imperial phytosociology.[6] From the 1930s pioneering ecologists like Charles Elton hypothesized disastrous takeovers or "colonizations" by plants (and other organisms) that people unwitting introduced into previously "virgin" landscapes, and catastrophic mingling of weed species there.[7]

[2] S. Reynolds, "Empires: A Problem of Comparative History," *Historical Research* 79 (2006), 152–62. Connectivity is the leitmotif of J. Burbank and F. Cooper, *Empires in World History* (Princeton, 2010).
[3] L. Ziska and J. Dukes, *Weed Biology and Climate Change* (Ames, IA, 2011), 109.
[4] On industrialization and empire, see Burbank and Cooper, *Empires*, 19. R. Zimdahl, *Fundamentals of Weed Science* (Amsterdam, 2013), 192 explains weed scientists' distinction of "introduction" from "invasion." B. Bennett, "A Global History of Species Introduction and Invasion," in *Environments of Empire*, ed. U. Kirchberger and B. Bennett (Chapel Hill, 2020), 224–33 argues for a "key shift" in imperial biotic transfers AD 1600–1900.
[5] F. Pearce, *The New Wild* (London, 2015), 35; E. Salisbury, *Weeds and Aliens* (London, 1961), 50–80; R. Mabey, *Weeds* (London, 2012), 136–7, 146–52.
[6] U. Kirchberger, "Introduction," in *Environments and Empires*, ed. Kirchberger and Bennett, 1–2, lamented the preponderance of British studies in environmental histories of empire.
[7] C. Elton, *The Ecology of Invasions by Animals and Plants* (London, 1958); D. Simberloff, *Invasive Species: What Everyone Needs to Know* (Oxford, 2013), 8–11. See also P. Coates, *American Perceptions of Immigrant and Invasive Species* (Berkeley, 2007), 1–6; Bennett, "A Global History," 233–4.

Elton eventually likened the effects of biological "invasions" to the 1945 detonations of two atom bombs, hugely destructive man-made events with incalculable ecological and moral repercussions. He considered that the unprecedented technological mastery of humans, especially north-western Europeans, was wreaking havoc on placid ecosystems, particularly colonial ones which had been separate and stable until then. The connectivity of twentieth-century empires made possible transmissions on a scale and at an intensity never seen before.

As so often, what seemed to twentieth- and twenty-first-century people unprecedented actually had deep roots in the early industrial age, in the early modern period, and even further back into European history.[8] The British empire of the eighteenth and nineteenth centuries had already created the conditions for several botanical explosions, some ardently desired by the colonists: for though imperial agents often extolled the possibilities, and for example eighteenth-century courtiers at St. Petersburg were enthusiastic about the potential for plant adoption that Catherine the Great's annexation of Crimea opened up, it was the English Victorians who were the greatest "acclimatizers" of foreign plants, a few of which got out of hand in the home country, or became "naturalized."[9] Even George Perkins Marsh, a hero of early environmental thinking who took a dim view of the ecological transformations caused by empires like Rome's, was enough "of his times," enough of a Victorian gentleman, to consider that the botanical introductions that occurred around the ancient Mediterranean were positive developments.[10] Regardless, the relationship between Britain and the plant life of its colonies was not just a matter of some passionate gardeners and daffy lovers of unfamiliar vegetation. For, beyond managing the global circulation of "exotic" (tropical, northern Atlantic) plants in early modern times, imperial Britain also imposed its agronomical tastes on far-flung colonies. In all the unlikely places where British grains were sown, numerous companion plants that the sowers did not consciously introduce also arose, or "exploded." Both knowledge and ignorance of plants, both control and the lack of it, enabled the colonizers to harness colonial nature to imperial British interests. Indeed, for Alfred Crosby, essential to all imperial success was the exportation of "portmanteau biota," a fully developed agroecological package that had coevolved

[8] Pearce, *The New Wild*, 40–51. The founding father of this type of analysis was A. Crosby, especially in *Ecological Imperialism* (Cambridge, 1986), on whose insights this chapter tries to build.
[9] A. Schönle, "Garden of the Empire: Catherine's Appropriation of the Crimea," *Slavic Review* 60 (2001), 5–8.
[10] G. Marsh, *Man and Nature* (New York, 1865), 56–74. See also M. Hall, "The Native, Naturalized, and Exotic," *Landscape Research* 28 (2003), 5–9.

over long periods and grown entangled, self-sustaining. Crosby considered that by 1400 Europe's plants and animals, including humans, were a formidable coevolved unit, the components of which mutually reinforced each other, giving them competitive advantages when they left Europe, and especially in the Americas.[11]

Perhaps the best example (and definitely the most beautifully rendered) of the botanical explosions set off unknowingly by British imperial agents comes from the south Pacific. In his marvelous observation of the changing landscape in northeastern New Zealand during the decades around 1900, Guthrie-Smith described the relentless encroachment of weeds introduced from Britain, as well as the adventures of his flock of sheep who favored them as food. In his memorable phrase, "the proverbial sun that never sets on" the imperial flag also "never sets on the chickweed, groundsel, dandelion, and veronicas that grow in every English garden and on every British garden-path" across the world.[12] He chronicled meticulously how sacks of grain, cattle hooves, sheep hair, the intestines of several vertebrates, wildfire, the gardens of intrepid Christian missionaries, pig snouts, people's clothes, floods, shepherds' packed lunches, and other unwitting participants in a grand movement of weed dissemination, conveyed the seeds of numerous European weeds across the New Zealand landscape.[13] His account would have seemed familiar to the seventeenth-century New England Indians who called the meadow weed plantain (*Plantago maior*) "Englishman's foot" in recognition of its intimate association with the settlement and agricultural successes of British colonists.[14] The British empire was one of weeds as much as of scientific agriculture, resource extraction, and transcontinental naval connection. In the 1940s, when Elton began to be alarmed by and to study his "explosions," it had been so for a long time.

Beyond the reasons of state, the great fomenter of weed dissemination in empires was trade. Premodern empires (like their modern successors) tended to forge enlarged commercial networks, systems of trade within

---

[11] B. Tobin, *Colonizing Nature* (Philadelphia, 2005), 9–10; P. Anker, *Imperial Ecologies* (Cambridge, MA, 2001), 1–3; J. Frawley and I. McCalman, "Invasion Ecologies: The Nature/Culture Challenge," in *Rethinking Invasion Ecologies from the Environmental Humanities*, ed. J. Frawley and I. McCalman (Abingdon, 2014), 4–5. A. Crosby, "Ecological Imperialism," *Texas Quarterly* 21 (1978), 117 defined Europe's "portmanteau biota" as "often mutually supportive plants, animals, and microlife which in its entirety can be accurately described as aggressive and opportunistic, an ecosystem simplified by ocean crossings and honed by thousands of years of competition in the unique environment created by the Old World Neolithic Revolution."

[12] H. Guthrie-Smith, *Tutira: The Story of a New Zealand Sheep Station* (Seattle, 1999), 236. For lists of the invaders keyed to the time of their invasion, see 242–5.

[13] Ibid., 236–94.   [14] W. Cronon, *Changes in the Land* (New Haven, 1983), 143.

which metropolis and peripheries exchanged goods, usually to the greater benefit of the hegemon.[15] In these bigger, more-than-regional markets, unwanted plants circulated more readily, for just as markets are epidemiological communities, they are also botanical communities, and a more cosmopolitan flora is one inevitable outcome of a more interconnected economic system. Inevitably, the best evidence for the impact of market integration on phytosociology is fairly recent. A nice example of how an increasingly integrated imperial market facilitated the dissemination of weeds comes from the industrializing United States.[16] In the nineteenth century the commercial seed trade permeated American markets with new species and new cultivars, and also new weeds able to insinuate themselves into the packages of cuttings, bulbs, and seeds that traveled by mail to remote destinations.[17]

But the nascent American market for domesticated plant seeds was not alone in driving weeds' success. Other kinds of markets were equally effective. Quite accurately Guthrie-Smith identified Napier, the provincial port and main market town of the Tutira area, "as the main centre of weed liberation."[18] At roughly the same time as farmers spread into north America numerous new unwanted plants by buying desired ones, and Guthrie-Smith carefully tabulated the movements of weeds in northwestern New Zealand, the importation of raw wool from Australia and other corners of the British empire to Tweedside, the finished cloth from which was highly prized, introduced hundreds of species of alien plants to northern Britain, even quite far from the Tweed river. For the wool waste called grey shoddy was a highly regarded soil fertilizer among British gardeners, and despite the brutal treatment of the fibers in the course of cloth production, it contained viable seeds of plants that had attached themselves to sheep in pastures thousands of kilometers away.[19] While enriching their flower beds and onion rows, gardeners were also providing new, promising refuges to tough foreign seeds and weeds.

Deeper in the past it is more difficult to discern evidence of the expansion of weed flora that accompanied the formation of imperial networks and their "disturbance corridors." But it is not impossible. The vast and dense connectivity of the Umayyad and Abbasid caliphates had demonstrable effects on the dissemination of plants, particularly from the tenth

[15] Kirchberger, "Introduction," 3–6 suggests network as a better model of imperial trade relations as it allows agency to more actors.
[16] Burbank and Cooper, *Empires*, 6 consider the nineteenth-century USA a territorial empire.
[17] R. Mack, "The Commercial Seed Trade: An Early Dispenser of Weeds in the United States," *Economic Botany* 55 (2001), 257–73. See also Guthrie-Smith, *Tutira*, 268.
[18] Guthrie-Smith, *Tutira*, 280.   [19] Salisbury, *Weeds and Aliens*, 138–9.

century onward. The caliphs in effect brought botanically distinct zones into contact, in a united commonwealth. They facilitated the westward migration of numerous Indian and Persian plants. The most famous among them are the citrus fruits, sugar cane, spinach, and rice that were being grown in the western Mediterranean by the thirteenth century, though an argument could be advanced for clover being the most important, since this potent nitrogen fixer restored the chemical balance to fields exhausted by grain cultivation. But we should not doubt that numerous obligate weeds accompanied the respectable immigrants of Arab agronomy, adapted to their specialized cultivations, or that opportunistic native weeds of the Mediterranean also honed their strategies to the new conditions, often irrigated, that the new crops entailed.[20] Thistles, for example, had become so ubiquitous in the Islamic Mediterranean by 1000 that weeders gave up, domesticated them, and grew them as a crop called cardoon.[21]

Earlier still, the first and last unification of the Mediterranean, and the empire's integration of several regions contiguous to the Romans' Very Own Sea (Mare Nostrum), produced still more premodern botanical upheavals and big breaks for weeds. Fritz Heichelheim's *Ancient Economic History*, first published in 1938, already hypothesized that the consequences of empire for ancient Italy included a vast uncontrolled influx of foreign plants, a vegetable counterinvasion that was not designed and almost wholly uncontrolled by the Roman hegemon.[22] Heichelheim's alarmed tone in describing this botanical counterthrust against Rome's legions was unwarranted, for most colonial powers generally are able to export their own systems of production and expectations, and end up bringing home far fewer weeds than they spread among their colonies along with the imperial agronomic order: this was certainly the case for the modern British and early modern Spanish empires, for instance.[23]

In fact, an enduring puzzle in imperial botanical history is the imbalance that tends to arise between the metropole's plants and weeds, usually

---

[20] A. Watson, *Agricultural Innovation in the Early Islamic World* (Cambridge, 2008). See also P. Squatriti, "Of Seeds, Seasons, and Seas," *Journal of Economic History* 74 (2014), 1205–20; T. Kjaergaard, "A Plant that Changed the World," *Landscape Research* 28 (2003), 43 (on clover, whose point of origin is not certain); and (on irrigation and weeds) Zimdahl, *Fundamentals*, 119.

[21] G. Sonnante et al., "The Domestication of Artichoke and Cardoon," *Annals of Botany* 100 (2007), 1097. It is still possible that cultivated cardoons were a Roman invention.

[22] F. Heichelheim, *Wirtschaftsgeschichte des Altertums* 1 (Leiden, 1938), 597–8, 742–3. See also W. Hondelmann, *Die Kulturpflanzen der griechisch-römischen Welt* (Berlin, 2002), 9.

[23] Salisbury, *Weeds and Aliens*, 86–8.

quite successful in the imperial peripheries, and the generally less assertive vegetation of the colonized regions.[24] Darwin himself liked to joke
about how Old World plants had thoroughly outcompeted New World
ones, and made themselves at home throughout the Americas, while few
American plants established themselves in Europe.[25] The transfer of so
many Mediterranean weeds to the Habsburg transatlantic colonies was an
important component to Crosby's "Columbian Exchange," and a partial
explanation for the European humans' triumph on the western coast of
the Atlantic Ocean.[26] In this early modern case the wanted and the
unwanted plants, combined, became imperial agents, enablers of the
human colonization that took place at the same time.[27] The apparent
botanical lopsidedness to the Columbian Exchange remains something of
a mystery, and may depend most of all on the Eurocentric assumptions
historians have made, yet there are no simple, singular explanations for
it.[28] Weed scientists note several preconditions that heighten a locale's
vulnerability to "alien" plants. Among them, the absence in the new
habitat of specialized pests and predators of the immigrant plants, the
less crowded and competitive ecosystems of the Americas, and their
shorter history of human land use, must have had an impact. But the far
greater success of European weeds outside Europe than other weeds
within western Eurasia is certainly related to the fact that, as William
Cronon put it lapidarily, "economic and ecological imperialisms reinforced each other."[29]

There is no evidence that the rulers of the most famous European
empire of all, the Roman one, had any inkling of how political, cultural,
economic, and social supremacy shaped the flows of plants within imperial territories, nor that they were aware of the environmental conditions
that eased the life of foreign vegetation in previously sheltered areas. Yet it
appears that Roman thinkers did not worry much about biological "invasions," or specifically about botanical "explosions," though these

[24] Bennett, "A Global History," 228–34.
[25] W. Beinert and K. Middleton, "Plant Transfers in Historical Perspective," *Environment and History* 10 (2004), 6. Bennett, "A Global History," 227 points out that after centuries of exporting them, around 1850 Europe became a net importer of exotic species.
[26] Crosby, *The Columbian Exchange*, 150, 158.
[27] J. McNeill, "Europe's Place in the Global History of Biological Exchange," *Landscape Research* 28 (2003), 33 stresses how exceptional was this case.
[28] Reflecting contemporary academic sympathies, recent work emphasizes the impact and agency of colonial plants in Europe: see, for example, M. Norton, *Sacred Gifts, Profane Pleasures* (Ithaca, 2008); E. Test, *Sacred Seeds* (Lincoln, NE, 2019).
[29] Simberloff, *Invasive Species*, 29–33. Cronon, *Changes in the Land*, 162. Also A. Ricciardi et al., "Invasion Science," *Trends in Ecology and Evolution* 32.11 (2017), 809 acknowl-
edged "socioeconomic conditions govern the susceptibility of a country to invasion and its potential as a source region."

certainly took place in the territories governed by Rome, and perhaps in the waters of the Mediterranean as well.[30] In this the Roman writers on vegetable matters followed Aristotle and Hellenistic theorists, for whom human-induced changes to the landscape and flora of their Mediterranean worlds were legitimate and beneficial. Indeed, they proved the ingenuity and power of the men (always men) who set them off, as the importation to the Mediterranean of cherries by Lucullus did. Successful botanical introductions reflected the introducer's subtle understanding of plant and place, an intrinsic compatibility that others had until then missed.

Though classical Latin literature has its fair share of hostile asides against "foreign" innovations, in the case of botanical introductions from afar writers like Varro, Pliny, and Columella seem not to have been worried, and to have cheerfully accepted into their backyard landscapes a wide array of plants unknown to their ancestors. Biological invasions were not feared as much as military ones also because botanists expected the local, familiar conditions to mollify the exotic species, which would adapt and thereby improve themselves, as well as the place where they grew. This expectation that plants could change their nature somewhat, with or without human blandishments, suggests that in Roman literate culture some instability in the essence or identity of vegetation was normal and even desirable, especially if it improved the land's agricultural productivity.[31]

For the achievement of disseminating previously unknown plants in Roman landscapes was celebrated especially if it somehow generated profits. In imperial Rome respect for wealth-creating introductions overcame any suspicion of "un-Roman" vegetation, even when the plant in question could be deemed luxurious and a threat to Roman virtue. Especially after Augustus's reign, it seems, any link between eastern Mediterranean despotism and manipulation of natural vegetation weakened, though good emperors should not soil their own hands with tasks like transplantation. But, more than the absence of strong ideas of

---

[30] P. Squatriti, "The Vegetative Mediterranean," in *A Companion to Mediterranean History*, ed. P. Horden and S. Kinoshita (Chichester, 2014), 32–6; B. Galil et al., "Mare Nostrum, Mare Quod Invaditur: The History of Bioinvasion in the Mediterranean Sea," in *Histories of Bioinvasion in the Mediterranean*, ed. A. Queiroz and S. Pooley (Cham, 2018), 21–49.

[31] J. Secord, "Overcoming Environmental Determinism. Introduced Species, Hybrid Plants and Animals, and Transformed Lands in the Hellenistic and Roman Worlds," in *The Routledge Handbook of Identity and the Environment in the Classical and Medieval Worlds*, ed. R. Futo Kennedy and M. Jones-Lewis (London, 2016), 210–20. Theophrastus, *Enquiry into Plants*, ed. A. Hort, 2 vols. (Cambridge, MA, 1916–26), v. 2, 8.8, 190 early on observed that "foreign" seeds take about three years to change into native types.

vegetational indigeneity, it was the Romans' admiration for the skill and know-how of those who refashioned the landscape and increased upon nature's productivity that determined an open attitude to biological invasions and the dissemination of plants far from their original ecological niches.[32]

By and large, it seems, the easy-going Romans were right, or at least less wrong than the panicked botanists and weed scientists of the twentieth century, who observed the mounting success of cosmopolitan weeds with dismay. One contemporary response has been increasingly nativist botanies, which ultimately have influenced American and European legislation, with their Weed Acts and Invasive Species Lists, and highway medians populated by "native" plants.[33] Instead the more relaxed attitude of Rome to the appearance of new species of plant in imperial landscapes may have better ecological foundations. For despite the early successes of most "exotic" volunteers after their arrival in new areas, exceedingly few foreign weeds manage to establish themselves as more than marginal presences in the long run. Without repeated re-introductions (which, of course, empires are good at providing), and without the support of the "portmanteau biota" with which they have coevolved at home, the vast majority of volunteer transplants fail within decades of their initial appearance in new lands.[34] It usually takes a great deal of human care to induce plants to make new homes for themselves in new ecological settings. And though ecological matters are always very complex, based on many layers of interdependence, and therefore hard to evaluate fully, it is also unclear that the dissemination of those weeds that do make themselves at home abroad is environmentally destructive, in the sense of reducing biodiversity (and through biodiversity, ecological resilience).[35] Perhaps the wisest imperialists of all were those who did not condemn the botanical mixtures their empires brought about.

[32] Secord, "Overcoming Environmental Determinism," 212–23; L. Totelin, "Botanizing Rulers and their Herbal Subjects," *Phoenix* 66 (2012), 131–40; E. Pollard, "Pliny's 'Natural History' and the Favian Templum Pacis," *Journal of World History* 20 (2009), 320–9. See C. Goodson, *Cultivating the City in Early Medieval Italy* (Cambridge, 2021), 157–9 on the Roman gardening ethos and the virtue of plant manipulation.

[33] M. Davis et al., "Don't Judge Species on Their Origins," *Nature* 474 (June 9, 2011), 153–4; Zimdahl, *Fundamentals*, 193; Mabey, *Weeds*, 122.

[34] E. Le Floc'h, "Invasive Plants of the Mediterranean Basin," in *Biogeography of Mediterranean Invasions*, ed. R. Groves and F. di Castro (Cambridge, 1991), 74–5 gives a nice example from Montpellier, 1686–1950. See Crosby, *Ecological Imperialism*, 89.

[35] E. Weber, *Invasive Plant Species of the World* (Wallingford, 2017), xi, omits twenty species (from the first edition's 450) because evidence of their "negative impacts is rather scarce." See also P. Hulme et al., "Evidence of Bias and Error in Understanding Plant Invasion Impact," *Trends in Ecology and Evolution* 28.4 (2013), 213. Resilience: L. Gunderson et al., "The Evolution of an Idea," in *Foundations of Ecological Resilience*, ed. L. Gunderson et al. (Washington, 2012), 435–40.

Weeds in the Carolingian Empire

A recent reassessment of the process by which humans came to prefer farming to other ways of making a living, namely of what used to be called the "Neolithic Revolution," has stressed the gradualness of the transition from hunting and gathering to sowing and plowing.[36] The fact that people took their time to become agriculturalists and long engaged in occasional farming only, mixing it in with more mobile ways of making a living, suggests that tilling the soil was far from an obvious choice, an ineluctable great leap forward in human evolution or economics. On the contrary, it seems that five thousand years ago conditions had to be pretty dire before humans gave up on their old flexible, often migratory methods of finding things to eat and places to take shelter. An unusual conjuncture of climatic, demographic, and other factors drove people to gather in communities to sow seeds on the same soil, year after year, and to live alongside the resulting fixed fields. Among the other factors, state formation was decisive. Scott argues that fixed-field, arable farming and "grain states" necessarily go together, and that the combination was not in earliest history, and never has been since, advantageous to most of humanity.

Among the disadvantages of specialized agriculture as it came, slowly, to be practiced in western Asia between 9500 and 5000 BC, was that it deskilled versatile hunter-gatherers until all they knew how to do was cultivate grain. Furthermore, this cultivation was laborious, much harder on human bodies than hunting and gathering and part-time farming seems to have been. Plowing, especially, represented a big increment in people's workload. Weeding was not far behind, but it was not as big a novelty, since prehistoric people had weeded their temporary fields and even stands of wild grasses whose seeds they intended to eat. But as Scott put it, sedentary communities farming the same fields created a "permanent feedlot" for parasites of different kinds, animal, microbial, and vegetable, all commensals of farmers. The result was poorer health, more malnutrition, and shorter human lifespans, as well as proliferating obligate weeds finely attuned to the vagaries of human manipulations of the soil. The result was also more social stratification and stronger central government.[37]

The reason why people put up with the new ways is not perfectly pellucid, but the "grain states" and the elites that ran them after about

[36] J. Scott, *Against the Grain* (New Haven, 2017), 12, 71, 96–7.
[37] Ibid., xiii, 45–55, 64–6, 71–4, 92–5, 107–9. Feedlot: 110, where Scott notes that "parasite" derives from the Greek for "beside the grain," and suggests Neolithic farmers were parasites too.

3500 BC were certainly involved. Their choice of crops, and resulting systems of cultivation and labor allocation, seem to have prevailed. The grains of choice were plants whose domestication created very visible seeds that would ripen at the same time, could be separated from their ear relatively smoothly, and resisted deterioration over the medium term. "Grain states" depended on regular harvests of these eminently quantifiable, taxable, and storable sorts of grain. Grains like barley or emmer wheat were vastly superior, from the point of view of a "grain state," to legumes (maturation of which is extremely uneven and spread out over the season), or tubers (hidden underground and thus of uncertain ripeness or quantity), or fruits (whose preservability is poor), or nuts (hard for humans to digest if eaten as a staple, with the noble exception of chestnuts, which, however, tend not to grow in the kinds of places agriculturalists and "grain states" like to live in).[38]

Despite the inevitable plagues that living in sedentary settlements and working the same restricted area of soil engendered, grain agriculture produced fairly reliable surpluses that sustained governments. But Scott also duly noted that the end of effective, large-scale government (for example, that of the Roman empire) set agriculturalists free to try their hand at less specialized living styles. A pattern of boom and bust in the formation of "grain states" and their dissolution meant that until relatively recently growing grain alone was not the normal human strategy, and it only prevailed when a burgeoning "grain state" was at the peak of its power and able to demand taxes and tribute in the most measurable, transportable, and preservable form, in other words when governments and elites could treat grain as a commodity.[39]

Scott's scheme has considerable applicability to early medieval history. If the Roman empire was just another (particularly successful) "grain state," then its decline and fall must have set off an array of improvements in the standard of living of the cultivators who happen to have survived the state's collapse and the reduction in its extraction of their surplus. One consequence should have been an increasingly flexible, more varied style of land use, with less focus on growing grains in fixed fields, and more exploitation of the uncultivated margin, of swamps, woodlands, bracken, and steppe landscapes. This more "natural" silvo-pastoral strategy might well have produced smaller surpluses, but it also produced more reliable returns on the labor people invested in the land, and greater resilience.[40]

---

[38] Ibid., 22, 113, 120–32.

[39] Ibid., 14–15, 184–6, 202–4, 209–13, and (in praise of dark ages) 213–19.

[40] Among several reconstructions that lean in this direction, see P. Squatriti, "Barbarizing the *Belpaese*," in *A Companion to Ostrogothic Italy*, ed. J. Arnold et al. (Leiden, 2016), 390–421.

Scott associated the post-"grain state" landscapes with barbarians. At the end of empire, as is well known, barbarians swarm, uninterested in fixed-field farming and the spoils of sedentarism. Curiously, to Scott, barbarians are just like weeds, opportunistic exploiters of the monomaniacal fascination for grain-growing that "grain states" inculcate in their subjects.[41] Yet in his account, weeds flourish when "grain states" do and barbarians when "grain states" don't, so whatever metaphorical similarity exists in their dependence on the choices and strategies of agriculturalists, weeds and barbarians have different historical settings. Weeds do well when empires wax, not when they decline and fall.

The Carolingian empire was the first barbarian empire in Europe's Middle Ages. It was also a kind of "grain state," encouraging (through its great monasteries especially) the "cerealization" of the empire's territories, or more growing of wheat, rye, and oats, and the regional circulation of grain surpluses from fields to various places of consumption. Therefore, the Carolingian empire was also a sponsor of weeds, of the obligate companions of the grains European peasants living under Carolingian authority increasingly sowed over the great estates of rulers, aristocrats, and ecclesiasts. Almost certainly Carolingian imperial hegemony was not as effective in propagating the best-adapted undesirable species of plant uniformly across its territory as had been the Roman empire, and definitely it lasted less long and covered less land. Yet the Carolingian empire was an aspirational "grain state" that launched "the caging of the peasantry" in Europe, with increases in peasants' agriculturalism, subjection to lords, and workload.[42] After the barbarian interlude of the sixth, seventh, and eighth centuries, when peasants were for the most part not taxed in grain by Rome's successor states, the Carolingian empire was more than a haphazard amalgamation of the barbarian polities of the Lombards, Bavarians, Aquitainians, and Saxons; it was a quite competent organizer of landscapes and their inhabitants, even if its organization was idiosyncratic and less centralized than that of other empires, and in consequence it, too, was an empire of weeds and of more attentive weeding.

For the political, social, and economic ferment of the eighth and ninth centuries in northwestern Europe, and the enhanced movement of people and things that the "practice of empire" stimulated, did establish novel conditions in several regions.[43] Particularly in the new agricultural

---

[41] Scott, *Against the Grain*, 221 ("weeds in the cultivated field are to domesticated crops as barbarians are to civilized life"), 223–9, 248–56.

[42] "Caging" is C. Wickham's metaphor for what happened to European agriculturalists in 800–1000: *The Inheritance of Rome* (London, 2009), 529–50.

[43] J. Davis, *Charlemagne's Practice of Empire* (Cambridge, 2015).

patterns of the ninth century, weeds found spaces into which to insinuate themselves, and these will receive the bulk of our attention in what follows; but the transfer of surplus produce from estates to emporia, the wider travels of the rulers' *missi*, or of high-ranking clergymen and Frankish aristocrats (with accompanying entourages), the tramping of armies and their supply trains, the surprisingly ubiquitous practice of rural migration, the forced population transfers (such as of Saxons into the Rhineland in 805), and the transportation of Rhenish quernstones or Roman Forumware pots far from their places of production also built useful "disturbance corridors" in Carolingian Europe.[44] Some weeds adapted to so much new-found mobility and flourished, while others languished.

Probably more than increased movement of people and things associated with running an imperial polity, it was the dynamism of the European agrarian economy in the eighth and especially the ninth century that created the biggest opportunities for weeds in Carolingian times: in this the Frankish empire differed somewhat from its earlier and later peers.[45] The Carolingian period saw conspicuous changes in Frankish agroecosystems, with inevitable repercussions for weed populations. The intensification of agricultural production, the expansion in arable grain cultivation, and, in at least a few regions, of rural settlement all had effects on both volunteer plants and Carolingian cultivars.[46]

Some general, necessarily tentative considerations will help to contextualize how shifts in farming practice during the Carolingian centuries affected weeds and were affected by them. Almost certainly the crop fields of Carolingian Europe, like most premodern fields, were far weedier than the fields of contemporary agribusiness, and possibly more than nineteenth-century American or European ones too, which tended to be sown in a manner that reduced weeds' spread (see below on broadcast

---

[44] Internal trade: O. Bruand, *Voyageurs et merchandises aux temps des carolingiens* (Brussels, 2002). Movement: M. Gravel, *Distances, rencontres, communications: réaliser l'empire sous Charlemagne et Louis le Pieux* (Turnhout, 2012), esp. 46–51, 71–92. Migration: J. Devroey, *La nature et le roi* (Paris, 2019), 351–8. Deportations: J. Nelson, *King and Emperor* (Berkeley, 2019), 405–7.

[45] Good synthesis in J. Devroey, *Économie rurale et société dans l'Europe franque (VIe–IXe siècles)* (Paris, 2003), 112–29. See also J. Quirós Castillo, "Agrarian Archaeology in Early Medieval Europe," *Quaternary International* 346 (2014), 1–6.

[46] Farming styles and weed populations: G. Jones et al., "Crops and Weeds," *Journal of Archaeological Science* 37 (2010), 70–7; C. Brun, "Biodiversity Changes in Highly Anthropogenic Environments (Cultivated and Ruderal) since the Neolithic in Eastern France," *The Holocene* 19.6 (2009), 867–8. Rural settlement in Berry and Saxony: N. Poirier, "La dynamique du peuplement et des espaces agraires médiévaux en Berry," *Archéologie médiévale* 40 (2010), 21–3; H. Nitz, "Feudal Woodland Colonization as a Strategy in the Carolingian Empire in the Conquest of Saxony," in *Villages, Fields, and Frontiers*, ed. B. Roberts and R. Glascock (Oxford, 1983), 171–84.

and drill sowing). Chemical fertilizers, cheap herbicides, the mechanization of seed-cleaning, and new systems of rotation have conspired against the ebullient society of weeds that had coevolved with European field crops in the *ancien régime*, limiting their numbers and variety.[47] And though higher weed populations likely prevailed in early medieval than in today's pastures as well, they probably did not in the more meticulous cultivations of gardens. For early medieval people lavished attention and work on gardens, either because of their privileged fiscal status or (in the case of monasteries) because manicuring them was thought to be a spiritual exercise, as good for the weeder as for the garden itself.[48] In many cultures, a "clean" field or garden is associated with positive outcomes and garners social capital to its tenders, even when the neatness is agronomically unnecessary or irrational.[49]

In addition to these general considerations, it matters to the history of weeds that many Carolingian farmers were not motivated by calculations of yield, instead measuring productivity in terms of labor inputs in relation to household needs; thus, as discussed in more detail in Chapter 3, they could tolerate some weeds in some seasons, because the crops lost thereby were less significant than the work that eliminating them would require.[50] Nevertheless, as in modern agribusiness, on Frankish farms and in Frankish gardens the presence of certain plants was resisted because they were deemed detrimental to the growth of desired vegetation. Despite all the differences across Frankish Europe in types and styles of cultivation, and in regional levels of weediness, all weeds gobbled up labor and limited crop growth.

Among the changes in agrarian practice that various specialists have reconstructed, particularly in the northwestern European Carolingian heartlands, the ninth-century intensification of land exploitation to increase surplus stands out. This intensification often seems to have been associated with bipartite estate management, or with the type of farm Anglophone scholars call manors. And it appears that the people

---

[47] Brun, "Biodiversity Changes," 867–8. Archaeophytes (see the introduction above), specialized by a longer coevolution with humans and thus dependent on the old style of cultivation, have suffered the biggest reductions.

[48] M. Montanari, *L'alimentazione contadina nell'alto medioevo* (Naples, 1979), 309–71; *The Rule of St. Benedict* 66, 48 insists both that monasteries should have gardens and that monks must labor with their hands. M. Goullet, "L'imaginaire du jardin monastique," *Pris-Ma* 26 (2010), 47–8 on spiritual gardening. Goodson, *Cultivating the City* is a guide to postclassical gardening.

[49] P. Halstead, *Two Oxen Ahead* (Chichester, 2014), 336, citing Mediterranean and Trobriand islander superstitions.

[50] Yields: J. Devroey, "La politique annonaire carolingienne comme question économique, religieuse, et morale," in *Settimane del CISAM* 63 (Spoleto, 2016), 303–5. Household production: Devroey, *Économie rurale*, 117.

who owned manors sought to organize land use in such a way that less lay fallow at any given moment than had been the case with two-field rotations, without, however, exhausting the soil. The technique involved in this more intensive exploitation of the same amount of land required rotating three types of cultivation across the manor's arable soil. In those places where it is attested, Carolingian enthusiasm for three-field rotations and its result, more productive cerealiculture, created new conditions for weeds.[51]

All rotations "create" weeds because they leave behind in harvested fields crop seeds of which the germination the following year produces unwanted plants. More frequent rotations create more weeds in this way. On top of this, on Carolingian farms for which accounting documents (polyptychs) survive, most of which seem to be bipartite estates, less familiar cereals were grown in the new rotations.[52] The greater dissemination of winter-sown rye and spring-sown oats helped obligate weeds that are associated with those crops to thrive, notably members of the Secalieta group and (though their remains are hard to distinguish from cultivated oats) wild oats (*Avena fatua*).[53] Where the oats were grown for animals, not humans, to consume, no weeding occurred, giving excellent opportunities for wild oats and, in northwestern Francia, also to rye brome (*Bromus secalinus*) and to a weed usually found in rye fields, cornflower (*Centaurea cyanus*).[54] Even grain fields sown to feed people, if overrun by such specialist weeds, might have

---

[51] Three-field rotation: A. Verhulst, *The Carolingian Economy* (Cambridge, 2002), 60–4; Y. Morimoto, "L'assolement triennial au haut Moyen Âge," in *Économie rurale et économie urbaine au Moyen Âge*, ed. J. Devroey and Y. Morimoto (Ghent, 1994), 91–125 and, more skeptically on its prevalence, J. Devroey and A. Nissen, "Early Middle Ages, 500–1000," in *Struggling with the Environment*, ed. E. Thoen and T. Soens (Turnhout, 2015), 43–4.

[52] Rotations and weeds: M. Ruas, "La parole des grains," in *Plantes exploitées, plantes cultivées*, ed. A. Durand (Aix, 2007), 159; Halstead, *Two Oxen*, 56, 68, 200–7. On rye and oats, G. Comet, "Les céréales du bas-empire au Moyen Âge," in *The Making Feudal Agricultures?*, ed. M. Barceló and F. Sigaut (Leiden, 2004), 147–9, 162–4.

[53] Secalieta (also in inauspicious landscapes): D. Etienne et al., "Searching for Ancient Forests," *The Holocene* 23.5 (2013), 685; C. Bakels, "Crops Produced in the Southern Netherlands and Northern France during the Early Medieval Period," *Vegetation History and Archaeobotany* 14 (2005), 395–7; M. Ruas, "Alimentation végétale, pratiques agricoles et environnement du VIIe au Xe siècle," in *Un village au temps de Charlemagne* (Paris, 1988), 209–10. Wild oats: Salisbury, *Weeds and Aliens* 154–5; A. Kreuz, "Frühgermanische Landwirtschaft und Ernährung," in *Germanen*, ed. G. Uelsberg and M. Wemhoff (Berlin, 2020), 126; U. Willerding, *Zur Geschichte der Unkräuter Mitteleuropas* (Neumünster, 1986), 52–4; K. Knörzer, *Geschichte der synanthropen Flora im Niederrheingebiet* (Mainz, 2007), 454. How crop variety influences weed diversity: C. Bakels, "Archaeobotanical Investigations in the Aisne Valley, Northern France, from the Neolithic to the Early Middle Ages," *Vegetation History and Archaeobotany* 8 (1999), 76.

[54] F. Sigaut, "L'evolution des techniques," in *The Making*, ed. Barceló and Sigaut, 23. Early medieval oat cultivation in the Frankish northwest, and brome, esp. at

their crops repurposed as fodder.[55] Indeed, on bipartite estates, the fallow land integral to rotations had to be carefuly tended, sometimes tilled, and its complex plant associations managed (or weeded) for the benefit of cattle. The less laborious "long fallows" of early modern times are attested only in a document from Nanteuil-la-Forêt dating to 900, and the various kinds of temporary or shifting cultivation that endured in Carolingian Francia also redoubled the opportunities for weeds and the obligations of weeders.[56] Certainly many details of eighth- and ninth-century manorial botany remain obscure, since few excavations of sites of production and of crop processing have been carried out (as opposed to those of storage sites). But there is no doubt that the more productive farming of the Carolingian period entailed much added labor, including more weeding and winnowing.

Three-field rotation also required more fences, to keep animals out of sown fields during the crops' vegetative cycle and restrict them to the fallow ones. Wandalbert of Prüm thought fences would be built in March and April, and reinforced with ditches in the latter month; ruderal weeds will have found more refuge along these impediments that kept hoes and plows away.[57] While we might imagine cattle and goats tethered to the fences, acting as living lawn mowers by clearing the spontaneous vegetation the growth of which this additional fencing facilitated, even their munching cannot have eliminated the weeds altogether. Rather, in the diverse regions stretched across Carolingian Europe where three-field rotations and small-scale animal husbandry went together, fences and ruminants selected those species of weeds that could flourish under the novel evolutionary pressures, limited by the prevailing climatic and geological conditions.

Technology was another important aspect of the early medieval intensification of production and consumption associated with the Carolingian

Vieux-les-Gaudines (south of Caen): M. Ruas et al., "Les avoines dans les productions agro-pastorales du nord-ouest de la France," in *Des hommes aux champs*, ed. V. Carpentier and C. Marcigny (Rennes, 2012), 334–5, 346–7, 355–6. *Centaurea*: A. Ferdière et al., *Histoire de l'agriculture en Gaule, 500 av. JC–1000 apr. JC* (Paris, 2006), 185.

[55] Halstead, *Two Oxen*, 192.

[56] Ruas, "La parole," 159–60; F. Sigaut, "Le labour, qu'est-ce que c'est?" in *Nous labourons* (Nantes, 2008), 24–6; Halstead, *Two Oxen*, 200–7; J. Devroey, "Mise en valeur du sol et cycles de culture dans le système domanial (VIIIe–Xe siècle) entre Seine et Rhin," in *Cultures temporaires et féodalité*, ed. R. Viader and C. Rendu (Toulouse, 2014), 33–57.

[57] Wandalbert, "De mensium duodecim," ed. E. Dümmler, *MGH Poetae* 2 (Berlin, 1884), 606–7; J. Henning, "Did the 'Agricultural Revolution' Go East with the Carolingian Conquest?" in *The Baiuvarii and Thuringii*, ed. J. Fries-Knoblauch (Woodbridge, 2014), 337–8. Drainage ditches still serve as reservoirs for weeds because farmers do not weed them: G. Zanin, "Definizione e classificazione delle malerbe," in *Malerbologia*, ed. P. Catizone and G. Zanin (Bologna, 2001), 50.

ascendancy.[58] Several machines gained a new prominence on Carolingian manors, investments or inputs that made sense to the estate lords who pursued expanded production and profits, particularly in the ninth century when the rewards of conquest and plunder were harder to come by.[59] One example is the scythe, which François Sigaut believes to have obtained new prominence in northwestern Europe after about AD 700, and to have spread in parallel to spring-sown oats as fodder for horses in Carolingian times.[60] In Roman Gaul the introduction of bigger iron scythes virtually conjured up a new vegetable formation, the meadow, and had a deep effect on vegetable sociology by selecting the kinds of plant that could endure repeated cuts at the height of the growing season while still offering farmers adequate fodder for their beasts.[61] The Carolingian dissemination of such technologies will have had parallel effects on the meadow community's desirable vegetation, but also of course on the undesirable one: weeds that clung to the ground and did not get in the way of the scythe had an advantage over tall ones, and over weeds the scythers sought to eliminate because they rendered the hay unpalatable to animals.

Though the "heavy plow" is not today considered to have had a history quite as linear or as revolutionary as Lynn White Jr. imagined, relevant innovations in plowing equipment certainly took place during the early Middle Ages, particularly in northwestern Europe.[62] In the ninth century, written records suggest, deep-digging iron plowshares and coulters cut open, mixed up, aerated, and drained more soil than hitherto, and the Frankish heartland in the old kingdoms of Neustria and Austrasia, and its manors, were at the forefront of these changes in the land. Indeed, the enormous (68 cm long) high-quality seventh-century steel coulter recently unearthed at Lyminge in Kent, which weighed more than five

[58] Sigaut, "L'evolution des techniques," 23–9.

[59] T. Reuter, "Plunder and Tribute in the Carolingian Empire," *Transactions of the Royal Historical Society* 35 (1985), 75–94, with comments by Nelson, *King and Emperor*, 461–2.

[60] F. Sigaut, "Crops and Agricultural Development in Western Europe," in *Plants and People: Choices and Diversity through Time*, ed. A. Chevalier et al. (Oxford, 2014), 109. See also P. Reigniez, "Histoire et techniques: l'outil agricole dans la periode du haut Moyen Âge," in *The Making*, ed. Barceló and Sigaut, 2004), 57, 91–6.

[61] L. Foxhall et al., "Human Ecology in the Classical Landscape," in *Classical Archaeology*, ed. S. Alcock and R. Osborne (Oxford, 2012), 112.

[62] Postclassical plowing history: A. Verhulst, "The 'Agricultural Revolution' of the Middle Ages Reconsidered," in *Law, Custom, and the Social Fabric in Medieval Europe*, ed. B. S. Bachrach and D. Nicholas (Kalamazoo, 1990), 17–24; J. Henning, "Germanisch-romanisch Agrarkontinuität und -diskontinuität in nordalpinen Kontinentaleuropa," in *Akkulturation*, ed. D. Hägermann et al., (Berlin, 2009), 401–15; G. Forni, "Innovazione e progresso nel mondo romano: il caso dell'agricoltura," in *Innovazione tecnica e progresso economico nel mondo romano*, ed. E. Lo Cascio (Bari, 2006), 145–79.

and a half kilograms, is thought to be a high-status gift to an English ruler from Francia, where such technologies were better established than in the British Isles.[63]

Throughout early medieval Europe soil-stirring machines equipped with such long steel coulters were surely an exception, almost exclusively reserved to large estates and surplus production, yet their mere existence suggests that postclassical plowing was a dynamic area of experimentation and adaptation of technologies. And whatever the details of their introduction and distribution in Carolingian Europe, various forms of "heavy plow" used in more and more fields made a difference to weeds because they transformed soil structure and field ecology. By affecting soil temperatures and composition (longer coulters brought to the surface minerals and other nutrients that shallower plows did not reach), the bigger, heavier plows gave new species of field weeds opportunities they lacked earlier when simple wooden ards scratched barely the top ten centimeters of soil: plants whose seeds were able to remain dormant for longer periods (generally, plants with bigger seeds) did best, like stinking chamomille (*Anthemis cotula*) and wild mustard (*Synapis arvensis*). By crushing roots, rhizomes, stolons, and tubers that had lain hidden from shallower-plowing machines, or by bringing them to the surface where atmospheric agents could finish them off, they also robbed previously dominant weed species of their edge: perennials and biennials were at a disadvantage where heavy plows dug the ground up.[64]

The popularization of the "heavy" plow refashioned the conditions of plant life also because bigger, heavier, deeper-gouging plows rendered cultivation viable in areas where clay soil discouraged farming with smaller and lighter equipment. In England, at roughly the same time as the Carolingian intensification took place, heavy clay soils came under cultivation, presumably thanks to new-style plows. Very promptly, stinking chamomille, a specialist in cultivated clay fields, sprang up in numbers, for the plows created a new landscape to which it was perfectly suited. But the improved drainage of the topsoil that the deeper furrows of Carolingian plows ensured also banished weeds that specialized in damp patches and were adapted to waterlogged soils.[65]

"Heavy" plows required strong traction, best supplied by large oxen and horses. However, to work well these animals required good fodder, a need important enough to alter agricultural strategies. For the strength

[63] G. Thomas et al., "Technology, Ritual, and Anglo-Saxon Agriculture," *Antiquity* 90.351 (2016), 742–58.
[64] Kreuz, "Frühgermanische Landwirtschaft und Ernährung," 132 on how scanty first- to fourth-century plowing gave weeds opportunities.
[65] M. McKerracher, "Bread and Surpluses," *Environmental Archaeology* 21 (2016), 97.

of a plow team determined how thorough was the tillage, which in turn affected how weedy a sown field could become: poorly tilled fields and untilled strips were the redoubt of weeds. Instead, perfectly tilled fields did not require subsequent manual clod-breaking prior to sowing, nor as much weeding after the crop had germinated. On the other hand, the new plowing methods created uneven surfaces that were hard for people to clear of unwanted plants once they had germinated: deep plowing piled up soil on the edge of the furrows, creating a ridge-and-furrow effect. Such ridged fields encouraged manual weed plucking, because the raised soil got in the way of scythes and hoes and slowed down weeding with tools, favoring weeds that were low and hard to handle because they were prickly or slender-stemmed and firm-rooted. Again, the spread of heavier plows shaped phytosociology, and Carolingian-era plowing techniques introduced new conditions for weed seeds and plants, which only some species could exploit.[66]

A further cause of weeds' success was the customary method of crop sowing. Carolingian broadcast sowing meant most field crops did not grow in neat rows, which meant that traversing a crop field after germination was a delicate business. Broadcast sowing, whereby a swinging arm and semi-closed fist distributed the seed, also allowed more unexamined seed on to the field than did drill sowing, in which sowers manipulated individual seeds and could discard suspect ones before placing them in holes "drilled" into the ground, often in tidy rows. The broadcast sower could choose how thickly to sow a field, depending on soil conditions and maybe seed availability, but also on a calculation of how many weeds could be accepted in a given time and place. For this method of sowing could leave more space unoccupied by crop seeds, and thus available for weeds to colonize, or could so cover the tilled soil with seeds that crops smothered competitors once they germinated.[67] The choice was shaped by the size of the farm and the ultimate destination of the crop, whether domestic consumption or market.[68]

---

[66] Tillage style and weeds: M. Jones, "Dormancy and the Plough," in *From Foragers to Farmers*, ed. A. Fairbairn and E. Weiss (Oxford, 2009), 60; Devroey and Nissen, "Early Middle Ages," 35–6; Zimdahl, *Fundamentals*, 264–7; A. Ferrero and P. Casini, "Mezzi meccanici," in *Malerbologia*, ed. Catizone and Zanin, 253; Halstead, *Two Oxen*, 12–17, 44–55. See also G. Hillman, "Phytosociology and Ancient Weed Floras," in *Modeling Ecological Change*, ed. D. Harris and K. Thomas (London, 1991), 28–31, based on observation of moldboard plows' introduction to Syria and Turkey in the 1970s.

[67] Sowing styles: Salisbury, *Weeds and Aliens*, 31, 40, 144; G. Comet, *Le paysan et son outil* (Rome, 1992), 152–4, 167–8; P. Anderson and F. Sigaut, "Reasons for Variability in Harvesting Techniques and Tools," in *Explaining and Exploring Diversity in Agricultural Technology*, ed. A. van Gijn et al. (Oxford, 2014), 86.

[68] Halstead, *Two Oxen*, 11–12, 28–9 on sowers' calculus.

Partly to encourage crops' root and stem growth, limit lodging (the toppling of grain stalks), and improve yields, heavily plowed or not, early medieval fields were by modern standards sparsely sown. This technique left more ground bare, greedily colonized by spontaneous plants, but the resulting fields were easier to move through without treading on the seedlings of the crop.[69] Still, wielding a hoe or other long tool in them required careful calibration of the worker's movements, and interventions had to fall in line with the growth cycles of the crops and of the targeted species of weed, in such a way as to diminish the damage inflicted on the former and maximize that inflicted on the latter. The late Roman agronomist Palladius, whose book on agricultural tasks enjoyed some fortune in Carolingian libraries, suggested a thoughtfully modulated calendar of hoeing to his readers, depending on the type of crop and its maturation rates (which he recognized would not be the same in every place). The tenth-century Byzantine *Geoponika* considered the hoe best against dog-tooth grass (*Cynodon dactylon*) in June, evidently because the weed's warmth-dependent (and thus slow to germinate) growth cycle left it vulnerable in fields of quicker-maturing grain. But the point here is that whether in late ancient Rome, Macedonian Byzantium, or Carolingian Europe, the added power and speed of weeding with a tool did not magically free wielders of it from all constraints. Even the most balanced, lightest, sharpest-edged hoe obliged people to pay attention, bend their backs, stoop, and sweat.[70]

At the end of the cropping cycle Carolingian harvesters faced many of the same constraints all pre-industrial harvesters faced.[71] But where deep plowing took place, sickle-wielding reapers, slowed by the uneven terrain formed by the deeper incisions of heavier plowshares, could notice and avoid more weeds. This attentiveness might save some labor during crop processing and reduce the number of weed seeds that found their way into granaries and silos alongside oat, rye, or wheat seeds, where they might enjoy protection until the next sowing season.[72] But fear of unfavorable weather created urgency, so a harvest team might remove the cut grains

---

[69] Devroey and Nissen, "Early Middle Ages," 52–3.

[70] Hoeing left the weed in the field as "green manure," so was done before the weed set seed. Estimates of premodern sowing density: J. Sadoks, *Crop Protection in Medieval Agriculture* (Leiden, 2013), 131, 134; P. Steen Henriksen, "Rye Cultivation in the Danish Iron Age," *Vegetation History and Archaeobotany* 12 (2003), 179–80. Many excellent observations on hoeing are in J. David, *L'outil* (Turnhout, 1997), 54, 101, 128, 145 and (as on most topics) in Comet, *Le paysan*, 167–70. Palladius, *Opus Agriculturae* 2.9–10, 2.14, 3.24, 4.3, 4.9, 5.1, 10.1. *Geoponika* 3.5, 3.10, tr. A. Dalby (Totnes, 2011), 106, 108. Gregory the Great (*Commentarii in Librum I Regum* 3.31) described hoes and their work subtly.

[71] On the premodern harvest, see the very compelling B. Shaw, *Bringing in the Sheaves* (Toronto, 2013). Also useful is Anderson and Sigaut, "Reasons," 85–92.

[72] Hillman, "Phytosociology," 30.

from the fields without too much fuss or sorting. And meteorology was not the only constraint, for on large estates with large plow teams the need for fodder obliged harvesters to stoop lower to cut the entire stalk off; this naturally affected the weeds, too, giving an advantage to ground-hugging plants able to elude the sickle.[73]

After harvest, farmers had to store crops safely, threshed or unthreshed, for further use. There was some room for innovation even in this timeless activity. In the 800s bigger grain stores appeared in several Carolingian settlements.[74] Though small underground silos continued to be popular, a new design for granaries also gained favor. The larger granaries, often raised, that archaeologists associate with Carolingian-sponsored intensifications and rural reorganizations, offered opportunities to weeds that mimic grain crops and "bank" their seeds in human reserves rather than in the ground, as is the custom of most weeds. Their contents were less scrupulously threshed and winnowed than those of the silos associated with domestic consumption. For such storage chambers served a more tightly integrated economy in which exchanges, even of bulky commodities like grain, played a bigger role, and enabled weeds that imitated well the seeds of stored and transported crops to hide in comfort in the granaries, or to hitch rides and move across space more effectively. The seeds of these weeds could now await re-sowing in safe conditions, or even colonize new terrains if they entered commercial circuits.[75]

Other Carolingian economic patterns also changed the odds of survival for weeds. The removal of arboreal cover appears to have accelerated during the Carolingian heyday, sometimes organized by monastic owners of great estates who left written traces of their endeavors.[76] Deforestation to create pasture or arable opened to light-dependent annual plants landscapes hitherto precluded to them, and if the loggers' intention was to favor some selected edible members of that category, namely crops,

[73] Halstead, *Two Oxen*, 117.
[74] S. Jesset, "Les formes de l'exploitation rurale du IXe au XIe siècle," in *Lumières de l'an mil en Orléanais* (Turnhout, 2004),91; E. Peytremann, *Archéologie de l'habitat rural dans le nord de la France du IVe au XIIe siècle* (Saint-Germain-en-Laye, 2003), 337, 356–7; G. Bianchi and S. Grassi, "Sistemi di stoccaggio nelle campagne italiane (sec. VII–XIII)," in *Horrea, Barns, and Silos: Storage and Incomes in Early Medieval Europe*, ed. A. Vigil-Escalera Guirado et al. (Bilbao, 2013), 85–6, 90–1; H. Zug Tucci, "Le derrate agricole," in *Settimane del CISAM* 37 (1990), 884–902.
[75] Trade and traffic: Bruand, *Voyageurs*; W. van Zeist et al., "Plant Husbandry and Vegetation of Early Medieval Douai," *Vegetation History and Archaeobotany* 3 (1994), 216; P. Crabtree et al., "Environmental Evidence from Early Medieval Antwerp," *Quaternary International* 460 (2017), 120.
[76] C. Grainge, "Assarting and the Dynamics of Rhineland Economies in the Ninth Century," *Agricultural History Review* 54 (2006), 10–13. Still worthwhile is the pioneering H. Nitz, "The Church as Colonist," *Journal of Historical Geography* 9 (1983), 105–26.

inevitably some hangers-on also benefited. The archaeobotanical evidence of this is reviewed more thoroughly in Chapter 2, but for now we should note how in the Eifel hills of eastern Belgium, during the eighth and ninth centuries, alder woodlands were cleared to make way for pastures in which flourished oxeye daisy (*Chrysanthemum leucanthemum*), ragged robin (*Lychnis flos-cuculi*), and brownwort (*Prunella vulgaris*).[77] Meanwhile, the extension of animal raising that accompanied the rise of the Carolingian dynasty in most of Europe required bigger pastures and, in the same areas, inaugurated a glorious period of increases in the populations of certain wild plants in the Poaceae (grasses) family.[78] The best adapted were weeds that could tolerate the harsh living conditions of pasture land, usually by being so brittle that when broken off by tooth or hoof (or plowing) they might regenerate from the remaining fragments, and by being able to germinate quickly and equally quickly produce many seeds that dispersed widely before the next phase in farmers' cultivation strategies redesigned conditions. Any plant that sought to flourish in Carolingian pastures also had to know how to cope with the novel soil chemistry that grazing animals' inadvertent and farmers' more conscious manuring created.[79] Where cattle and sheep raising declined in the ninth and tenth centuries, as in mainland Italy, phytosociological change also took place, though in an opposite direction.[80] Shadier, wooded pig pasture permitted weeds to prevail that were resistant to rutting snouts and tolerant of exposure to less light.

The weeds that found eighth- and ninth-century economic activities most congenial, that adapted best and evolved fastest, were not everywhere the same, of course. But the point here is that a valid generalization can be made, namely that the doings of Carolingian lords and farmers had an impact on the phytosociology of the empire's fields, just as the agricultural strategies of early modern English or Spanish colonists did in the New World, as Arab farmers did in western Eurasia, or Roman veterans did across the Mediterranean basin. Carolingian agropastoral economies

---

[77] C. Herbig and C. Sirocko, "Palaeobotanical Evidence of Agricultural Activities in the Eifel Region during the Holocene," *Vegetation History and Archaeobotany* 22 (2013), 460.

[78] Pastures: Jesset, "Les formes," 91. Poaceae: Herbig and Sirocko, "Palaeobotanical Evidence," 459. Animal husbandry patterns: P. Crabtree, "Agricultural Innovation and Socio-Economic Change in Early Medieval Europe," *World Archaeology* 42.1 (2010), 129–33.

[79] Candidates whose ecological curricula match these requirements include creeping buttercup (*Ranunculus repens*), quackgrass (*Agropyron repens*), and silverweed (*Potentilla anserina*): Hillman, "Phytosociology," 29. On the difference manure made: R. Jones, "Manure and the Medieval Social Order," in *Land and People*, ed. M. Allen et al. (Oxford, 2009), 216–17.

[80] Synthesis of archaeozoological data: F. Salvadori, "The Transition from Late Antiquity to the Early Middle Ages in Italy," *Quaternary International* 499 (2019), 38–9.

formed novel ecosystems in which specific kinds of weeds grew well, while others struggled.

Yet we should not imagine that Carolingian landlords and peasants had all the agency, and weeds quietly and passively adapted to the agricultural conditions of empire. Sometimes weeds struck back and created conditions to which humans had to adjust their strategies for profit maximization or survival. In a thrilling study of tumbleweed in 1930s Montana, Fiege developed the concept of "mobile nature." To Fiege the mechanics of wild plants' seed dispersal in windy steppe conditions remained an ineluctable ecological fact that commercial alfalfa farming, rugged individualism, and private property rights were unequipped to control. Tumbleweeds were a category of wild plant perfectly adjusted to local conditions, able to use the wind to spin large balls of fiber laden with seeds; since these balls were light enough to be blown considerable distances across the relatively open local landscapes, they conferred on tumbleweeds a peculiar mobility, an ability to pop up where they had not been before and to colonize virgin soils. Montanan farmers' increasingly desperate efforts to prevent the windborne spread of weeds whose tough stem structure impeded mowing, and whose vigorous growth deprived the lucerne crop of vital resources, including water, introduced social change. The weeds drove farmers in Montana to pool labor in weed-control cooperatives, to solicit and then welcome state interventions, and to limit the exclusive rights of landowners too lazy or negligent to take care of tumbleweed in their own fields.[81] In other words humble tumbleweeds subverted some of the loftiest social and cultural assumptions of capitalist westerners.

Little of Carolingian Europe appears to have been quite as arid as Dust Bowl Montana, and few of the various species of plant that rely on large, dry, rolling diaspores are native to western Europe.[82] In addition, few early medieval landscapes can have been quite as monotonous as the monocropped alfalfa fields of twentieth-century Montana. However, in some parts of central Europe, more structured forms of landholding became established under Carolingian rule, and throughout the empire property rights over land were strengthened. In Carolingian Europe, what Peytremann has called a "more trenchant assertion of property in land" came along with larger settlements, more definite limits to the built space

---

[81] M. Fiege, "The Weedy West," *Western Historical Quarterly* 36 (2005), 23–47.
[82] In Montana the bugbear was Russian thistle (*Kali tragus*), introduced to the American west in the 1870s in contaminated flaxseed: Fiege, "The Weedy West," 30. Aldo Leopold's essay "Cheat Takes Over," republished in *A Sand County Almanac* (New York, 1949), 154–8, tells a similar story of western pastures overrun by invasive species, particularly *Bromus tectorum*.

of villages (set off from the cultivated space), stricter delimitation of people's living quarters (vs. storage space, for instance), bigger churches, longer use of cemeteries, and greater stability all around.[83] The empire, as we have seen, became increasingly cerealicultural over the course of its life, and the large estates revealed by ninth-century polyptychs seem prevalently given over to wheat, rye, barley, and oats. Moreover, the intensified rotations of Carolingian farming, with attendant increases in fencing, ditches, and other physical impediments to movement, in some areas created conditions not unlike those the Montanan settlers created for tumbleweed.[84]

Weeds as usual darted across the new landscape, even if Carolingian Europe did not resemble 1930s Montana. The eighth- and ninth-century "mobile nature," in the form of creeping stolons or rhizomes or blowing pappi (the featherlike bristles that carry some seeds) may not have been as spectacular as meter-high balls of tumbleweed. But in its utter lack of respect for human conventions, and opportunistic exploitation for its own purposes of the conditions those conventions created on the ground, Carolingian "mobile nature," too, exerted pressure on people. Carolingian peasants, certainly, and maybe also Carolingian landowners, were incited to think of their landscapes as an integrated whole. The mobile weeds reminded everyone of "the shared experience of ecological connections."[85] Farming strategies, theories of ownership, commercial routes, neighborly connections, and weed ecology were interwoven. Fixed boundaries, customary dues, and labor calendars had to consider environmental facts like weeds' seasonal rhythms, their techniques of dispersal, and their irrepressible movement across space. Weeds distilled nature's mobility and thereby destabilized the sedentary assumptions of Carolingian agriculturalists.

Conclusion

Empires cannot help it: they fashion new conditions for vegetation. In their modern and premodern territories crop plants move by design, becoming a trace element of the imperial economic project and its homogenizing power. The diffusion of citrus cultivation (in the early Middle Ages, principally lemons and bitter oranges) from south Asia to Andalusia in the caliphate is only one example. But within imperial space some plants circulate by mistake, without humans intending them to. Several

---

[83] Peytremann, *Archéologie* 356–7: "une affirmation plus nette de la propriété foncière."
[84] Henning, "Did the 'Agricultural Revolution' Go East?", 336–8.
[85] Fiege, "The Weedy West," 25.

of these volunteer travelers are the weeds which have adapted to the field conditions necessary for the growth of popular crops. Others are weeds that flourish on the edges of imperial landscapes, on the borders of fields, along roadways and canals, in the shadow of walls, alongside middens near houses. Each weed is keenly honed to the environmental conditions that the economic activity of imperial people creates. Their propagation is a side effect of the larger free-trade zones and common markets of empire.

In the Carolingian case an increase in economic activity, meaning more intensive and extensive agriculture, also stimulated weeds. But this happened in a peculiarly Carolingian way, affected by the particularities of the Franks' empire. Amidst these, its short duration, and the preceding integration the Romans had brought about over the western portions of Frankish Europe, certainly matter.[86] Another important characteristic of the Carolingian polity was that despite the increased movement of people and goods it facilitated, it did not cause mass migration of peasants who completely reconfigured landscapes, unlike ancient or early modern imperial systems based on "settler colonialism."[87] But probably the most relevant idiosyncrasy of the Carolingian empire in this context was its Lilliputian scale, among empires. This was usefully underlined some years ago by Richard Hodges: however enormous by early medieval European standards, the empire Charlemagne laboriously assembled was miniscule compared to the Habsburg, British, or Ottoman empires of early modern times, or to its contemporary Tang empire in China or the caliphate.[88] In part because of its relatively modest scale, Carolingian Europe was also more geographically homogeneous than most empires, giving weeds fewer chances to prove their mettle and mobility. Its impact on phytosociology was correspondingly slighter.

That, of course, does not mean the impact was inconsequential. Increases in the cultivation of oats, rye, and wheat, discernible in the

---

[86] If Rome's control of the Mediterranean had collapsed with the Gracchi, its impact on the area's vegetation would have been slight: the pace of plant colonizations is slower than that of human ones. See Le Floc'h, "Invasive Plants." For the botanical impoverishment Rome's demise brought to northwestern Europe, see A. Livarda, "Spicing up Life in Northwestern Europe," *Vegetation History and Archaeobotany* 20 (2011), 146–7, 158–9; M. van der Veen et al., "New Food Plants in Roman Britain," *Environmental Archaeology* 13 (2008), 21–4.

[87] Bennett, "A Global History," 228 on "first phase settler colonialism" and its ecological impact before the 1800s. A case of new settlement and colonization: Nitz, "Feudal Woodland Colonization," 171–84.

[88] R. Hodges, *Dark Age Economics* (London, 2012), 117–20. J. Moreland, "The Carolingian Empire," in *Empires*, ed. S. Alcock (Cambridge, 2002), 415–18 nicely locates the Frankish one within broader imperial histories.

pollen and macrofossil records of several eighth- and ninth-century sites, probably reflect the tastes and demand of a new imperial elite. Membership in the Carolingian community, or "ecclesia," was after all a liturgical fact, and participation required distinctive kinds of grain, able to produce very pale and "shiny" hosts.[89] Yet Crosby's "portmanteau biota" do not appear to have been exported from a Frankish core area to the conquered peripheries of Europe, and the hard task of governing, from Aquitaine to Bavaria, from Saxony to Tuscany, was not obviously facilitated by the transfer of a Carolingian agroecological package into those regions. In fact, the new cultivations mostly extended and expanded older shifts and trends in land use, without many signs of large-scale botanical transfer accompanying the diffusion of the distinctive economic patterns of northwestern Europe.

In a sense, failure to replicate the ecological transformations of other empires actually enhances the significance of the Carolingians' looser, smaller hegemony. The Carolingian case underscores how various was the exercise of premodern imperial power. Even if no palaeobotanical evidence for "explosions" of the sort that worried empire-watchers in the twentieth century currently exists for Carolingian Europe, and if much eighth- and ninth-century land use remained mixed and silvopastoral, nevertheless the ecological and phytosociological ramifications of more cereal cultivation, more market integration, and more thoroughgoing land exploitation were important. Some weeds lost ground, while others took advantage of the technologies and techniques of agrarian intensification, of the wine and grain trade, and became nuisances. That, for any agrarian population, including imperial ones, always meant more work, and sometimes different work. Given the dynamism of the Carolingian agrarian world, cultivators had to be flexible and adjust their management strategies, fundamentally their toil, to a fast-evolving weedy landscape. While the Carolingian empire did not sponsor a "Carolingian Exchange" or shape a homogeneous landscape of a few species of weeds from the north to the Ionian Sea, it did create novel conditions in various regional agroecosystems. However short-lived and Lilliputian it was, the Carolingian empire shifted the dialectic of relations between humans and plants in Europe

[89] M. de Jong, "The Empire as Ecclesia," in *The Uses of the Past in the Early Middle Ages*, ed. Y. Hen and M. Innes (Cambridge, 2009); R. Kramer, *Rethinking Authority in the Carolingian Empire* (Amsterdam, 2019), 37–8; P. Squatriti, "The Material Eucharist in the Early Middle Ages," forthcoming.

2   Weeds on the Ground

In the past few decades, a happy conjuncture of technological development and new cultural interests has revolutionized medieval archaeology.
As a result, the material culture of early medieval Europe is now better
documented than it was into the 1980s, when high-status sites, mostly
burials, dominated the archaeological record. A quarter century ago, little
or nothing was known of what careful laboratory analysis of soils cored
from bogs and river banks now reveals about postclassical pollen deposi-
tion, and therefore of past plant life. Meticulous sieving of organic matter
discovered during excavation of wells, middens, granaries, and other
humble structures now routinely turns up preserved, identifiable seeds
and bits of plants that flourished centuries ago, providing clues to how
early medieval agroecosystems functioned. We also used to be more
ignorant than we are now about the housing and equipment peasants
used, including their weeding tools.

In spite of some big bald patches in the coverage available, particularly in
the south and east of Carolingian Europe, it is nowadays possible to survey
the archaeological attestations to the activities of weeds and of the people
who sought to remove them. The astounding, detailed views into the most
basic ecological and economic processes of the early medieval period
afforded to us by archaeobotany are perhaps for now clearer and richer
than the archaeology of rural implements, and thus deserve more space in
any survey. But an attempt to consider synoptically, on the basis of the
archaeological record, what can be made out about real weeds on the
ground, and strategies to control their growth, is well worthwhile. As subsequent chapters will demonstrate, the comparison of weed history reconstructed from archaeological proxies with the story told by Carolingian
writers suggests that farmers and writers confronted quite different weeds.

An Archaeology of Weeds and Weeding

The archaeology of Carolingian agricultural tools is still today imperfect,
and may remain so for some time. For early medieval rural work

implements wore out with use, depriving modern researchers of finds, and especially of finds in reasonable condition. Tools in any case tended to be recycled at the end of their useful life. But archaeologists have lately made progress toward uncovering some of the toolkit of rural people during the early Middle Ages. At present the orthodoxies of Georges Duby, who considered the early medieval period technologically impoverished and thought its farmers had been reduced to Neolithic levels of equipment, are no longer fashionable.[1] A more sanguine evaluation of postclassical peasants' endowment with tools prevails. This rehabilitation of early medieval agricultural technologies derives from a re-evaluation of the teleological presuppositions on which twentieth-century technological history rested, and a similar reassessment of Duby's preference for a technological awakening to coincide with demographic, social, and cultural changes after the year 1000, which required the previous period to have been underdeveloped. Alongside a concerted critique of the positions held by this influential pioneer of medieval rural history, new respect for the "world of wood" has further elevated early medieval rustic techniques in modern consideration.[2] Wooden tools can be perfectly effective in premodern farming, and it is sobering to consider that until well into the 1800s no one in Europe was able to manufacture an iron pitchfork head as light and balanced as a fully wooden one, or that only after 1950 did aluminum-tined rakes overtake wooden rakes' efficacy.[3] Unfortunately for modern scholars, the refined and cleverly fashioned implements that most Europeans used most of the time during the first two millennia AD leave few archaeological traces.

Yet the rehabilitation of early medieval farming equipment also derives from more and better rural archaeology. Such work has produced evidence of the kinds of rustic tools Duby, on the basis of his reading of the written sources, thought rare or absent.[4] Equally important has been the patient archival research of scholars like Joachim Henning, who surveyed

---

[1] G. Duby, *Rural Economy and Country Life in the Medieval West* (Columbia, SC, 1968), 19–22; G. Duby, *The Early Growth of the European Economy* (London, 1974), 13–17. See also J. Henning, "Germanisch-romanische Agrarkontinuität und -diskontinuität im nordalpinen Kontinentaleuropa," in *Akkulturation*, ed. D. Hägermann et al. (Berlin, 2004), 418–19, and his "Revolution or Relapse?" in *The Langobards before the Frankish Conquest*, ed. G. Ausenda et al. (San Marino, 2009), 150, 161–3; P. Reigniez, "Histoire et techniques," in *The Making of Feudal Agricultures?*, ed. M. Barceló and F. Sigaut (Leiden, 2004), 80; J. Devroey, *Économie rurale et société dans l'Europe franque (Vie–IXe siècles)* (Paris, 2003), 124–9.
[2] J. Radkau, *Wood: A History* (New York, 2011).
[3] J. David, *L'outil* (Turnhout, 1997), 91.
[4] The pictorial record, which Duby did consider, would instead have suggested Carolingian farmers had more and bigger metal tools than their predecessors (or Byzantine contemporaries): P. Mane, *Le travail à la campagne au Moyen Âge* (Paris, 2006), 289–91.

the inventories and dusty recesses of minor provincial museums in remote parts of Europe to produce extensive catalogues of early medieval rural equipment and elaborate typologies of their metal parts (the components that survive best, though rural frugality meant little was forgotten or cast aside, even as parts wore down and lost their efficacy, and broken shards of tool found new lives at the smithy). What has emerged is an early medieval countryside far better equipped with iron spades, gouges, sickles, axes, scythes, and plowshares than Duby ever imagined.[5]

A handful of sophisticated archaeological studies proves the firebrand occasionally helped people to clear away unwanted plants from Carolingian-era landscapes.[6] Yet the most important early medieval weeding equipment turned up in archaeological investigations consisted basically of hoes and billhooks; presumably rakes mattered too, though as these were wooden they survive much less perfectly.[7] These implements were not significantly different in design than their ancient ancestors, because they were versatile. For, like any tool, past and present, while it might have a primary purpose, early medieval rustic equipment could be deployed in several contexts. For instance, because they were able to serve, in a pinch, as weapons, billhooks had a gender: they were masculine tools, sometimes buried with their male owners, a mark of status as well as of manhood.[8] Hoes were much less clearly male, or honorable, though early medieval iconography, building on the first-century BC apocryphal *Life of Adam and Eve* and the idea that the provision of work instruments was part of God's providence and magnanimity, consistently assigned them to the first man, Adam; in this way, hoes became the quintessential work implement, the symbol of how all men had been assigned to toil in the fields after Adam's lapse.[9] But since in most agrarian societies weeding is a task for subaltern people, particularly for women and children, the real weeding hoe was a lighter tool, different from the mattock men used to break up the sod and render it friable.[10]

[5] J. Henning, *Südosteuropa zwischen Antike und Mittelalter* (Berlin, 1987). See also Henning, "Did the 'Agricultural Revolution' Go East with Carolingian Conquest?" in *The Baiuwarii and Thuringi*, ed. J. Fries-Knoblauch et al. (Woodbridge, 2014), 339–46.
[6] M. Buonincontri et al., "Shaping Mediterranean Landscapes," *The Holocene* 30 (2020). In general, see F. Sigaut, *L'agriculture et le feu* (Paris, 1975). Following Roman agronomy, some Carolingians recognized the utility of fire to prevent "destructive growth" in fields (see Hrabanus Maurus, *De Universo* 19.1, ed. J. Migne, *PL* 111 (Paris, 1864), 503, who goes beyond his model, Virgil, in crediting fire's role against weeds). But their lack of notice for this technique is puzzling.
[7] Henning, *Südosteuropa*, 76–86, 93–6.   [8] Reigniez, "Histoire et techniques," 81–2.
[9] S. Piron, "Ève au fuseau, Adam jardinier," in *Adam: la nature humaine avant et après*, ed. I. Rosier-Catach and G. Bruguglia (Paris, 2016), 293–4; Mane, *Le travail*, 97.
[10] Weeders' status: J. Zadoks, *Crop Protection in Medieval Agriculture* (Leiden, 2013), 105. Light hoes: Henning, *Südosteuropa*, 81–3. In the miniatures accompanying the text of Genesis in the mid-ninth-century Vivian bible, discussed in Chapter 5 below, Adam has a hoe in his hands. Because this Carolingian Genesis illumination does not show the

Notker's story of Pippin the Hunchback, whom Charlemagne's messengers found weeding the monastic garden, underlines such gender and labor hierarchies: Pippin was old and frail, and thus prevented from the heavier work ("maiora opera") that young monks did in the fields. Hence he weeded with his three-pronged hoe. Age and monastic status feminized him.[11]

The gendered nature of weeding tools and work may help to explain why in polyptychs the fairly meticulous listings of labor that dependent peasants with diverse status owed to their (ecclesiastical) landlords excluded weeding. Male work, especially plowing and portage, predominates among the peasant "manoperae" that ninth-century landlords kept track of in their accounts because female work, like weeding fields or bundling the sheaves of grain, however onerous and decisive for the outcome at harvest time, was presumed: it came together with the work of male heads of household.[12] The polyptychs thus reflected not the perceived economic value of labor but the social hierarchy in the domestic unit of production from which that labor derived.[13]

For this reason, it is worth contemplating again the most effective weeding machine of the early medieval period, the plow. Whether it involved a simple wooden ard with shallow draft in the topsoil, or a complex, moldboard plow with asymmetrical share and long steel coulter, on wheels, plowing equipment changed the odds of survival for field weeds (as detailed in Chapter 1). The dissemination of bigger, heavier, and deeper-cutting plows in the second half of the first millennium also helped spare peasant time and labor, specifically male time and labor.[14] For plowing, whether with light or heavy equipment, was the work of men. More efficient plowing tools saved men time. They liberated men from some of the drudgery that preparing fields entailed by cutting down on the number of crossings the plowman had to perform on the same field. But it appears women, the weeders of choice in most rural communities, derived few benefits from this. Their work in the field, aimed at weeds that grew among the crops, was only indirectly affected by the period's innovations in plowing. Thoroughly, deeply plowed fields

---

ground broken up by Adam's tool, it is possible he is imagined weeding, not hoeing the soil.

[11] Notker, *Gesta Karoli Magni* 2.12, ed. H. Haefele, *MGHSRG* n.s. 12 (Berlin, 1959), 73.

[12] Carolingian demands on labor: J. Devroey, *Puissants et misérables* (Brussels, 2006), 509–10, 537–46.

[13] On labor dues: Y. Morimoto, "In ebdomada operetur, quicquid precipitur ei," in *Études sur l'économie rurale du haut Moyen Âge*, ed. Y. Morimoto (Brussels, 2008), 381–96; R. Fossier, *Polyptyques et censiers* (Turnhout, 1978), 31–2. On weeding in polyptychs: A. Longnon, *Polyptyque de l'abbaye de Saint-Germain des Prés redigé au temps de l'abbé Irmiron* 1 (Paris, 1895), 161–2.

[14] J. Devroey and A. Nissen, "Early Middle Ages, 500–1000," in *Struggling with the Environment*, ed. E. Thoen and T. Soens (Turnhout, 2015), 35–6, 41–3.

permitted fewer weeds to grow, but also encouraged new species to prevail, adapted to the chemical and physical conditions in the soil that new plowing techniques created. Hence some targeted weeding was still required to help the crop reach maturity, and Carolingian-era plowing technology had a gendered impact on weeding. More efficacious tools freed males from work (plowing with oxen) far more than they did females (weeding with hoes and hands).[15]

If archaeologically based reconstructions of early medieval weeding tools (and people's endowment with them) are more sophisticated now than they were a few decades ago, the transformations in the archaeobotany of the same period have been truly stunning. Late twentieth-century and early twenty-first-century European environmental anxieties, worries about rising average temperatures, extreme meteorological events, impoverished biodiversity, and reductions in the habitats of numerous species probably motivated much of this research.[16] A lot of it took place in the context of salvage archaeology, as new housing complexes, train lines, or commercial structures (arguably closely related to the same environmental changes that alarmed Europeans and stimulated interest in vegetation history) were built over sites neglected for centuries. It was on the verge of transformations that would sequester their archaeological secrets for the foreseeable future, or obliterate them outright, that archaeologists began to study these landscapes.

However, the worries that spurred so much fertile archaeological and archaeobotanical research also overrode the high costs of specialized fieldwork and lab analyses entailed by dealing scientifically with fossil pollen grains and spores, or waterlogged or carbonized seeds and plant parts. Both sorts of palaeobotanical data have their pitfalls and limitations, but archaeologists' increasing willingness to delve into them has had illuminating results, not just for the early medieval period.[17] Meticulous analyses of variations over time in deposits of spores and pollen grains, usually in damp places, or in the species composition of fossil plant remains in places where people lived, now reveal something of

[15] Medieval plowing: F. Sigaut, "Le labour, qu'est-ce que c'est?" in *Nous labourons* (Nantes, 2007), 25–6. A. Olmstead and P. Rhode, *Creating Abundance* (Cambridge, 2008), 12–13 point out that in the USA in the 1800s, improved plowing tools gave men more time, but they spent this extra time working on their fields.
[16] Eco-anxiety and research: A. Durand, "L'émergence d'outils empruntés aux sciences biologiques végétales en archéologie médiévale en France," in *Trente ans d'archéologie médiévale en France*, ed. J. Chapelot (Caen, 2010), 29–32; J. Devroey, *La nature et le roi* (Paris, 2019), 11–12.
[17] See, in fact, the helpful introduction to archaeobotanical methods, pitfalls, and results, applied to Roman times, in M. van der Veen, "Archaeobotany: The Archaeology of Human–Plant Interactions," in *The Science of Roman History*, ed. W. Scheidel (Princeton, 2018), 53–60.

how Europe's agrarian societies fit into postclassical ecologies.[18] As a good proportion of the new botanically informed archaeology is rural, another benefit of the recent uptick in archaeobotanical research is the light it sheds on the production and consumption systems of Europe's "people without history," to use the phrase Eric Wolf applied to *ancien régime* peasants.[19]

Weeds have a surprisingly high profile in archaeobotany. Partly that is because they were ubiquitous, as well as prominent, in most past agroecosystems and therefore in most assemblages of plant remains, and particularly in those associated with crop processing prior to consumption. It is also related to the fact that weeds are important proxies for archaeobotanists, for their presence indicates the prevalence of specific agricultural practices or other environmental conditions in the period with which they are associated. For example, the Functional Interpretation of Botanical Surveys method probes weed species' characteristics to reconstruct the agricultural practices that facilitated their growth and dissemination in the past.[20] Indeed, the size of common weed seeds tells of soil productivity and manuring, the stable isotopes within them carry the signatures of irrigation and soil enrichment practices, the prevalence of different species speaks to soil chemistry and physics, while the type of weed found in grain stores may reveal the provenance and circulation of crops associated with it (as now does aDNA from the seeds), and fluctuations in the abundance of pollen of species like ribwort plantain (*Plantago lanceolata*) reveal rhythms in past deforestation, since that weed quickly occupies land cleared of woods in temperate climates.[21] For few organisms are as sensitive or responsive to environmental variables as are weeds. Thus, the disappearance over the course of a century of pollens from ruderal weeds at a given site suggests a reduction of human activity there relevant to historical demography, while a relative increase in the remains of spring-germinating weeds in people's

---

[18] Archaeobotanical contributions: J. Quirós Castillo, "Agrarian Archaeology in Early Medieval Europe," *Quaternary International* 346 (2014), 2–3. Devroey, *Économie rurale*, 102 thought a true history of early medieval grain cultivation would finally become possible thanks to archaeobotanical tools.

[19] E. Wolf, *Europe and the People without History* (Berkeley, 1982).

[20] G. Jones, "Weed Ecology as a Method for the Archaeobotanical Recognition of Crop Husbandry Practices," *Acta Archaeobotanica* 42 (2002), 185–92. See also A. Wolff et al., "In the Ruins," *Weed Science* 70.2 (2022), 6–13.

[21] G. Jones et al., "Crops and Weeds: The Role of Weed Functional Ecology in the Identification of Crop Husbandry Methods," *Journal of Archaeological Science* 37 (2010), 70–7; Devroey and Nissen, "Early Middle Ages," 41; A. Ferdière et al., *Histoire de l'agriculture en Gaule, 500 av. J-C–1000 apr. J-C* (Paris, 2006), 185; L. Lodwick, "Arable Weed Seeds as Indicators of Cereal Provenance," *Vegetation History and Archaeobotany* 27 (2018), 801–15; A. Bogaard et al., "An Index of Weed Size for Assessing the Soil Productivity of Ancient Crops," *Vegetation History and Archaeobotany* 7 (1998), 17–22.

grain silos signals a new agricultural strategy, perhaps the introduction of oats into the rotations of a farming community, and the presence of weeds with a propensity for long periods of underground dormancy indicates specific (deep) plowing techniques that are significant for the history of technology.[22] There are, in sum, an array of reasons why weeds win so much attention from archaeobotanical researchers.

British archaeobotanists have been particularly successful in accumulating data and analyzing it. For Anglo-Saxon England, specifically for "mid-Saxon" times (AD 650–900), Mark McKerracher counted 137 assemblages of plant remains from 96 sites, generating more or less comparable data on vegetation, including weeds. Across England, it seems, expanding agriculture, more manuring, and a shift to growing more free-threshing grains facilitated conspicuous increases in nitrophilous henbane (*Hycoscyamus niger*) and stinging nettles (*Urtica urens*) in the eighth and ninth centuries.[23] Unfortunately, the early medieval situation across the channel is not as well documented or analyzed. While a massive, Europe-wide database of archaeological pollens is being assembled, it is not complete.[24] And even after years of fine fieldwork, there are still extremely few published archaeobotanically informed investigations focused on the period of Frankish hegemony in Europe.

A fully satisfactory, archaeobotanically informed general synthesis of Carolingian period weed history would in any case be difficult. For "average" conditions existed nowhere in Carolingian Europe. The empire of the Carolingians encompassed a substantial slice of western Eurasia, and if they never transformed it into a "Frankish ecosystem" that was partly because the area is ecologically uneven or diverse.[25] Aside from the obvious climatic differences between its northern and southern provinces, each region of the empire had its own particular geology and its own hydrological regime and vegetation. Even if it lacked the geographical heterogeneity of the Roman empire or caliphate, the Carolingian empire is best considered a constellation of botanical microregions, within which two contiguous fields could produce quite distinct floras, different mixtures of cultivated and wild, as was true in all premodern territories.[26]

But by comparing scattered microregional insights, we can discern the contours of the possible. It is clear that the environmental variety of

[22] M. Jones, "Dormancy and the Plough," in *From Foragers to Farmers*, ed. A. Fairbairn and E. Weiss (Oxford, 2009), 58–63.
[23] M. McKerracher, *Anglo-Saxon Crops and Weeds* (Oxford, 2019), 18, 97–103, 127–8.
[24] The europeanpollendatabase.net run by an Aix-Marseille university team is already a useful tool, searchable by species, region, and period.
[25] Devroey, *La nature*, 14, "écosystème franc."
[26] P. Steen Henriksen, "Rye Cultivation in the Danish Iron Age," *Vegetation History and Archaeobotany* 12 (2003), 179.

Carolingian Europe dictated equal variety in botanical and human adaptations, or agroecosystems. In addition, it seems that Frankish hegemony did not effect change everywhere, creating homogeneous landscapes: its imperial ecological footprint was smaller than that of early modern or modern empires. Thus, in the Basque foothills of the Pyrenees, cereal cultivation was slight, while nettles were exceptionally abundant, and in another Carolingian periphery, in Tuscany, Carolingian innovations like growing more oats are tenuously attested (the difficulty of telling *Avena sativa* seeds apart from wild oats may partially account for this).[27] Even in the Frankish heartlands, for instance in the Eifel's volcanic sectors or on the Brie plateau, the palaeobotanical indicators of Carolingian-driven changes in the land are imperfectly recorded, perhaps because the changes were small.[28] The same is true for a marginal landscape like that of Müstair, an imperial abbey in a saddle at more than 1,270 meters above sea level in the eastern Alps that governed access to the Reschen and Stelvio passes and to the Inn and Adda rivers, and therefore controlled communications between Bavaria and eastern Lombardy, thus meriting Charlemagne's patronage: its Carolingian inhabitants had minimal impact on the surrounding vegetation, to judge from carpological proxies.[29] Regional variety, and the endurance of pre-Carolingian ways, must be factored into any reconstructions.

The pointillist portrait sketched below recognizes regional environmental difference and, at the same time, tries to represent something more general about weeds' Carolingian history. It proceeds through discussion of examples. It arranges palaeobotanical data on weeds into northern and southern Carolingian spheres of influence, while also seeking to keep in mind the local circumstances that led to the formation of each botanical assemblage. The aim, ultimately, is to evaluate whether something of what grew on the ground, in the real villages and farms that made up the empire, reflected the consistent, quite uniform weedology of Carolingian literate culture.

---

[27] Pyrenees: S. Pérez-Díaz et al., "A Palaeoenvironmental and Palaeoeconomic Approach to the Early Middle Age Record from the Village of Gasleiz," *Vegetation History and Archaeobotany* 24 (2015), 687–92. Tuscany: M. Buonincontri et al., "Farming in a Rural Settlement in Central Italy," *Vegetation History and Archaeobotany* 23 (2014), 783–4; M. Buonincontri et al., "Multiproxy Approach to the Study of Medieval Food Habits in Tuscany," *Archaeological and Anthropological Sciences* 9 (2017), 664–5.

[28] Eifel: C. Herbig and F. Sirocko, "Palaeobotanical Evidence of Agricultural Activities in the Eifel Region during the Holocene," *Vegetation History and Archaeobotany* 22 (2013), 458. Brie: T. Bonin, "Le site de Chessy et l'occupation du sol en Île-de-France (VIe–Xe siècles)," *Archéologie médiévale* 29 (2000), 51–4.

[29] C. Brombacher et al., "Bronzezeitliche und mittelalterliche Pflanzenfunde aus dem Kloster St. Johann in Müstair," in *Müstair, Kloster St. Johann* 4, ed. H. Sennhauser (Zurich, 2007), 86–7.

Weeds of the North

More abundant precipitation and, especially, more evenly distributed precipitation throughout the year, set the northern sections of the Carolingian empire apart from its southern provinces. From the Loire to the Rhine, and east of that great river, in order to succeed plants had to know how to survive cold winters and how to make the most of shorter summers and less solar irradiation. Competitiveness had as much to do with leaves quick to photosynthesize as with deep taproots, effective at soaking up dampness. Within this vast zone, even species adapted to loess soils like Queen Anne's lace (*Orlaya grandiflora*) had to cope with cool average temperatures: a thermophilous nature was a disadvantage.[30]

Also relevant to the dissemination of weeds were Carolingian economic patterns and agricultural strategies. For instance, in the ninth century by Orléans on the Loire, more structured settlement, with bigger buildings and raised granaries, suggests what Carolingian large estates looked like: they deeply reshuffled vegetation by creating new pastures and pushing agriculture out into previously wild lands, according to studies of the local pollen record.[31] Further southwest, in the Morvan hills near Autun, pollens from several bogs suggest that the second half of the first millennium AD coincides with increased human pressure on woodland, and open areas increased at several sites around 800. Fungi that favor cattle excrement for their growth, and whose spores are abundant, reveal one purpose of clearing the Morvan beech forest.[32] That various weedy members of the Caucalidion group, especially *Neslia paniculata* and *Legousia speculumveneris*, did so well in the vicinity of the great Carolingian abbey of Reichenau during the ninth century suggests there was demographically driven pressure on arable land: for these weeds prevail only on poor soils, and their success is best explicable if people were farming increasingly "marginal" areas, something we can presume they did only when the areas with more fertile soils were already occupied.[33]

As rural settlement north of the Loire also concentrated into denser clusters, and grain growing expanded, particularly rye and oats, in some

---

[30] C. Bakels, *The Western European Loess Belt* (Dordrecht 2009), 167–8.
[31] S. Jesset, "Les formes de l'exploitation rurale du IXe au XIe siècle," in *Lumières de l'an mil en Orléanais* (Turnhout, 2004), 91.
[32] I. Jouffroy-Bapicot et al., "7000 Years of Vegetation History and Landscape Changes in the Morvan Mountains (France)," *The Holocene* 23.12 (2013), 1897–9. Peat compacting made dating of pollen and spores arduous at some sites.
[33] M. Rösch and J. Lechterbeck, "Seven Millennia of Human Impact Reflected in a High Resolution Pollen Profile from the Profundal Sediments of Litzelsee, Lake Constance Region, Germany," *Vegetation History and Archaeobotany* 25 (2016), 353. See also M. Rösch, "Evidence for Rare Crop Weeds of the Caucalidion Group in Southwestern Germany since the Bronze Age," *Vegetation History and Archaeobotany* 27 (2018), 75–84.

areas at the expense of woodland, inevitably some obligate weeds benefited.[34] But in what is now the Netherlands, robust palynological traces of ninth- and tenth-century increases in rye cultivation curiously do not align with increases in pollens of rye's constant companion elsewhere, namely cornflower (*Centaurea cyanus*). A single seed survives from the well-excavated village of Kootwijk, while the nearby trading post of Dorestad produced no remains of cornflower either. Instead, in the rye fields of the ninth- to tenth-century Low Countries, ribwort plantain (*Plantago lanceolata*), red sorrel (*Rumex acetosella*), corn spurry (*Spergula arvense*), wild buckwheat (*Fallopia convulvus*), and German knotweed (*Scleranthus annuus*) flourished.[35] Red sorrel and knotweed also did well at Douai, judging from pollens dated AD 850–950, and surprising amounts of curry dock (*Rumex crispus*) were found there among charred grain remains.[36] Rather like ribwort plantain, the growing presence of *Rumex* can signal the creation and extension of pastures, as it responds well to grazing.[37] In the grain stores of the monastery of Cysoing, founded near Lille around 854 by Gisela, daughter of Louis the Pious, despite the presence of rye in respectable amounts, a single cornflower seed was discovered: instead there were surprising amounts of the seed of timothy grass (*Phleum pratense*) mixed in with the wheat, barley, rye, and oats.[38] Because of its hardiness and nutritional value, such grass is favored by people who need to feed large herbivores.

Cornflowers, the tough stems of which dull harvesters' sickles in grain fields, slowing down a time-sensitive operation and thus was much resented by *ancien régime* farmers, was, however, a significant nuisance on the Mitteleuropean farms along the Danube.[39] There red sorrel and knotweed also made their mark. Yet, on balance, it is the relatively slight

---

[34] M. Rösch, "The History of Cereals in the Territory of the Former Duchy of Swabia (Herzogtum Schwaben) from the Roman to the Postmedieval Period," *Vegetation History and Archaeobotany* 1 (1991), 221–2; C. Bakels, "Crops Produced in the Southern Netherlands and Northern France during the Early Medieval Period," *Vegetation History and Archaeobotany* 14 (2005), 395–7; Devroey, *Économie rurale*, 105–7, 117–24.

[35] C. Bakels, "The Early History of the Cornflower (*Centaurea cyanus*) in the Netherlands," *Acta Palaeobotanica* 52.1 (2012), 28–9; J. Pals and B. Van Geel, "Rye Cultivation and the Presence of Cornflower," *Berichten van de Rijkdienst voor het Oudheidkundig Bodemonderzoek* 26 (1976), 200–1.

[36] W. van Zeist et al., "Plant Husbandry and Vegetation of Early Medieval Douai, Northern France," *Vegetation History and Archaeobotany* 3 (1994), 216.

[37] As observed by L. Sadori et al., "Climate, Environment and Society in Southern Italy during the Last 2000 Years," *Quaternary Science Reviews* 136 (2016), 178.

[38] D. Censier et al., "Indices de productions au sein d'une communauté religieuse carolingienne," *Archéologie médiévale* 48 (2018), 115.

[39] Blunt sickles: Bakels, "The Early History," 30. Mitteleuropa: U. Willerding, *Zur Geschichte der Unkräuter Mitteleuropas* (Neumünster, 1986), 82–90 (*C. cyanus*), 234–7 (*R. acetosella*), 244–6 (*S. annuus*).

footprint in the Carolingian heartlands of cornflower, a weed finely attuned to north European rye cultivation in the high Middle Ages, that is most remarkable.[40] It is confirmed also by excavations at Sermersheim, near Colmar in Alsace, and by cores from volcanic lakes in the Eifel south of Aachen. Though rye and cornflower pollens do appear in the Eifel before AD 800, the Carolingian period's main signature there was vast increases of grassland plants like daisies (*Chrysanthemum leucanthemum*), woundwort (*Prunella vulgaris*), and ragged robin (*Lychnis flos-cuculi*): these were the botanical winners in this corner of empire.[41] From the eighth century intensified occupation of the loess terrace at Sermersheim brought more cereal and legume cultivation, and the attendant weeds. Field gromwell (*Lithospermum arvense*) was the commonest, but corncockle (*Agrostemma githago*) was also somewhat successful. The fill of a Carolingian-era well there instead suggests the settlement was infested principally by stinging nettles, which made up 37 percent of the submerged weed finds.[42]

Along the Seine river, too, weed populations responded to Carolingian human activity in archaeobotanically visible ways. At the village of Villiers-le-Sec, near Saint-Denis, the cultivation of grains had not changed much from Merovingian times, but between the eighth and the tenth century more broad beans, peas, flax, and vines grew than before.[43] Deforestation extended the arable area, while chicory (*Chicorium intybus*), dandelions (*Taraxacum* sp.), and nettles adorned the settlement, according to pollens recovered from the site.[44] In the grain stores, archaeologists discovered the remains of grainfield weeds like white charlock (*Raphanus raphanistrum*) and horticultural weeds like silverweed (*Potentilla anserina*) or knotgrass (*Polygonum aviculare*).[45] Upstream from Paris, on the plain of Troyes, macroremains found in settlements datable to the Caroligian period suggest small increases in the cultivation of rye and oats

---

[40] High Middle Ages: Bakels, "The Early History," 30.

[41] Herbig and Sirocko, "Palaeobotanical Evidence," 458–9.

[42] E. Peytremann and S. Wiethold, "L'apport de la carpologie à l'étude du site du premier Moyen Âge (VIe–XIIe siècle) de Sermersheim (Bas-Rhin)," in *Des hommes aux champs*, ed. V. Carpentier and C. Marcigny (Rennes, 2012), 201, 204–6. Gromwell and corncockle flourished in Bavaria, too: M. Rösch, "The History of Crops and Weeds in South-Western Germany from the Neolithic Period to Modern Times," *Vegetation History and Archaeobotany* 7 (1998), 118, 120.

[43] E. Peytremann, *Archéologie de l'habitat rurale dans le nord de la France du IVe au XIIe siècle* (Saint-Germain-en-Laye, 2003), 338–41.

[44] P. Guilbert, "Étude des pollens prélevées dans es couches archéologiques de Villiers-le-Sec," in *Un village au temps de Charlemagne* (Paris, 1988), 197.

[45] M. Ruas, "Alimentation végétale, pratiques agricoles et environnement du VIIe au Xe siècle," in *Un village au temps de Charlemagne* (Paris, 1988), 209; M. Ruas, "Près, prairies, pâtures: éclairages archéobotaniques," in *Près et pâtures en Europe occidentale*, ed. F. Brumont (Toulouse, 2008), 38.

(and bigger ones in viticulture), with the resulting specialist weeds of those crops.[46] Further downstream on the river, south of Rouen, at Tournedos, the obligate weeds of barley, oats, rye, and wheat, and of flax showed up: they were able to navigate the three-field rotations that had recently been introduced to fields there.[47]

Corncockle and cornflower were significant weeds at Villiers-le-Sec, and corncockle also at Sermersheim, as we have seen, but overall they did not have the protagonist's role on the northern stage of bad plants. Since much of our information, in carbonized or otherwise mineralized form, derives from Carolingian grain stores, it is possible that these plants are under-represented in the record because they were purposefully excluded from those spaces by meticulous threshers and winnowers. In fact the palynology is more generous with them, and suggests that corncockle, at least, made inroads during the Carolingian period in the Indre valley south of Tours (where, however, it was mostly members of the Cichorioideae subfamily that expanded their range and numbers, while Carolingian cattle and oxen placidly grazed among them) and around Lake Constance.[48]

The susprising expansion of that very resilient grain einkorn (*Triticum monococcum*) in the region of Troyes in early medieval times could be related to this species' ability to smother weeds: after harvest its clingy husks added to the toils of whoever prepared it for human consumption, but its competitive edge in the field meant at least that it would reach storage spaces in purer form, without much sorting.[49] That some cultivators at Troyes valued crops that took care of themselves and stymied their weedy competitors indicates that they participated in a culture that appreciated "clean" harvests. Indeed, elsewhere it seems that Carolingian sieving and winnowing practices were very stringent: at Serris, another dependency of Saint-Denis, like Villiers-le-Sec, and at Goudelancourt just east of Laon, preserved ninth-century wheat stores were remarkable for their purity.[50] But as the silos of the royally connected abbey at Cysoing show, not everyone was so diligent. So it remains possible, too,

---

[46] F. Toulemond et al., "A Brief History of Plants in North-Eastern France," *Vegetation History and Archaeobotany* 30 (2021), 15–17.

[47] Peytremann, *Archéologie*, 338.

[48] A. Querrien et al., "Évolution et exploitation du paysage végétale au Moyen Âge," in *Trente ans*, ed. Chapelot, 42; Rösch and Lechterbeck, "Seven Millennia," 352.

[49] Toulemond et al., "A Brief History," 16; P. Halstead, *Two Oxen Ahead* (Chichester, 2014), 236.

[50] Bakels, *The Western European Loess Belt*, 219. Teilleul near Rennes, with 13 percent weeds in ninth-century grain stores, was different: M. Ruas and B. Pradat, "Les semences découvertes," in *Les habitats carolingiens de Montours et La Chapelle-Saint-Aubert*, ed. I. Catteddu (Paris, 2001), 66–8.

that Carolingian weeders were particularly sedulous in pursuit of the unwanted plants in their croplands, that heavy plows made life difficult for companion species, or that denser sowing succeeded in crowding out weeds, especially cornflower and corncockle, producing a relatively homogeneous harvest in eighth- and ninth-century fields.[51]

Weeds of the South

In the southern portion of the Europe Charlemagne gradually assembled during the late eighth century, the Mediterranean climate exercised its control on plant life. Though modulated by relief and numerous other microregional geographic factors, the long summer drought and the concentration of most precipitation in just a few months were everywhere important constraints. An ability to cope with the seasonal distribution of moisture mattered more than the capacity to absorb solar energy, the opposite of the characteristics that adapted plants to continental European climatic conditions.[52]

To succeed in Carolingian southern Europe, weeds also had to learn how to navigate the agricultural conditions engendered by intensifying consumption and production. This was a fact of eighth- and ninth-century botanical life well beyond the Carolingian sphere, in Byzantine south Italy as well.[53] More attentive animal husbandry, woodland use, and arable exploitation seem to have characterized the eighth century in much of western Eurasia. But it is still fair to say that empire in its Carolingian form did exercise some homogenizing magnetism on the southern provinces, assimilating them a little into a broader European economic pattern.[54]

Yet in the southern, coastal region of Tuscany, not far from Rome, one of the great beneficiaries of the Carolingian stimulus package, the centuries-long economic slump launched by late antiquity persisted.[55] There, scanty agropastoral activities, for the most part close to the Tyrrhenian ports, continued unaffected by Frankish invasions, imperial coronations, coinage

---

[51] J. Zadoks, *Crop Protection in Medieval Agriculture*, 131–3; D. Postles, "Cleaning the Medieval Arable," *Agricultural History Review* 37 (1989), 140. How tolerant of weeds peasants are is also shaped by how much land they have to weed: see Halstead, *Two Oxen*, 233.
[52] H. Allen, *Mediterranean Ecogeography* (Harlow, 2001), 115–17, 163.
[53] P. Arthur et al., "Roads to Recovery," *Antiquity* 86 (2012), 444–55.
[54] M. Rottoli, "Crop Diversity between Central Europe and the Mediterranean," in *Plants and People: Choices and Diversity through Time*, ed. A. Chevalier et al. (Oxford, 2014), 75–81. See also M. Rottoli, "Reflections on Early Medieval Resources in North Italy," *Quaternary International* 346 (2014), 21–4.
[55] P. Delogu, "Rome in the Ninth Century," in *Post-Roman Towns, Trade and Settlement in Europe and Byzantium* 1, ed. J. Henning (Berlin, 2007), 105–22.

reform, and the economic integration of long-distance trade.[56] In the Maremma weeds were not influenced by the Carolingian empire. Just as the shriveling of agriculture in the sixth century had reduced obligate weeds' opportunities, in the lightly frequented wastelands between the Aurelian and Cassian consular roads, Carolingian-era ecologies were too little agricultural to generate weeds.[57]

Nearby, however, different situations prevailed. The growing rural settlements of the Colline Metallifere, increasingly willing to clear the area's wooded valleys, including by fire, and increasingly equipped with big, perhaps lordly grain storage spaces, were good places for bad plants.[58] The gradual shift from growing tough, self-reliant grains like emmer to growing more barley, rye, and oats, as well as grass pea (*Lathyrus sativus*), allowed ruderal weeds to expand their presence during the eighth and ninth centuries. The carbonized plant remains in the surviving grain stores at Miranduolo suggest that crops were winnowed prior to entering any silo. Indeed, at that hilltop settlement south of Siena, the Carolingian period coincided with larger-seeded, more demanding crops, and seems to have introduced more stringent winnowing practices, with consequent reductions in the numbers of intruder seeds found in the silos dated to after AD 850.[59] Still, enough mimics of grain seeds, especially of the grass family (*Poaceae*), insinuated themselves to suggest that field weeds were steadfast companions of the standard grain and legume cultivations. Thirteen species of weeds made up on average 5.3 percent of what could be recovered from eighth- and ninth-century grain stores at Miranduolo: corncockle (*Agrostemma githago*) and ryegrass (likely *Lolium multiflorum*, an annual subspecies of the Lolium genus that infests winter-sown crops and vegetables) were the most numerous. Furthermore, as the crop seeds became bigger over time, so did the weeds' seeds.[60] Also, at Miranduolo the risk aversion of peasants remained strong enough during the Carolingian epoch that wild oats seem to have been tolerated in fields,

[56] G. Di Pasquale et al., "Human-derived Landscape Changes on the Northern Etruria Coast (Western Italy) between Roman Times and the Late Middle Ages," *The Holocene* 24.11 (2014), 1498.
[57] E. Vaccaro, *Sites and Pots: Settlement and Economy in Southern Tuscany* (Oxford, 2011).
[58] Fire: Buonincontri et al., "Shaping Mediterranean Landscapes," 1428–9. Storage: G. Bianchi and F. Grassi, "Sistemi di stoccaggio nella campagna italiana (secc. VIII–XIII)," in *Horrea, Barns, and Silos: Storage and Incomes in Early Medieval Europe*, ed. A. Vigil-Escalera Guirado et al. (Bilbao, 2013), 77. G. Bianchi, "Recenti ricerche nelle Colline Metallifere ed alcune riflessioni sul modello toscano," *Archeologia medievale* 42 (2015), 9–26 cautions against generalizing southern Tuscan economic changes and argues that assertive lords came only after the end of Carolingian authority.
[59] Buonincontri et al., "Farming in a Rural Settlement," 779–84.
[60] Ibid., 785. See also the article's "Supplementary Material 1."

since in the last resort this wily mimic weed could feed domestic animals, or even people.

Further north, in the Po valley, heartland of the Lombard kingdom and the most important colony acquired by Charlemagne, similar economic developments left some archaeobotanical signs. During the ninth century, rye, particularly, but also oats and even sorghum, accelerated their diffusion. On the hillsides where farmers grew sorghum, weeds with fast lifecycles, able to keep up with sorghum's pressing schedule, or with spring-sown oats, multiplied their numbers. Weeds with more leisurely habits fit into agroecosystems dedicated to winter-sown wheat, barley, or rye.

A site high in the central Alps, where summer farming and pasturing had taken root in the early Iron Age, shows some signs of "intensification" in the pollens dated AD 500–900. At Barch, high above Lake Como, in the (roughly) Carolingian period, arboreal pollens declined as settlement stabilized, and though dairying was the main economic activity, around some mires volunteers like red sorrel (*Rumex acetosa*) and ribwort plantain (*Plantago lanceolata*), but also poisonous wolf's bane (*Acontium*), grew vigorously.[61] Even on the most difficult terrains weeds responded to the prompts of human agropastoral strategies.

In Mediterranean Francia rye was not as popular among Carolingian-era cultivators as it was in Lombardy.[62] Only in a few plains do pollens of rye show up. A similar limited diffusion of oats, and restriction to some lowlands, emerges from various palynological studies. However, at the outset of the eighth century, shepherds who spent at least part of the year high in the Pyrenees evidently did favor rye: at Orri d'En Corbill, some 1,950 meters above sea level, rye was the grain of choice, likely the only one hardy enough to tolerate the cool temperatures of the mountainsides below the shepherds' summer pastures.[63] But since Carolingian miners and loggers decisively altered the Pyrenean woodlands, for instance eliminating boxwood in some valleys of the Ariège, we should not underestimate the ability of even marginal figures, like shepherds, to effect botanical change.[64] In the

---

[61] D. Moe and F. Fedele, "Alpe Borghetto," *Vegetation History and Archaeobotany* 28 (2019), 152–3, 156.

[62] G. Comet, "Les céréales du bas-empire au Moyen Âge," in *The Making of Feudal Agricultures?*, ed. M. Barceló and F. Sigaut, 151; Devroey, *Économie rurale* 103; J. Devroey, "La céréaliculture dans le monde franque," *Settimane del CISAM* 37 (Spoleto, 1990)," 233–6; M. Ruas, "Aspects of Early Medieval Farming from Sites in Mediterranean France," *Vegetation History and Archaeobotany* 14 (2005) 404–6.

[63] M. Ruas, "Les plantes consommées au Moyen Âge en France méridionale d'après les semences archéologiques," *Archéologie du Midi médiévale* 15–16 (1998), 197–200.

[64] M. Saulnier et al., "A Study of Late Holocene Local Vegetation Dynamics and Responses to Land Use Changes in an Ancient Charcoal Making Woodland in the Central Pyrenees (Ariége, France), Using Pedoanthracology," *Vegetation History and Archaeobotany* 29 (2020), 249–58.

Languedoc, the introduction of more cattle-raising, and the resulting need for pasture, elevated the economic importance of wetlands and gave a boost to leguminous burclover (*Medicago* genus), and in settlements exploiting recently cleared woodland rust fungi specialized in infesting broad beans.[65] For the rest, southern France was more stable and less experimental in its agricultural practices than either Italy or northern France. Early medieval Roussillon, in the area between the Têt and Tech rivers, did not take up rye or oat cultivation, and remained loyal to barley and wheat, though millet, grown in small quantities, was added to the upland peasants' arsenal of grain cultivation; the spectrum of legumes likewise remained steady.[66] Such dedication to traditional cultivations, like wheats and barley, created fewer chances for botanical invaders, and left the weeds of antiquity in control of the ground in Mediterranean Francia. Corncockle (*Agrostemma githago*), the seed of which could get mixed up in stores of several kinds of wheat, particularly emmer (*Triticum turgidum*), enjoyed continued prominence.[67] But, carried forth by a millennium-long wave of adoption, unhulled grains waxed in popularity, and in the last centuries before the turn of the second millennium einkorn wheat (*Triticum monococcum*), increasingly marginalized by growers, became a weed in most southern French fields.[68]

Conclusion

Carolingian agroecosystems, in sum, favored certain weeds and volunteer plants, marginalizing others. By introducing or just encouraging new patterns of production, Carolingian landowners promoted some phyto-social mobility and, especially in Lombardy and the areas of Neustria and Austrasia, new phytosociological arrangements emerged in response to their demands. However, the advances of rye in Carolingian fields appear not to have unleashed a pan-European invasion of cornflower, as one might have expected, and oats' raised profile, as food and as fodder, had only the mildest stimulating effects on wild oats (insofar as *Avena fatua* may be identified with confidence). Carolingian archaeobotany, then, offers some surprises.

---

[65] Ruas, "Aspects," 412.
[66] J. Ros et al., "Archaeobotanical Contribution to the History of Farming Practices in Medieval Northern Catalonia (8th–14th c.)," in *Archaeology and History of Peasantries* 1, ed. J. Quiros Castillo (Bilbao, 2020), 171–2.
[67] L. Firbank, "*Agrostemma Githago* L.," *Journal of Ecology* 76 (1988), 232–46; M. Ruas, "La parole des grains," in *Plantes exploitées, plantes cultivées*, ed. A. Durand (Aix, 2007), 163.
[68] Ruas, "La parole, 165; Devroey, *Économie rurale*, 105.

Among them is certainly the fact that the species archaeobotanically proven to have succeeded in Carolingian times are not those, to be discussed in detail in subsequent chapters, that enjoyed the limelight in Carolingian texts. This observation raises the question of Carolingian empiricism. Already some decades ago, Butzer suggested that certain Carolingian writers, at least, were agronomically well informed and that, in particular, Wandalbert of Prüm's calendrical listing of cultivation tasks, composed in the 840s, was a reasonable adjustment to real north European conditions of Mediterranean-inspired agronomical manuals.[69] Entering the debate over the accuracy of Carolingian writing about natural phenomena from a different angle, Eastwood proposed that there was considerable affinity between the empirical study of the night skies of Carolingian Europe and the respectful study of the authoritative books on astronomical phenomena, such as Isidore's and Bede's.[70] The natural sciences, in other words, were an integral part of the cultural renascence engendered by Carolingian patronage. Though the renascence aimed at the improvement of Europeans' Christianity, it encouraged an observant attitude toward the natural world. Charlemagne's own curiosity about astral movements, recorded by Einhard, was based on observation of the stars, as well as on manuals of computus.

Yet maybe what applied to the highest elements of creation did not always apply to some of the most down to earth. Alcuin's letter in response to Charlemagne's questions on astronomy had pointed out the vast distance between natural phenomena like stars and herbs; when he humbly recognized human ignorance of both, he identified their sole common denominator.[71] "You ask me, an old man with weak faculties, to scrutinize the skies, one who cannot even explain terrestrial affairs, to expound the course of the stars erring randomly across the heavens, one who cannot even sort out the natures of the herbs sprouting from the soil." Oddly similar in recognizing the limits of human understanding, recently Corrie Bakels underlined the complete incongruence between the medieval agricultural world revealed by palynological and carpological tools and the agricultural world known from texts. Ultimately, Bakels

---

[69] K. Butzer, "The Classical Tradition of Agronomical Science," in *Science in Western and Eastern Civilization in Carolingian Times*, ed. P. Butzer and D. Lohrmann (Basel, 1993), 540, 558, 562–4, 578.

[70] Bruce Eastwood, *Ordering the Heavens: Roman Astronomy and Cosmology in the Carolingian Renaissance* (Leiden: Brill, 2000).

[71] Alcuin, "Epistolae" 155, ed. Dümmler, *MGH Epistolae* 4 (Berlin, 1895), 250: "hortans seniorem fragili sensu caelestia scrutare, qui terrenorum necdum didicit rationes, stellarum in caelo errantium vagabundos exponere cursus, qui herbarum in terra nascentium naturas nequaquam agnoscere valet."

took an agnostic stance on which world best approximated past botanical conditions, recognizing limitations in both.[72]

It could be the differences between ethereal stars in the sky above and terrestrial plants on the ground underneath people's feet that explain the discordance between the apparent openness to empiricism of Carolingian astronomers and the lack of interest that Carolingian writers and texts seem to evince for the bad plants that actually propagated themselves in Europe's fields and gardens. For, as we will see in the next chapters, the protagonists of Carolingian weed science were not the main pests on Carolingian farms identified here. Neither the spiny weeds, like briars or thistles, nor the duplicitous ones, like darnel, that colonized the imaginations of Carolingian writers appear to have had much agronomic or economic relevance. Arguably this is true also of stinging nettles (*Urtica urens*), whose fossil pollen presence is respectable at several sites in Carolingian Europe, but whose capacity to cause damage to agriculture is not proportional to the attention lavished on it by clerical writers.

Certainly darnel, or *Lolium temulentum*, the weed with the most fearsome textual reputation, crops up very seldom in early medieval palaeobotanical records: carbonized seeds were found in sixth-century granaries at Monte Barro near Como and in some seventh-century Swiss peasant grain stores, and its pollen left signals in the vicinity of the thoroughly investigated ninth-century settlement of Villiers-le-Sec; at Cysoing in the later ninth century one silo contained twenty-five fragments of *Lolium* (probably the annual species *L. multiflorum*, which is not toxic and can become decent fodder, and which surfaced at roughly the same time in Miranduolo in Tuscany).[73] Though this is a nice demonstration of darnel's ecological versatility and of a vigorous aptitude for quite different soil and climate conditions, it is hardly the record of a triumphant invasive species or successful instrument of the devil. Rather, in early medieval record, it is darnel's archaeobotanical absence that is most striking. On the ground, in the fields of Carolingian Europe, darnel appears to have been almost unknown.[74]

Had the creators of Carolingian weed discourse prioritized scrutiny of the nearby gardens and fields, rather than Christian exegesis, the wicked plants they wrote about might have been different. They might have

---

[72] Bakels, *The Western European Loess Belt*, 212–13.

[73] E. Castiglioni et al., "I resti archeobotanici," in *Archeologia a Monte Barro* 2 (Lecco, 2001), 233; Guilbert, "Étude des pollens," 197; Censier et al., "Indices," fig. 6. Darnel makes up 3.6 percent of mid-Saxon English assemblages: McKerracher, *Anglo-Saxon Crops*, 182.

[74] Darnel remained a tiny presence in the medieval lower Rhine region: K. Knörzer, *Geschichte der synanthropen Flora im Niederrheingebiet* (Mainz, 2007), 89.

noticed more the tall, slightly hairy stems of corncockle (*Agrostemma githago*), a weed whose toxic seeds reached maturity alongside grain, which harvesters gathered with the sheaves of their crop, which winnowers easily confused with crop seeds (adequate winnowing required repeated fine sieving), and which appears to have been present wherever Europeans manipulated the soil.[75] They might also have chronicled the qualities of wild oats (*Avena fatua*), a weed capable of robbing its cultivated cousin of space, light, and nutrients, without generating seeds anywhere near as comestible for humans and their domesticates.

It is, of course, feasible that recovery biases in archaeobotanical samples mask the relevance of undesirable plants, and indeed much of the evidence derives from archaeologically investigated grain stores, which is not a perfect reflection of what grew in the fields. In some cases, it seems, exceptionally finicky winnowing purified the seeds that made their way into granaries and silos, but since at least some weed seeds tend to stay with the harvested crop despite the most fastidious sieving, this is at most a remote possibility. Thus, until more archaeobotanical evidence emerges to illuminate Carolingian crop processing, and sites preserving the byproduct of winnowing become known, the likeliest explanation for the paucity of darnel, and of the other weeds that colonized the Carolingian imagination, is that actually they were not much of a pest to farmers.[76]

The apparent disjuncture between the weeds on the ground and those that found their way on to the parchment page suggests that agronomy and theology for the most part developed separately. Though Carolingian scribes copied some agronomical manuals, and though some secular readers, like Count Ekkehard (+844), kept them in their libraries, the two disciplines did not cross-pollinate much.[77] The exemplary Latin one could learn from Palladius was more important than his considerations on when to weed the grain field, what bad plants to watch out for, and which elimination technique suited which noxious herb. Duly armed with improved Latin, literate Carolingians could turn from agronomy and weed science to the biblical readings and spiritual cultivation that mattered most to them. Thus, this investigation of the archaeobotanical evidence for weeds in Carolingian Europe in some sense supports Richard Hoffmann's generalization that a very big "recurring gap" separated literate

[75] Sieving: Halstead, *Two Oxen*, 156.
[76] Thanks to Marijke van der Veen for clarifying this for me.
[77] J. Gaulin, "Traditions et pratiques de la littérature agronomique pendant le haut Moyen Âge," in *Settimane del CISAM* (Spoleto, 1990), 109–111, 121–3, 129; Butzer, "The Classical Tradition," 553–4, 573–5. Ekkehard: F. Guizard-Duchamp, *Les terres du sauvage dans le monde franque (IVe–IXe siècle)* (Rennes, 2009), 55.

expressions of Christian ideology and "the experience and work of human beings in the material world."[78] But if the weeds on the ground in eighth- and ninth-century Europe were different from the ones that worried Carolingian writers, still the weeds in texts were well grounded. The cultural humus that nurtured them was colored by political and religious concerns, most of all by the distinctive Carolingian sense of how to rightly order a Christian society on earth. That sense encompassed a botany in which all plants were created good, and if some seemed bad, their phyto-social mobility proved how contingent was fallen humanity's evaluation of them.

---

[78] R. Hoffmann, *An Environmental History of Medieval Europe* (Cambridge, 2014), 86–7.

3 The Time of Weeds

Weeds had their rhythms, their own calendars. Depending on the species, they might germinate early in the growing season, or later. They might bloom and set their seed rapidly, or take their time, calculating that delay improved the next generation's chances of survival. Some meticulously matched the pace of growth of crop plants in hopes of having their seeds harvested along with the grains and receiving free housing in a silo or granary over the winter. Most weeds, however, spent most of their lives buried underground, in diverse communities of organisms there, as part of the topsoil's seed bank.[1] Dormant, they waited patiently, sometimes for several years, for the right moisture conditions, for the glimmer of light that might be created by a human activity like plowing, or for the ground temperature to reach perfection. At that exact moment they began to grow roots, stems, and later leaves.

Weeds' time-keeping mechanisms are so finely tuned that palaeobotanists use their remains to discern whether farmers sowed their crops in autumn or spring, to reconstruct past farming practices.[2] For weeds' infamous "opportunism" in practice means they have to be especially vigilant, always aware of the development of the seasons and the passage of time. Quick response to environmental stimuli is (and always was) one of their hallmarks. It has shaped their evolution.[3]

Perhaps a little less quick, but also quite vigilant, alert to the opportunities created by the bad plants' growth and development, were weeders. They carefully calibrated their interventions to the sogginess or hardness of the soil, as these affected the ease of uprooting their targets. They timed their weeding to coincide with the lack of other pressing tasks. They

---

[1] M. Jones, "Dormancy and the Plough," in *From Foragers to Farmers*, ed. A. Fairbairn and E. Weiss (Oxford, 2009), 59.

[2] For an example of land-use reconstruction in ninth- and tenth-century Switzerland based on weeds, see C. Brombacher et al., "Bronzezeitliche und mittelalterliche Pflanzenfunde aus dem Kloster St. Johann in Müstair," in *Müstair, Kloster St. Johann* 4, ed. H. Sennhauser (Zurich, 2007), 96.

[3] H. Baker, "The Evolution of Weeds," *Annual Review of Ecological Systems* 5 (1974), 2–17; E. Russell, *Evolutionary History* (Cambridge, 2011), 38–40, 50–2.

73

delayed until they were certain the crops could withstand the trampling and stirring of the ground that weeding caused. They sped up work against weeds whose growth cycles put them in direct competition with crops. They used hoes, or rakes, or hands, or plows to deal with different weeds at different times of the year.[4]

The herbalists who recognized the positive characteristics in some bad plants were also extremely attentive to vegetable time. Like the early medieval agronomists who advised weeding dog's tooth grass (*Cynodon dactylon*) when the moon was waning, so as to dissuade that pesky weed from ever growing again in the same place, the medicinal herb gatherers sought to pluck their herbs at precisely the right time.[5] The ninth-century redaction of the (mostly Plinian) herbal cures called today the St. Gall Botany, after the manuscript's place of residence for the past 1,200 years, is remarkable for its thoughtful adaptation of ancient Mediterranean prescriptions to early medieval continental (and maybe alpine) conditions.[6] The writer's attention to mountain gentian, a plant not much considered by Pliny, his source, is a sign of such adaptation and of early medieval empiricism.[7] Hence it is more relevant that this herbal does not modify the traditional temporal indicators for gathering wild plants. The time when a weed ceased to be a weed was a medical-scientific fact, immutable: one should only pick such plants before sunrise or after sunset in order to gain access to their medicinal qualities and, presumably, elude their weedy ones.[8] A major source of botanical science for Carolingian readers, Pseudo-Apuleius' herbal, widely disseminated in the Carolingian era, is even stricter about timing: to acquire their potency one must pick thistles at dawn, but only when the moon is in Capricorn.[9]

In sum weeds were (and are) bounded chronologically as much as they are spatially. We are accustomed to calling weeds "plants out of place," and tend to lose sight of their temporality. In Carolingian Europe, weediness was an expression of time just as it was of place, and weeds were plants growing at the wrong *time* more than in the wrong place. This strong chronological dimension to weediness contributed to the bad plants' fluctuating status. Forged by time, in the early Middle Ages

[4] Examples of such modulation of weeding work: Palladius *Opus Agriculturae* 2.9, 2.14, 4.3, 4.9, 5.1; *Geoponika*, tr. A. Dalby (Totnes, 2011), 2.24, 89; 2.38, 94; 3.3, 106; 10.87, 232.
[5] *Geoponika* 3.5, 106; Palladius 10.1 thought manuring a plowed grain field under a waning moon in September liberated it from weeds.
[6] M. Niederer, *Der St. Galler "Botanicus": Ein frühmittlelaterliches Herbar* (Bern, 2005), 9–11, 23–34.
[7] E. Landgraf, "Ein frühmittelalterlicher Botanicus," *Kyklos* 1 (1928), 119–20.
[8] Niederer, *Der St. Galler "Botanicus"*, 104.
[9] "Pseudoapulei Herbarius" 110, ed. E. Howald and H. Sigerist, in *Corpus Medicorum Latinorum* 4 (Leipzig, 1927), 195.

weed identity was malleable and depended on prevailing conditions; it was a "situational construct," rather like human identity.[10] Thus, as noted above, in Carolingian rotations, the very same plant that one year was a pampered field crop became, through its escaped seeds, an infesting weed the following (fallow) season, or the next time the field was sown with a different crop.

The Carolingian people who thought about or coped with weeds knew how important considerations of time were in weedology and reacted accordingly. This chapter therefore examines weeds as temporal phenomena. It seeks to show that the inexorable passage of time was integral to early medieval weeds, to thinking about them, and to their management. And since the beginning of time was a crucial moment in weed history and development, as these were conceived by Carolingian writers, the question of weed origins is a fitting place to start a discussion of weeds in time.

The Original Weed

We know about the Word, but in the beginning was there the Weed, too? In most secular and mainstream religious cosmologies today, this question might seem idle, but it was not so in late antiquity. Then, as Christians grappled with their growing power, and as they discovered the immense diversity that existed among themselves, understanding where weeds had come from, and why, was an important matter. Indeed, it had been an issue for both Mediterranean polytheists and monotheists to chew over for centuries before the Roman emperors converted to Christianity and changed the fortunes of that religion.

The greatest Latin theologian of late Roman times, Augustine of Hippo, acknowledged that Genesis, in its explanation of how the natural world had come into being, was reticent and obscure about the origin of weeds. This obscurity troubled him because, as Greenblatt observed, Augustine desperately wanted to protect God from responsibility for the creation's flaws, and weeds could be numbered among them.[11] Augustine's theological career began just before 390, with most of it concentrated after 393 when he became bishop in the coastal city of Hippo, west of the African provincial capital at Carthage. From his earliest elucubration on weeds in his commentary *On Genesis against the*

[10] P. Geary, "Ethnic Identity as a Situational Construct in the Early Middle Ages," *Mitteilungen der anthropologischen Gesellschaft in Wien* 113 (1983), 15–26.
[11] S. Greenblatt, *The Rise and Fall of Adam and Eve* (New York, 2017), 110. The links between late antique exegesis and ecology are nicely explored in J. Kreiner, *Legions of Pigs in the Early Medieval West* (New Haven, 2020), 46–57.

Manicheans, composed in 388–9, until the 420s, when he was an international celebrity whose opinions on grace, free will, and the nature of creation were considered carefully by people in Rome and Alexandria as well as Carthage, Augustine returned again and again to the subject of how some plants were bad.[12] His "weedology" followed essentially two tracks, depending on his theological purpose. Thus, to Augustine, as to so many others, weeds were good to think with because they were especially supple and adaptable to different discourses, whether of inclusion/exclusion in the community of the righteous or of the nature of created matter and its proper use by Christians.

In the later 380s when he first discussed weeds, Augustine was a recovering Manichean. For, as a young man, from 373 to 382, the future champion of Latin Christian orthodoxy had been won over by the religion named after Mani. Fourth-century observers considered Manicheanism a form of Christianity, and even Augustine sometimes treated it as a deviant or heretical Christian sect.[13] Nowadays Manichean belief in two divine principles seems antithetical to Christian monotheism, but, like early Christians, Manicheans worried about the presence of evil in the world, and how one might live well amidst imperfection. For Manicheans, the physical, material components of creation were most problematic, associated with the inferior divine force and at loggerheads with the positive, utterly immaterial divinity associated with light. Manichean rejection of matter and material enjoyments simplified the task of humans on earth, whose living should be ascetical and whose engagement with physical creation limited to the barest minimum. Even after he turned skeptical of Mani's cosmology, this Manichean concern with the origin of all the manifest imperfections in material creation left Augustine with a persistent curiosity about what God had been up to when he created the world. At Milan, where he had moved in search of career opportunities, Augustine became disillusioned with Mani's teachings because they were incompatible with the best contemporary natural science, and seemed incapable of explaining the nature of the world around him. In the mid-380s the North African turned to more neoplatonic explanations of the origin and nature of the universe.[14]

Partly, one suspects, to distance himself from his previous affiliation, which was well known in Africa through his *Confessions* (of around 400) as

---

[12] On Augustine's growing reputation in the early 400s, see P. Brown, *Augustine of Hippo* (Berkeley, 2000), 462.

[13] J. Lassère, *Africa, quasi Roma (256 av. J-C–711 ap. J-C)* (Paris, 2015), 565–7; R. Lane Fox, *Augustine: Conversion to Confessions* (New York, 2015), 92–3.

[14] Lane Fox, *Augustine*, 228–33; H. Chadwick, *Augustine of Hippo* (Oxford, 2009), 16; J. Lancel, *Saint Augustin* (Paris, 1999), 88.

well as by word of mouth before that autobiography's publication, Augustine dedicated his new Christian self to study of the text his co-religionists considered the most authoritative exposition on the creation of the physical world and its vegetation.[15] According to Genesis 1.11–12, God had created all plants together, once and for all, on the third day. Moreover, God had determined that all this verdure was "good." This telegraphic rendition in Genesis of how the world had come into being reduced the act of vegetative creation to sixty Latin words, and thereby left open a lot of questions. With his characteristic intellectual vigor and agility, Augustine sorted through the narrative to develop a satisfying and, as it turned out, highly influential interpretation of weeds' origins that was compatible with what Genesis said.[16]

His was not the first intervention on the subject, of course. In classical antiquity various authors had pondered plants that harm people and why they existed. According to a venerable pagan tradition, for example, the gods had put weeds on earth both to punish humans for their impudence and to challenge them a bit, or to improve them by stimulating human striving: in other words, weeding could make people, not just the land, better. This view of what weeds were doing in the world shared with the Hebrew scriptural one, and eventually also with Augustine's, a deep anthropocentrism. The presumption throughout was that vegetation served human purposes, whether plants collaborated actively with people's economic purposes or whether they taught people lessons in humility or resilience.

Virgil's *Georgics* contain the most elaborate and (for Latin readers like Augustine) also the best-known version of the pagan explanation for weeds' persistence and ubiquity.[17] But the myth of Zeus' anger when Prometheus stole fire from the gods' residence and spread this technology across earth, thereby elevating humans to almost-godly status, and the subsequent punitive expedition of Pandora to earth, equipped with an ominous "box" whence all manner of mischief (including weeds) sprang forth among humans, was known in some of the earliest compositions in the classical canon.[18] Unlike Hesiod, who alluded in a dozen lines of his

---

[15] Even in the 390s Augustine had to confront repeated insinuations about his "manicheanizing": Chadwick, *Augustine*, 56.

[16] See A. Scafi, *Mapping Paradise* (Chicago, 2006), 34–47 for an orientation to early Christian doubts about Eden and Genesis, and Augustine's popular solutions to many of them.

[17] Virgil, *Georgics* 1.121–34.

[18] Hesiod, "Works and Days" 40–1, in *Theogony, Works and Days, Testimonia*, ed. G. Most (Cambridge, MA, 2006), 88–97 (in *Theogony* Pandora has no pythos when sent to humankind). Aristarchos taught the ancients to equate Hesiod's "jar" full of trouble with the two jars Homer said Zeus kept, filled with Evil and Good to dole out according to

"Works and Days" to the contents of Pandora's jar, Virgil was more curt with the myth. While he referred briefly to the Prometheus story in his account of the beginning of things, in far greater detail Augustus' favorite poet presented a bygone golden age, when Saturn reigned, as a time of workless bliss when people lived from the earth's abundance.[19] When Jupiter arranged a coup d'état at Saturn's expense, he also intervened, somewhat capriciously, to ensure that ease did not spawn lethargy among early humans. He made agriculture challenging, just as he put poison in snakes, gave wolves a rapacious nature, and endowed the seas with waves.[20] This Olympian social and environmental engineering would sharpen human wits and stimulate ingenuity, since there would be plenty of need for it in the new age over which Jupiter presided. Under the Jupiterean regime, primitive people, no longer able to feed themselves on acorns, turned to cultivating grain. This fateful decision led to the spread of fungal parasites and, of course, to weeds. With poetic precision Virgil specified that thistles were the first problem plant, followed by burr-bearing ones and caltrop. Then, among "shining" crops, "unhappy darnel" and "sterile wild oats" began to predominate, requiring a redoubling of effort on the part of the luckless cultivators who sought only to feed themselves.[21]

Augustine, who loved Virgil's poems, flatly rejected the Age of Saturn and its contented simplicity. He likewise deconstructed Virgil's chronology of the earliest times and the development of agriculture, along with weeds. In Augustine's rendition of these events, Virgil's golden age emerged as a rather "pedestrian episode in Italian agricultural history," compressed in its significance by the far longer history outlined in Genesis: Jupiter's subversion of his father, Saturn, merely proved how depressingly human pagan divinities actually were, while Romulus' and

his whim: I. Musäus, *Der Pandoramythos bei Hesiod und seine Rezeption bis Erasmus von Rotterdam* (Göttingen, 2004), 135. See also Greenblatt, *The Rise and Fall*, 121–2; J. McGregor, *Back to the Garden* (New Haven, 2015), 130–1.

[19] The loss of fire in *Georgics* 1.131 evokes the Prometheus myth. The Pandora story was surprisingly unpopular in classical literature and almost unnoticed in Latin texts: aside from Virgil, Horace mentioned it. In Christian circles, Gregory of Nazianzus alone paid much attention to it: Musäus, *Der Pandoramythos*, 9, 135–49, 165–72. See also G. Clark, "Paradise for Pagans?" in *Paradise in Antiquity*, ed. M. Bockmuehl and G. Stroumsa (Cambridge, 2010), 168–73; Greenblatt, *The Rise and Fall*, 110–13.

[20] On the Christian reception of the idea that necessity mothered invention (so agricultural hardships were a divine gift), see C. Glacken, *Traces on the Rhodian Shore* (Berkeley, 1967), 185, 191–2.

[21] *Georgics* 1.147–59. Virgil also considered thieving birds, overarching tree branches, and drought threats to the grain harvest. Virgil's account of earliest human evolution in *Aeneid* 8.316–27 was less agricultural: hunter-gatherers' lives worsened just because they did.

Remus' murderous exchanges were remote and pallid evocations of the far earlier and more significant ones of Cain and Abel.[22]

But if Augustine's interpretation of the classical account of humans' adoption of agriculture and the appearance of weeds was part of his broader polemic with paganism, the soon-to-be-bishop of Hippo's own explanation for the emergence of weeds had more to do with immediate, local affairs in North Africa in the 380s. *On Genesis against the Manicheans* acknowledged the perplexity of those who asked how anyone could consider the creation good when it teemed with noxious plants and useless trees.[23] These doubters, presumably with Manichean antimaterialist sympathies, wondered how "hideous and sterile" vegetation became established in God's good world. Indeed, some of these skeptical folk may have known the Manichean *Letter of Foundation*, which revealed that vegetation originated in demonic ejaculations and was really no better than any other part of created matter.[24] In Augustine's North African circles several people might ask, tauntingly, "who ordained the birth of so many weeds, prickly or poisonous, which are not good to eat, and such multitudes of trees that bear no fruit?" Where then did the weeds come from if a good God had created everything?[25]

In response to this question, the freshly converted Augustine advanced the straightforward answer that human sin had earned a divine curse over the earth, so "prickly plants appeared."[26] They were far from useless, however. Even poisonous plants were educational, reminding humans of how different nature had been in the beginning.[27] Likewise, trees that failed to deliver fruits people could eat taught a lesson about spiritual sterility. Wrapping up his solution to the quandaries of weeds, Augustine appealed to farmers' knowledge: experienced cultivators, he claimed, should understand that unwanted plants (he specifically evoked the "thorns and thistles" of Genesis 3.18) were not there by nature, but

---

[22] S. MacCormack, *The Shadows of Poetry* (Berkeley, 1998), 177–80, 208–10.

[23] J. Coyle, "Genesi adversos Manichaeos, de," in *Augustine through the Ages*, ed. A. Fitzgerald (Grand Rapids, 1999), 378–9.

[24] See Lane Fox, *Augustine*, 104–6. Augustine knew the *Letter*.

[25] Augustine, *De Genesi contra Manichaeos* 1.13.19, 85–6, with "post peccatum autem vidimus multa horrida et infructuosa de terra nasci" and "quis iussit nasci tantas herbas vel spinosas vel venenosas quae ad pabulum non proficiunt, et tam multa ligna quae fructum nullum ferunt?"

[26] A hexameral standard: F. Egleston Robbins, *The Hexameral Literature* (Chicago, 1912), 4–5.

[27] Augustine, *De Genesi contra Manichaeos* 1.13.19, 85 ("herbae autem venenosae ad poenam vel exercitationem mortalium creatae sunt"), 2.27.41, p. 166; also *De Genesi ad Litteram* 2.38, 373. Brown, *Augustine*, 504–5 discusses neoplatonic sensitivity to the divine majesty of nature, its reminder to humans of the creator's power and wisdom. Boosted by Romans 1.20, this "theologia naturalis" became influential among Christians: Glacken, *Traces*, 160–2.

artificially, as part of the divine chastisement of fallen humanity.[28] They were in the deepest sense unnatural.

Among Augustine's ruminations on the subject of weeds, *On Genesis against the Manicheans* is perhaps the least imaginative. Though the North African sage had, apparently, read Ambrose's six sermons on the creation narrative in Genesis shortly after these were delivered in Milan in 387, he did not incorporate much of Ambrose's *Hexaemeron* into his first Genesis commentary, written shortly thereafter. Yet the Milanese archbishop's text was a watershed in Latin Christian thinking about the days of creation. It offered a far more profound and thorough account of what God was up to than had been available before. Ambrose's vast learning permitted him to mine the earlier (AD 378) *Hexaemeron* written in Greek by Basil of Caesarea: indeed, to some extent Ambrose's was a paraphrase of Basil's biblical exegesis. What made Basil's *Hexaemeron* exciting, aside from its acuity, was its incorporation of contemporary scientific, and therefore also botanical, knowledge. While Christian exegetes of the "six days of creation" (hexameron) had always dipped into classical scientific texts to bolster their interpretations, Basil did so more systematically and with more technical competence than his predecessors. The result was a hexameral text that Ambrose thought worth making available to western Roman Christian readers several decades before Eustathius finished a complete Latin translation of Basil's Greek, in the early fifth century.

Both Augustine's growing awareness of this fresh fourth-century hexameral literature, and his waning anxiety about Manichean critiques of the cosmology of Genesis, enabled him to enrich his weed exegesis in the years after he finished *On Genesis against the Manicheans*. One of the biggest differences between Augustine's more mature writings about weeds and his earliest forays in the field is his abandonment of the idea that weeds are didactic, a set of plants God introduced to the world after human sin in Eden in order to remind people of their stumbling history. Instead, Augustine adopted Basil's, and Ambrose's, idea that the bad plants sprouting throughout the world were actually not so bad. In fact, they had important roles to play in the proper functioning of God's creation. The surprisingly modern-sounding notion that plants people abhorred really served important ecological purposes and delivered unexpected social benefits was older than Christian hexameral musing. Adumbrated in Plato's *Timaeus* (77C), it featured in the earliest Greek

---

[28] Augustine, *De Genesi contra Manichaeos* 2.17.41, 166. In ibid., 1.16.25, 92–3 Augustine applied to apparently useless animals (mice, frogs, flies, maggots) reasoning other hexaemeralists had reserved to plants: human ignorance of natural processes blinds us to the beauty and ecological utility of "pests."

treatises on botany, and was taken up with zeal by the Roman encyclopedist Pliny, in whose *Natural History* were listed all the botanical facts
available to a first-century polymath.[29] But to the Church Fathers the
ecological (and medical) utility of weeds had a slightly different, less
environmental valence. They proved God's creation was indeed good
from the start, or at least was the product of a beneficent and rational
creator who did not need to go back over his work, introducing correc-
tions to it in light of errant human behavior.[30]

Augustine's contribution to the emerging Christian weedology was, as
so often with him, scintillating and persuasive. His eloquence and ability
to express complex ideas crisply persuaded many later generations of
readers, for instance about the physical existence of Eden, a real place
on earth, or about the Edenic garden's plants being the same ones that
one could observe growing across the rest of the world.[31] Thus what
Augustine had to say about weeds proved exceptionally influential, even
if we should recall that their future impact was not part of these compositions when Augustine wrote his three commentaries on Genesis (one was
never completed) or treatises against Donatism, and in the process developed a mature Latin Christian weed discourse.

Especially in his great literal commentary on Genesis, the *De Genesi
ad Litteram* of 401–15 (but mostly, it seems, written in 412[32]),
Augustine offered new perspectives to Latin readers. He built on
Basil's insight that to expect all creation to serve human ends is
a provincial, small-minded way to look at the universe: God did not
create everything just to satisfy people's bellies.[33] It was foolish therefore to become indignant when some plants failed to deliver benefits to
people and others delivered measurable harm. Such plants served
other purposes, many of which remained opaque to humans, who
should be content to recognize the immense complexity of the universe

[29] K. Gronau, *Posidonius und die jüdisch-christliche Genesisexegese* (Leipzig, 1914), 99–110
and the introduction in Basil of Caesarea, *Homélies sur l'Hexaéméron*, ed. S. Giet (Paris,
1949), 53–69 list Basil's sources. Augustine was less invested in ancient scientific literature: Brown, *Augustine*, 276. See also V. Burrus, *Ancient Christian Ecopoetics*
(Philadelphia, 2019), 28–35.

[30] Ambrose's belief that God added thorns to Eden's roses after the Fall ("Exameron" 3.11,
in *Sancti Ambrosii Opera*, ed. G. Schenkl (Vienna, 1896), 91) is an exception.

[31] A. Scafi, "Epilogue: A Heaven on Earth," in *Paradise in Antiquity*, ed. Blockmuehl and
Stroumsa, 212–13; Clark, "Paradise for Pagans?", 171; Scafi, *Mapping Paradise*, 34–6,
45–6; Brown, *Augustine*, 501.

[32] P. Hombert, *Nouvelles recherches de chronologie augustinienne* (Paris, 2000), 135.

[33] Such neoplatonic relativism was unpopular in Christian Alexandria: Burrus, *Ancient
Christian Ecopoetics*, 40. On too bellycentric readings of Genesis, see Basil, *Homélies sur
l'Hexaéméron* 5.4, 292 (=Eustathius, *Ancienne version latine des neuf homélies sur
l'Hexaéméron de Basile de Césarée* 5.6, ed. E. Amand de Mendieta and S. Rudberg
(Berlin, 1958), 60).

in such cases.[34] Thus (following Basil and Ambrose), Augustine proposed that plants that seemed hostile were not so in truth, but performed ecologically valuable functions, such as providing food to certain birds and animals: "for there exist animals that easily and sweetly feed on both the tender and the dry thorns and thistles."[35] But compared with Basil and Ambrose, who specified the animal species involved (starlings, quails, deer) and the "noxious" plants they consumed (hellebore, hemlock, poppies), Augustine generalized.[36]

Still, he was much more specific than his Christian predecessors had been on what made some plants obnoxious.[37] Convinced finally by Genesis that all botanical creation was accomplished on the third day, Augustine now deduced that weeds too had first sprouted then, all plants already "making seed" and "fruit according to its kind."[38] As God deemed these plants good, Augustine divined that their bad qualities had simply not become apparent until later.[39] For in God's country plants went about their business, growing leaves, making flowers, and setting seeds according to the divine mandate. There, people had just not been aware of any weediness. Human sin, the expulsion from Eden, and the ensuing need to feed themselves by the sweat of their brows had changed people's perspective. Hitherto innocuous plants with important positions in Eden's healthy ecosystem began to look unfriendly, even dangerous, to humans.

In effect weeds, and particularly "thorns and thistles," appeared when Adam had to begin to bend creation to his agricultural purposes. Not plants' biology, nor even their ecological role, but only human perception had changed after the expulsion from Eden. Plants that did not participate actively in the new economic projects of fallen humanity were now a nuisance or menace. To Augustine it was the greedy gaze of farmers that transformed the innocent vegetation that God created on the third day into infesting weeds in the real world.

The alarming ability of weeds like "thorns and thistles" to entangle Adam after his fall from grace derived from the goal of his earthly striving.

---

[34] Augustine of Hippo, *De Genesi ad Litteram* 3.18.27, 83. Lactantius, *De Ira Dei* 13.10 dismissed the Stoic argument that seemingly useless organisms have utility humans have not yet discerned, but will one day.

[35] Augustine, *De Genesi ad Litteram* 3.18, 84.

[36] Basil, *Homélies* 5.4, 292–4; Ambrose, "Exameron," 3.9, 84–6. See also Egleston Robbins, *The Hexameral Literature*, 51–2.

[37] Augustine, *De Genesi ad Litteram* 3.18.28, 83–4.

[38] Ibid., 5.6.17, 147–9. *De Genesi ad Litteram* 8.3.6, 234–5 states the plants of Eden were the same as everyday plants.

[39] Lane Fox, *Augustine*, 346 points out that Augustine made similar arguments about the appearance of evil on earth in his 392 debate with Fortunatus.

Sin compelled people to seek sustenance in agriculture, and their consequent distortion of nature necessarily altered human relations with plants. Augustine's acute critique of too-anthropocentric botanical evaluations, as we have seen, depended on earlier exegetes' insights. But they led Augustine to consider that when Adam tended to Eden (Genesis 2.15), the thorns, toxins, and hypercompetitive behavior of some plants had not presented any problems. Adam and Eve's activity in managing the garden of Eden was not yet labor of the sort they would have to engage in after the Fall, and a glimmer of their original pleasant tending to plants was visible in the joy that certain modern farmers experienced when amidst their fields.[40] The earliest "working and caring for" the garden was an agreeable pastime in which plants cooperated with humans to perfect God's creation.[41] No weeding was necessary, for there *were* no weeds in God's garden. In postlapsarian fields, on the other hand, it would be foolish, and Manichean, to refrain from rooting out undesirable plants.[42]

Carolingian Beginnings

Carolingian exegetes too pondered the origin of weeds, and the associated matter of why noxious plants covered the ground around them. In the eighth and ninth centuries, these questions retained importance for cosmology and the divine structure of the world. Even endowed with the necessary clarifications of late antique Christian exegesis, the book of Genesis, early medieval Europe's main guide to the origin of weeds, furnished a somewhat confusing account of their emergence on earth, so there was a lot of explaining to do.[43] But, as we saw in the previous section, by the time of Charlemagne theologians could read and evaluate several learned opinions on the topic, amassing thereby an arsenal of Christian, orthodox answers.

---

[40] Augustine, *De Genesi ad Litteram* 8.8.15, 242–3.

[41] In both the Vulgate and Vetus Latina the relevant verbs were "operaretur" and "custodiret." McGregor, *Back to the Garden*, 105 points out the relevant Hebrew verb ("avad") is also used of religious worship. See also M. Lauwers, "Le 'travail' sans la domination?" in *Penser la paysannerie médiévale, un défi impossible?*, ed. A. Dierkens et al. (Paris, 2017), 321–2; S. Piron, "Ève au fuseau, Adam jardinier," in *Adam: la nature humaine avant et après*, ed. I. Rosier-Catach and G. Briguglia (Paris, 2016), 302–3, 305–7.

[42] Augustine of Hippo, *Civitas Dei* 1.20, lest "virgultum evellere nefas ducimus et Manichaeorum errori insanissime adquiescimus." See M. Marder, *The Philosopher's Plant: An Intellectual Herbarium* (New York, 2014), 68–71.

[43] Genesis in Carolingian Christianity: J. Contreni, "The Patristic Legacy to c. 1000," in *New Cambridge History of the Bible* 2, ed. R. Marsden and E. A. Matter (Cambridge, 2012), 507, 525–34; D. Ganz, "Carolingian Bibles," in ibid., 327; S. Shimahara, *Haymon d'Auxerre, exégète carolingien* (Turnhout, 2013), 460–1.

The growing uniformity of biblical text in Carolingian times, and the gradual retreat of the Vetus Latina, removed one source of potential uncertainty. A difficulty early Christian exegetes had confronted when trying to sort out how God had created the world's vegetation was textual. Everyone agreed the Hebrew scriptures were divinely inspired and therefore truthful. But not everyone agreed on what the scriptures said about those generative earliest days. For instance, Augustine deemed the Septuagint a divinely inspired text, and hence preferred the Latin translation of that Greek version of the Hebrew now known as the Vetus Latina. At first, he cheered on the work of his fellow Church Father Jerome, who abandoned Rome in 385 and moved to the Holy Land to complete a new, streamlined, more authoritative redaction of the Vetus Latina text. But when Jerome's knowledge of Hebrew advanced to a level where he could compare the Septuagint and Hebrew versions of God's word, Jerome decided to embark on a more radical retranslation of the Hebrew into Latin. His Vulgate thus often departed from the familiar Latin of the Vetus Latina, alarming and disappointing Augustine, who in fact generally quoted the older text.[44] He was not alone. In fact, both Vulgate and Vetus Latina Genesis texts circulated until Carolingian times, when Jerome's version finally became the undisputed canonical one.[45]

Regarding vegetative creation in Genesis, Jerome's and Augustine's preferred versions of events differed somewhat. The North African's affection for the Vetus Latina led him to encounter in Genesis 1.12 an earth that germinated "edible herbs bearing seeds according to their kind" and "fruitful trees making fruits" likewise according to species. Later in that book, God sentenced Adam to eat "the hay of the field" (Genesis 3.18).[46] Instead, Jerome's determination that the Hebrew Bible was uncorrupted persuaded him the earth was to germinate "green herbs that make seeds and fruit-bearing trees that make fruit according to their kind," elevating a chromatic above a gastronomic qualifier for earliest

[44] R. Teske, "Genesis Accounts of Creation," in *Augustine through the Ages*, ed. Fitzgerald, 379; Lane Fox, *Augustine*. 487–8; Lancel, *Saint Augustin*, 590; F. van Liere, *An Introduction to the Medieval Bible* (Cambridge, 2014), 81–8. Letters between Jerome and Augustine about differences in translation revolved around botany (whether "kykayon" was actually "cucurbita"): 88.

[45] Van Liere, *An Introduction*, 81–2. Biblical text was less stable in manuscript cultures, but divergences among various Vetus Latina editions of Genesis 1 and 3 were inconsequential.

[46] *Bibliorum Sacrorum Latinae Versiones Antiquae* 1, ed. P. Sabatier (Paris, 1751), 9, 20: "germinet terra herbam pabuli, ferentem semen secundum genus, et secundum similitudinem, et lignum fructiferum faciens fructum, cuius semen sit in ipsum secundum similitudinem suam super terram" and "spinas et tribulos germinabit tibi, et edes feonum agri."

plants. He also assigned Adam to eat "the herbs of the earth," a less agricultural diet, better suited to wild ruminants than the tamer vegetarian one designated by the Vetus Latina.[47] All told, though, such divergences were minor compared with what some other exegetes saw in the Hebrew, the wording of which in Genesis 1.11 is ambiguous enough to suggest God might have created three kinds of plants (greens, herbs, and trees) rather than two (green herbs and trees).[48] At least with regards to how many categories of vegetation God created, the Vetus Latina and Vulgate agreed.[49]

These tribulations did not concern the Carolingians, who turned with ever greater confidence to the Vulgate and its "green herbs" that were to be fallen humans' main food. Despite this consensus, the issue of weeds' origins was tangled and the late ancient theological tradition about it was not unanimous; therefore, in Carolingian times more than one solution could circulate. For instance, rather like the younger Augustine, a few thinkers took this to mean that the original good earth did not generate such unpleasant plants. The manifest existence in postlapsarian conditions of weeds was thus explainable as a punishment for Adam's transgression. Weeds had not been part of God's original design but were created afterwards to chastise humans for their disregard of divine precepts.[50]

In the Insular exegetical tradition, particularly in Bede's analysis of Genesis and in the so-called Reference Bible (an Irish biblical commentary in dialogue form, quite popular in Francia), it had seemed unlikely that Edenic perfection included obviously imperfect plants. Perhaps impressed by his English teacher Alcuin, Hrabanus Maurus determined that the Anglo-Irish interpretation of how weeds came to earth had merit: they were put there upon Adam's introduction to earth to teach him, and his descendants, a lesson.[51] For it was the Carolingian polymath

---

[47] *Biblia Sacra iuxta Vulgata Versionem*, ed. R. Weber and R. Gryson (Stuttgart, 2007), 4, 8: "germinet terra herbam virentem et facientem semen et lignum pomiferum faciens fructum iuxta genus suum" and "et comedes herbas terrae."

[48] M. Alexandre, *Le commencement du livre de Genèse I–IV: la version grecque de la Septante et sa reception* (Paris, 1988), 122–3.

[49] Augustine, *De Genesi contra Manichaeos* 1.31, 99, 1.40, 109 distinguished between "herbis seminalibus" and "herbis viridis," seedy and leafy plants.

[50] F. Guizard-Duchamp, *Les terres du sauvage dans le monde franc (IVe–IX siècle)* (Rennes, 2009), 64–6.

[51] Insular thinking: *The Reference Bible* 12.1, ed. G. MacGinty (Turnhout, 2000), 49 (regarding trees); Bede, "Libri Quatuor in Principium Genesis" 1.29, 3.17, in *Bedae Venerabilis Opera* 2.3, ed. C. Jones (Turnhout, 1960), 30, 68. See also Alcuin, "Interrogationes et Responsiones in Genesin" 79, ed. J. Migne, *PL* 100 (Paris, 1863), 524 and his "Carmina" 115, 346, with M. Fox, "Alcuin the Exegete," in *The Study of the Bible in the Carolingian Era*, ed. C. Chazelle and B. Van Name Edwards (Turnhout, 2003), 39–51.

Hrabanus who most clearly articulated the theory that God had created "thorns and thistles," and by implication other infesting plants that hampered human agriculturalists, long after that third day when vegetation had first sprung up.[52] Before him, Claudius of Turin (who died around 827, and though distrusted by several Carolingian thinkers, participated in their "discourse community") entertained the possibility that spiny weeds were an invention God conjured up after Adam sinned, in order to curse a previously verdant land: evidently, in the early ninth century some people still had doubts on the subject.[53] Walafrid Strabo, gifted student of Hrabanus at Fulda, alluded to the postlapsarian invention of weeds in a poem about Christmas and its seasonal undoing of the "original curse," expressed by the retreat of spiny plants.[54] The doubts lingered, too, through the end of the century, as Remigius of Auxerre's *Exposition on Genesis* attests.[55] Thus, some of the most celebrated Carolingian exegetes were quite ambivalent about whether "thorns and thistles" had been a postlapsarian afterthought of the creator. Yet most other Carolingian commentators found the idea awkward because it implied that God's creation was incomplete at the end of the sixth day, or even that God had overlooked some details, like a sloppy architect, and the first earthly structure had required amendment.

The record of discussions at the Council of Paris (825) offers a rare instance where the broader Carolingian church came close to agreeing with the notion that new species of plant could arise even after God had finished creating earthly vegetation. The clergy gathered there determined that sometimes miracles could engender unprecedented plants. In this case it seemed worthwhile to forget that all plants on earth had been created on the third day, once and for all, because the new botanical species ("herba quaedam nova specie") permitted the council to correct both iconoclasts and idolaters, and keep to the middle ground on the issue of the correct Christian use of images.[56] The source attesting to the spontaneous growth of the unprecedented plant was Eusebius, who

[52] Hrabanus Maurus, "Commentaria in Genesim" 1.19, ed. J. Migne, *PL* 107 (Paris, 1864), 497.
[53] Claudius of Turin, "Commentarii in Genesim" 1, ed. J. Migne, *PL* 50 (Paris, 1859), 898, with M. Gorman, "The Commentary on Genesis of Claudius of Turin and Biblical Studies under Louis the Pious," *Speculum* 72 (1997), 279.
[54] Walafrid Strabo, "Carmina" 25, ed. E. Dümmler, *MGH Poetae* 2 (Berlin, 1884), 381.
[55] Remigius, *Expositio super Genesim* 3.17, ed. B. Van Name Edwards (Turnhout, 1999), 62–3.
[56] "Concilium Parisiense" 1, ed. A. Werminghoff, *MGH Legum Sectio III* 2.2 (Hanover, 1908), 484, citing Eusebius, *Die Kirchengeschichte* 7.18, ed. E. Schwartz and T. Mommsen 2.2 (Berlin, 1999), 673. On plants' ability to absorb the virtue of the things they grew over, see V. Flint, *The Rise of Magic in Early Medieval Europe* (Princeton, 1991), 270.

claimed to be an eyewitness, and the story involved a statue of Jesus in Caesarea, at the base of which suddenly grew a new and beneficent plant, much used by the locals to cure disease, so the small detour from accepted opinion on the completeness of creation when God took his rest seemed justifiable to the assembled Carolingian clergymen.

For the rest, learned Franks who pondered the origins of uncooperative plants disagreed that vegetable creation took more than a day to finish. This was the safer, canonical position, one that did not call into question the wisdom and perfection of God's creative activity, and that aligned with what the Fathers (mostly) had maintained. It was destined to enjoy a long afterlife: in 1735, when he published the *Systema Naturae*, his still-authoritative classification of all plants by genus and species, the great Swedish naturalist Carl Linnaeus expected the total number of species he could include to be the same as the total number made on the third day. Though his successful experiments to cross two species of dandelion and produce a third species later persuaded him this expectation was wrong, the founder of modern plant taxonomy continued to believe that God had fixed the number of genuses, even if species could interbreed and thus multiply.[57]

Similarly convinced that all vegetation arose in one fell swoop when God ordained it, many educated Carolingians took a relativizing, almost "post-human" and Augustinian stance to account for weeds' origin: not all creation was there to please humans, so one should not wonder at the existence within it of plants that displeased them. This humbler view had, as we saw in the preceding section, been eloquently set out by Basil of Caesarea in much-admired sermons, and by Ambrose in his influential Genesis commentary, which deeply affected Augustine's reading of the creation narrative. In this mighty wake, many leading Carolingian exegetes, like Wigbod and Angelomus, as well as ultimately Claudius of Turin and Remigius of Auxerre, wrote about plants that seemed "sterile," even poisonous, to people, but were important resources to birds and other animals, who fed and rested on them.[58] In other terms, to wonder why God placed pernicious plants on earth was to forget that earth was not merely a human playground. Before humans became mortal, and susceptible to plant toxins or plant armor, poisonous and just obnoxious weeds had, unnoticed by them, been doing the same things they continued to do into the present: they supported the ecosystem.

[57] N. Kingsbury, *Hybrid* (Chicago, 2009), 73.
[58] Wigbod, "Quaestiones in Octateuchum," ed. J. Migne, *PL* 96 (Paris, 1862), 1126–7; Claudius, "Commentarii in Genesim" 1, 898; Angelomus, "Commentarius in Genesin" 1.11–13, ed. J. Migne, *PL* 115 (Paris, 1881), 120; Remigius, *Expositio super Genesim* 3.17, 63.

Augustine had developed this insight into the cultural construction of the weed out of the economic necessities of human life. His Carolingian readers adapted this thinking. As Haimo of Auxerre put it, writing around 850, the "thorns" that certainly grew luxuriantly in Eden did not then hinder human activities, including the recreational gardening of Genesis 2.15.[59] Still more popular in eighth- and ninth-century exegesis was Augustine's (and others') suggestion that even after the Fall weeds were a culturally useful component in creation. The didactic service of weeds to humans, their ability to remind people of the early transgression and the consequent imperfection of human environments, appears in numerous Carolingian scriptural commentaries. Even for Hrabanus Maurus the thorns in humans' fields were less a punishment than a kind of monument, an enduring reminder, of what had transpired; and to Angelomus, apparently unfruitful or sterile trees and poisonous grasses in the postlapsarian world both reminded of and warned against sin.[60] Persistent, inescapable, slightly menacing, weeds made great teachers. They imparted understanding of the order of things.

When eighth- and ninth-century scholars thought about the cosmological place of weeds, they could choose among several authorities to guide them.[61] But essentially Carolingian ideas about the origins of bad plants were Christian late antique ideas, sometimes filtered through Dark Age texts like Isidore's or Bede's. Whereas their late antique predecessors knew alternative accounts of where weeds came from, and developed their Genesis-based version in polemic with some of the other natural histories, Carolingian authors ignored Pandora's box and any botanical side-effects produced by the end of the Age of Saturn when they reconstructed weeds' origins.[62] If a simplistic reading of God's infliction of weeds on Adam's progeny might suggest parallels with the pagan narratives, Carolingian audiences betray no awareness of them. For example, Virgil's elaborate explanation of the original weed gained no traction. However enthusiastic Carolingian consumption of Virgil was, his version of the deep history of weeds persuaded none.[63] By the eighth century,

[59] Haimo of Auxerre, "Commentarius in Genesim" 3.17, ed. J. Migne, PL 131 (Paris, 1884), 67: "spinae vero antea erant, quia inter reliquas arbores et virgultas spinas Deus creavit, sed non ad hoc ut homini laborem inferrent, quae post peccatum ad laborem et afflictionem humano genere datae sunt." See Shimahara, Haymon, 71–2, 160–83. On Genesis 2.15, see Lauwers, "Le 'travail' sans la domination?," 321–2.

[60] Hrabanus, "Commentaria in Genesim" 1.19, 497; Angelomus, "Commentarius in Genesin" 1.11–13, 120.

[61] For instance, they did not follow Lactantius, De Ira Dei 13.9–14 in his analysis of how harmful things arose on earth.

[62] Neglect of Pandora: Musäus, Der Pandoramythos.

[63] Georgics was the eleventh most-copied book in Carolingian scriptoria: J. Gaulin, "Traditions et pratiques de la littérature agronomique pendant le haut Moyen Âge," Settimane del CISAM 37 (Spoleto, 1990), 116.

Genesis, carefully considered, acutely expounded by the Fathers, and mediated by some Insular authorities, shed all the light one needed to understand where weeds had come from and when.

Weeds and the Carolingian Calendar

Weed time had several dimensions. One could ponder the cosmic question of when weeds had first arisen, but one could also wonder about their seasonality on earth, specifically in one's own northwestern Eurasian part of it. To the Carolingians, where weeds fit in the calendar by which humans kept track of the passage of time was a political question, because a reform of the calendar, intimately related to the computation of correct Easter observance, was among the several idealistic initiatives Charlemagne launched as part of the "correctio" of the 790s.[64] This involved firstly drawing up and then disseminating what scholars sometimes call the *Reichskalender*, a compendium of historical, astronomical, astrological, agronomic, and other data about each month and its days. Secondly, the calendar reform involved spreading through Frankish Europe knowledge of computus, the science of reckoning time in relation to the Christian holidays that reached its apogee in the eighth century.[65] The object was to get Charlemagne's subjects on the same schedule, part of the broader Carolingian push for greater uniformity among imperial territories and populations. As we shall see, weeds and weeding had a role to play in this chronological project.

Time-keeping was a topic of enduring interest to Charlemagne. Indeed, around 800 how to do it right was far from a settled matter in Europe: in the 780s court scholars had debated the correct calculation of when to observe Easter, and some of the continuing uncertainties and bafflements that keeping track of the passage of time engendered are visible in the Frankish king's correspondence with Alcuin from the last years of the eighth century: eight surviving letters from AD 798–799 deal with calendrical and time-measuring matters. As late as 809 Charlemagne, by then an aged emperor, posed anxious questions about gauging the passage of time to the scholars at his Aachen court, and even thereafter multiple versions of computus tables circulated.[66] So it makes

[64] J. Palmer, "Calculating Time and the End of Time in the Carolingian World," *English Historical Review* 126 (2011), 1307–31.
[65] See A. Borst, *Die karolingische Kalenderreform* (Hanover 1998), 234–41. Palmer, "Calculating Time," 1326–30 stresses the variety of opinions Carolingian computists held, and the lack of any court-sponsored dogma.
[66] D. Lohrmann, "Alkuins Korrespondenz mit Karl dem Grossen über Kalender und Astronomie," in *Science in Western and Eastern Civilization in Carolingian Times*, ed. P. Butzer and D. Lohrmann (Basel, 1993), 79–114; K. Springsfeld, "Karl der Grosse,

sense that several years after his royal patron's death, most likely in the early 820s, when Einhard wrote the definitive biography of the great ruler, he noted Charlemagne's lifelong interest in calendrical matters: "he studied the liberal arts most assiduously ... and [with Alcuin] he spent much time and effort learning rhetoric and dialectic, and especially though astronomy; he studied the art of computus and with thoughtful attention most carefully investigated the movements of the planets."[67]

After this general observation on his hero's curiosity about time-related matters, Einhard also claimed that a short time after he became emperor, Charlemagne sought to change the commonly used names for the months (as well as for the winds) and "impose names in his own language."[68] For until 800 it seems the Franks had called the twelve months by a mix of classical Latin or "barbarous" (and hence pagan) names. Einhard implied that Charlemagne disapproved of such usage, particularly after he took on the imperial office and grew more interested in more homogeneous and more explicitly Christian norms and practices across the realm: the relevant section of his biography emphasizes extant discrepancies in customs and Charlemagne's desire for codification and unification. The freshly crowned emperor, Einhard suggested, believed a properly ordered and God-pleasing society should use a single set of vernacular Frankish words for the year's subdivisions, and these labels should reflect eternal truths like the passage of the seasons, Christian belief, and especially peasant labor. Hence January would become Wintermonth (Wintarmanoth), April Eastermonth (Ostarmanoth), November Autumnmonth (Herbistmanoth), and December Holymonth (Heilagmanoth), and all subjects would henceforth (in Einhard's fantasy, at any rate) pronounce the new, unfamiliar words as a mark of their loyalty, of participation in a community bounded by its shared time-keeping practices.[69]

Alkuin, und die Zeitrechnung," *Berichte zur Wissenschaftsgeschichte* 27 (2004), 55–8; B. Englisch, "Karolingische Reformkalender und die Fixierung des christlichen Zeitrechnung," in *Computus and Its Cultural Context in the Latin West*, ed. I. Warntjens and D. Ó Cróinín (Turnhout, 2010), 238–58; J. Fried, *Charlemagne* (Cambridge, MA, 2016), 238, 276, 399–400, 488–91.

[67] Einhard, *Vita Karoli* 25, ed. G. Pertz, *MGH in Usum Scholarum* (Hanover, 1845), 24–5: "artes liberales studiosissime coluit ... apud quem [Alcuinum] et rhetoricae et dialecticae, praecipue tamen astronomiae ediscendae, plurimum et temporis et laboris impertivit. Discebat artem computandi, et intentione sagaci syderum cursus curiosissime rimabatur."

[68] Einhard, *Vita Karoli* 29, 27–8: "propriam linguam vocabula imposuit," in a segment which also stressed Charlemagne's dedication to "old time" Frankish culture and language, balancing his new Roman connection from ch. 28. On Charlemagne's native language(s), see J. Nelson, *King and Emperor* (Berkeley, 2019), 68.

[69] How use of foreign words ("code switching") forges unity among the cognoscenti is treated by J. Adams, *Bilingualism and the Latin Language* (Cambridge, 2003), 19–20,

Yet the majority of Charlemagne's new month names derived from farming operations associated with the warmer, and thus in northwestern Europe busier, part of the agricultural year.[70] In the new listing of months, May became Pasturemonth (Winnemanoth), June Plowingmonth (Brachmanoth), July Haymakingmonth (Hewimanoth), and October Vintagemonth (Windumemanoth). Maybe recognizing the ambiguities that human categorization produced when applied to natural variety, Charlemagne's proposed monthly routine thus juxtaposed a pasture-month (May) with a fallow-month (June), supposing the latter to be the time when unplanted fields were plowed in order to aerate the soil and, naturally, reduce weed growth. Immediately thereafter came the month when peasants made hay (July).[71] It is possible that in this ordering of activities the May-time pasturing of cattle was expected to take place on the same fallow fields to be plowed under in June, though hay-making obviously took place in separate areas. In effect, as we shall see in Chapter 6, the distinction between rough pasture and fallow land was hard to make on the ground, spatially, however reasonable it sounded when expressed temporally, as it was in Charlemagne's succession of month names. The same vegetation grew on both kinds of field, acting as pasture in May but as weeds in June, when one might want to plow and even plant fallow fields.

While Charlemagne's calendar reform, the most ambitious in Europe since Caesar and Augustus, had considerable success and can still be discerned behind the current global system for keeping track of time's passage, his attempt to rename the months seems to have persuaded no one.[72] Outside Einhard's biography it left no traces in texts, and people (at least literate people) in the Carolingian empire continued to call the months by their Julian names. Einhard had his reasons for presenting the new names as an accomplishment of the emperor, not least the fact that his literary model, Suetonius, ascribed the renaming of the month Sextilis (as August) to the Roman senate's desire to honor the first emperor, Augustus. That such rulerly intervention into how people named the months was in fact rare in antiquity and unprecedented in postclassical

402–5; E. Roberts, "Boundary Clauses and the Use of the Vernacular in Eastern Frankish Charters, c. 750–c. 900," *Historical Research* 91 (2018), 599–603.
[70] Calendar reform: C. Hammer, *Charlemagne's Months and Their Bavarian Labors* (Oxford, 1997), 10–14. D. Starostine, "\In die festivitatis," *Early Medieval Europe* 14 (2006), 465–86 argues for the pre-eminence of agricultural over religious time in Carolingian time-keeping practices. R. McKitterick, *Charlemagne* (Cambridge, 2008), 325–6 thinks the religious and agricultural calendars were easily fused. Issues of language: R. Bergmann, "Volkssprächige Wörter innerhalb lateinische Texte," in *Die althochdeutsche und altsächsische Glossographie* 1, ed. R. Bergmann and S. Stricker (Berlin, 2009), 977.
[71] Hammer, *Charlemagne's Months*, 11.   [72] Fried, *Charlemagne*, 550.

Europe, as was the association of potentates with calendrical observance and time-reckoning mechanisms, cannot have been lost on the author of the *Life of Charles*. Einhard made a point about Charlemagne's fitness to rule by remembering his correction of his subjects' month-naming. Perhaps he knew that it was not just Augustus, but also another exceptional forerunner of Charlemagne, the Hebrew reformer-king Josiah, who had tinkered with his people's time-keeping and thereby improved their religious observance (II Kings 23.5). And as Einhard inserted the information about the month names in a section of his biography evoking the "nativist" and "Germanicizing" policies of Charlemagne, he advanced his case for the unique nature of Carolingian authority, which was simultaneously Roman and Frankish (and maybe Hebrew). There was much more to the purification of Carolingian month names than a simple desire to tidy up.[73]

Regardless, Einhard's refined literary and political purposes seem not to have been widely appreciated in the ninth century. Indeed, Carolingian *Reichskalender* dating from after 800 themselves ignored the Frankish vernacular names that, according to Einhard, Charlemagne championed, though they incoporated a vast amount of information about each month, including its name in several languages other than Charlemagne's "own language," the Frankish one.

In the *Reichskalender* the month of August, which Einhard said Charlemagne wanted to rechristen "Aranmanoth," or Harvestmonth, preserved Roman imperial memories (perhaps more effectively than Einhard's subtle evocation of Augustan precedent) that could be useful in ninth-century Francia: drawing on Macrobius, the Carolingian calendar explained this month was named after Augustus by the Roman senate because on its first day Augustus overcame Antony and Cleopatra, thereby securing Rome's imperial rule.[74] More curious even than this bit of learned lore is the preservation in the *Reichskalender* of the Old English name for August, "Weodmonath," or Weedmonth. But from the first drafting of the new Carolingian calendar, evidently at Lorsch in 789, the Venerable Bede's influential *De Temporibus Ratione* had been an important source, which explains why the Carolingian imperial calendar retained the information about early English words. In chapter 15 of his computistical treatise, Bede recorded the fact that "the ancient English people" had called the month of August Weedmonth "because in that time they are most abundant."[75]

---

[73] Borst, *Die karolingische Kalenderreform*, 235; C. Parolo, *Immagini del tempo degli uomini, immagini del tempo degli dei* (Oxford, 2017), 8–9, 159–60.

[74] *Der karolingische Reichskalender*, ed. A. Borst, *MGH Libri Memoriales* 2.2 (Hanover, 2001), 1151.

[75] Bede, *De Temporibus Ratione*, ed. C. Jones (Turnhout, 1977), 331–2: "antiqui autem anglorum populi ... mensis Augustus Weodmonath vocatur. Weodmonath mensis

Bede thus transmitted to the Carolingian calendrical scholars a little Anglo-Saxon erudition connecting the height of the summer with the proliferation of weeds (and not any old weeds: Bede used the Gospel's "zizania," discussed in the next chapter, to ensure his readers knew these plants were truly bad). Of course, although the English Weedmonth appears eccentric in early medieval Europe, Anglo-Saxon England was hardly the only pre-industrial polity to name a section of the year after weeds, that inevitable fact of agricultural life.[76] But Bede's lexical information did not interest Carolingian readers. Despite Charlemagne's apparent enthusiasm for month names that alluded to peasant work in ancient Germanic languages, August remained August and nobody in Francia seems to have linked it with weeds or weeding. Thus, Wandalbert of Prüm's poem "On the Twelve Months," written around 848, called the eighth month August as it had been called for more than eight centuries, though the poet in a sense echoed Charlemagne by remarking that gathering crops was the sole preoccupation of peasants during these thirty-one days of the year.[77] Both the *Reichskalender* and Wandalbert were wrong, for in most of Europe, and most of Charlemagne's empire, harvesting grain tended to happen in July. Both calendar-reformers and poet in any case idealized, for when one actually gathered the crops depended on a host of unpredictable factors, beginning with the summer weather, but including the average temperatures in spring (when most grains germinate), the presence of rusts or other pests, and the availability of labor.[78]

Still, the "imperial" calendar's neglect of the ancient Anglo-Saxon idea that weeds were meaningful enough to name months after, and the general Carolingian association between August and tidy harvests, is significant. It was related to an imperial ideology according to which righteous rulers brought order to nature. The wild autonomy of weeds was inappropriate to the controlled rhythms of the Carolingian year, and the Carolingian calendar reflected this, as did Wandalbert's poem, which

---

zizaniorum quod ea tunc maxime abundant." Bede's observation was preserved in Old English time-keeping tools like *Das altenglische Martyrologium* 2, ed. G. Kotzor (Munich, 1981), 164, from the late 800s. On Bede's influence on the "imperial" calendar, see Borst, *Die karolingische Kalenderreform*, 56–7; for the Lorsch prototype, see ibid., 247–98.

[76] W. Cronon, *Changes in the Land* (New Haven, 1983), 43 discusses the southern (corn-growing) New England native calendar, and Weedingmonth, quite unlike the northern hunters' month names.

[77] Wandalbert of Prüm, "De Mensium Duodecim," ed. E. Dümmler, *MGH Poetae* 2 (Berlin, 1884), 611–12.

[78] Hammer, *Charlemagne's Months*, 6–9, 19–25 thinks the mistiming of rustic operations in Charlemagne's labors derives from the classical models employed.

nowhere refers to the very basic "labor of the month" that weeding crops represented.[79]

Weeds and Their Labors

Ecologically, at least, the Carolingians were right. The archaic English association of the eighth month with weeds is odd, for even in England, August is not especially weedy, certainly no weedier than July or September. In addition, the species of plant Bede identified as "weod," the darnel he rendered in Latin as "zizania," would be well past its prime by then, since darnel is a mimic of wheat and reaches maturity with the cereal it infests.[80] The details of early medieval Anglo-Saxon agrarian strategies are imperfectly known, but high medieval English farmers weeded in June and July, when their crops were mature enough to withstand the jostling, but also young enough to benefit from the reduced competition. The feast of St. John (June 24) was an important marker in the medieval weed calendar, and not just in England: indeed, to empha-size the feast's importance for early medieval Europeans, Hubert Mordek has called it a "summertime Christmas." June 24 was a special time partly because of the popularity of John the Baptist's cult and partly because (in northwestern Europe, anyway) it marked the beginning of the "good" season when the land was bountiful and generous, the specter of famine receded a bit, and everyone could anticipate soon bringing in their harvests.[81] The importance of St. John's day to the Frankish weeding calendar emerges from a story Gregory of Tours related about a woman who took her weeding hoe to her field on that feast day, and was struck with painful incapacitation when she began to weed. Her transgression of the holiday testifies to Frankish weeding habits, as well as to the power of St. Martin, who liberated her from her crippling pain after a few months.[82]

Instead, ancient Rome's agronomists, when in calendrical mode, sug-gested that weeding was an activity of the months between October and

---

[79] For evidence that "On the Twelve Months" is less realistic than poetic, see K. Butzer, "The Classical Tradition of Agronomical Science," in *Science in Western and Eastern Civilization in Carolingian Times*, ed. P. Butzer and D. Lohrmann (Basel, 1993), 562–4, 574, 577–8.

[80] Medieval English farming: D. Postles, "Cleaning the Medieval Arable," *Agricultural History Review* 37 (1989), 136.

[81] The feast of St. John: Postles, "Cleaning," 130; P. Mane, *Le travail à la campagne au Moyen Âge* (Paris, 2006), 150; A. Delatte, *Herbarius* (Brussels, 1961), 69–71. See also H. Mordek, "Karls des Grossen zweites Kapitular von Herstal und die Hungersnote der Jahre 778/779," *Deutsches Archiv für Erforschung des Mittelalters* 61 (2005), 14–15.

[82] Gregory of Tours, *De Virtutibus Beati Martini Episcopi*, ed. B. Krusch, in *MGH Scriptores Rerum Merovingicarum* 1.2 (Hanover, 1885), 628.

April, reflecting their Mediterranean orientation but also a broader truth
about the advisability of doing away with weeds during crops' early
growth, when their capture of moisture, nutrients, and sunlight is most
damaging to tender, immature grains.[83] Further moving Roman weed-
consciousness away from August, the somewhat obscure weed goddess
Runcina, derided by Augustine as proof of the useless proliferation of
polytheistic protectors, was venerated during the winter "sementivae
feriae," which usually fell in January and had absolutely nothing to do
with the peak month of summer.[84]

Though much weeding in Carolingian texts is metaphorical, it too
suggests that no ninth-century Frank expected weeds to be most obvious
in August. Like other Carolingian commentators, Smaragdus of St.-
Mihiel considered weeding a task that prepared fields for sowing, and
thus came in the immediate vicinity of that operation, in either early
autumn or early spring. He observed that no sane farmer would sow his
crop in a field crowded by weeds, and a prior purification increased the
likelihood of a good yield.[85] As noted, weeding is not really a preparatory
task, except perhaps when the plow is employed to grind unwanted
vegetation into the soil. In most cases weeding comes after the crops'
germination and accompanies the early development of the desirable
plants, so Samaragdus was agronomically inaccurate. Yet he did locate
the work in time, and delimit its relevance within the agricultural year.
Like other Carolingian writers he did not think weeds most abundant at
the height of summer.

Unpersuaded by the special weediness of August, the Carolingians
nevertheless accepted the idea that weeds sprang forth most luxuriantly
at specified times of year, and made people notice them most then, creating
an obligation to labor. Carolingian depictions of the "labors of the months"
developed a motif by which ninth-century painters represented the norma-
tive passage of time through peasant work. The iconography of laboring
farmworkers was considered an improvement over the pagan zodiacal
signs. Those that survive today do not suggest high summer was the time
of weeds and weeding in the ninth-century learned imaginary.[86] The very
beautiful single illuminated leaf from a mid-tenth-century sacramentary
now kept in Berlin's Staatsbibliothek (MS theol. lat. fol. 192, Fragment) is

---

[83] Palladius, *Opus Agriculturae* books 6–9 (outlining the May–August tasks) lack references
to weeds and weeding.

[84] Runcina: Augustine, *De Civitate Dei* 4.8. She is otherwise little attested: R. Phillips,
"Runcina," *Brill's New Pauly* 12 (Leiden, 2008), 781.

[85] Smaragdus of St.-Mihiel, *Expositio in Regulam S. Benedicti* 1, ed. A. Spannagel and
P. Englebert (Siegburg, 1974), 32 wrote of spiritual weeding, sowing, and reaping.

[86] J. Nelson, "The Church and a Revaluation of Work in the Ninth Century," in *The Use and
Abuse of Time in Christian History*, ed. R. Swanson (Woodbridge, 2002), 35–43.

unique in the (sensu lato) Carolingian pictorial canon for its image of weeding, a task it binds to the month of June, not August (see this book's cover).[87] Other Carolingian "labors of the months" ignore weeds and the toil they created, and this particular subject attracted Carolingian painters only when they needed to represent Adam's misfortunes right after his expulsion from Eden.[88] Even the gifted illuminator of the Utrecht Psalter, whose interest in rural toil surfaces in numerous pictures alongside the psalms' text, never represented weeding. In this neglect, on the one hand, Carolingian painters scrupulously imitated the classical "labors of the months" iconography, insofar as it can still be discerned, mostly in mosaic pavements of the third to sixth century.[89] But, on the other hand, it is also possible that an iconography dominated by male forms of rural work found it difficult to integrate weeding, a task that, as we have seen, was often left to women and children in agrarian Europe. Either way, if the painters were not particularly concerned with locating the time of weeds, Carolingian writers were fairly consistent in depicting spring as the weedy season, and therefore as the time of weeding. August, as Charlemagne's calendar claimed, was when the harvest happened.[90]

Suggestively, centuries after the Berlin sacramentary was painted, high and late medieval calendars from England and France continued to represent June as the thistle-cutting month, so the peasant carefully cutting the thistle-like plant may lie at the beginning of an artistic tradition.[91] It may also represent a fact of rural life for northwestern Europeans during the early Middle Ages, namely that in grain fields they faced a formidable competitor, deep-rooted thistles able to rob grains of nutrients during their key phase of growth to maturity, and liable later to get in the way of sickle-wielding harvesters if allowed to develop through the summer. Eliminating thistles in June, when the offending plants were immature and easier to handle, was an investment of labor that paid off on large estates, concerned with marketable surpluses and what modern economists might call rationality.

---

[87] See https://digital.staatsbibliothek-berlin.de/werkansicht?PPN=PPN656898992&PHYSID=PHYS_0007&DMDID=DMDLOG_0001, accessed November 21, 2019. Though the labors corresponding to each month differ in various versions (A. Borst, *Der Streit um den karolingischen Kalender* (Hanover, 2004), 96), none depicts weeding.

[88] See Chapter 5 on the iconography of Adam weeding.

[89] Parolo, *Immagini*, 132, 274 notes that at St. Mary's (dated to c. AD 568) in Beth She'an February is depicted as a peasant with a hoe. On medieval representations of weeding, see Mane, *Le travail*, 41–5, 149–51, 289–91.

[90] On the representation of Carolingian rural labor in time, see the excellent table 1 in Hammer, *Charlemagne's Months*, 84–5. The Utrecht Psalter (Utrecht University Library, MS 32) is splendidly available at https://bc.library.uu.nl/utrecht-psalter.html.

[91] J. Zadoks, *Crop Protection in Medieval Agriculture* (Leiden, 2013), 107; Mane, *Le travail*, 150.

Weeding Time

In an "organic economy" clearing crop fields of undesirable plants was an activity that tended to require one or two bursts of labor, of varying length according to the size of the plot one weeded, rather than multiple interventions scattered across the crop's entire growing cycle; harvest time was in any case definitely not weeding time. The tenth-century Byzantine agronomical treatise called *Geoponika* accepted that in the case of some crops, like millet, weeders might have to intervene several times prior to harvest, but carefully modulated all weeding according to the proclivities of the targeted plant, and strongly advised against interfering with crop fields between the seedlings' germination and when the grain stalks were in ear.[92] To some extent the anonymous author's wisdom replicated that of the ancient writers whose advice the *Geoponika* compiled and organized for tenth-century purposes: weeding by hoe fields of young grain, the stalks of which had barely developed four leaves, as opposed to plucking the weeds there by hand, was discouraged by Roman authorities on agriculture like Palladius.[93]

Thus, the field weeds that most preoccupied the powerful in Francia would have benefited from peasants' attention between late spring and early summer, especially in May and June, when both winter-sown grains like wheat or rye, and spring-sown ones like oats, developed.[94] Later, when the crop plants had established themselves and overshadowed any late-sprouting competitors, the urgency for and benefit of investing in work to clear weeds declined: in fact, such late weeding might deprive the animals who would graze on the stubble after harvest of precious nutrition.[95] Unfortunately, the polyptychs that form the basis of most Carolingian agrarian history do not offer any proof of this; indeed, though they are punctilious about dues owed and property owned, they never specifically mention weeding work, nor its timing on the large estates whose activities they portray.

Luckily, weeds grew in other contexts too, outside the grain fields and manors that concern the polyptychs. Adalhard of Corbie, the great ninth-century expert on monastic living, knew weeds well enough not to

[92] *Geoponika* 2.24, 89; 2.38, 94.   [93] Palladius, *Opus Agriculturae* 2.9, 4.3.
[94] Labor bursts: M. van der Veen, "The Materiality of Plants," *World Archaeology* 46 (2014), 804; but J. Devroey, "La céréaliculture dans le monde franc," *Settimane del CISAM* 37 (Spoleto, 1990), 245 disagrees. Charlemagne's names for May and June (pasture- and plowing-month) ignored this schedule.
[95] In the Toluca valley, east of Mexico City, anthropologists found farmers tolerate weeds that grow after corn has reached thigh height, because such plants supply valuable fodder to their milk cows, and rooting them out requires labor needed for other tasks as the corn ripens: L. Vieyra-Odilon and H. Vibrans, "Weeds as Crops: The Value of Maize Field Weeds in the Valley of Toluca, Mexico," *Economic Botany* 55 (2001), 426–43.

imagine they would all sprout forth during one month. His discussion of weeding the monastic garden reveals a gardener's intimacy with plants, including the undesirable ones. For monastic gardens were special places, more pampered and protected than the cereal fields where cultivators might weed intensively for a few days, during the early phases in the crops' life, and forget about the matter thereafter.[96] In monastic gardens, instead, and probably other early medieval vegetable patches, the labor was diffused in time, an ongoing concern. While it created people–plant attachments like the ones Strabo celebrated in *Hortulus*, the fact of continuous weeding also lightened each episode of work. For this reason, weeding the garden could be the preserve of the old and frail monks, when more vigorous work detained the young and hale.[97] In a same-sex community, they were the honorary women and children, fit for essential but less prestigious work than plowing or reaping.

Adalhard suggested Corbie's head gardener would know "when the time comes when it is necessary to rid the garden of noxious plants." He also identified a time-frame: "from mid-April up to the middle of October."[98] In ninth-century Corbie such an ample understanding of the right time for weeding had repercussions for the peasants in nearby settlements, who were expected to act as weeders ("sarculatores") whenever the head gardener determined they should, in exchange for bread, beer, and legumes.[99] It appears that in monastic contexts the need to eliminate "noxious" plants from gardens was not associated with one short month of the year. Writers expected weeds to grow throughout the warm season, and to require human attention for the duration. Prudently, they created a schedule in which weeders' labor remained available as long as possible.

Conclusion

As Rosamond McKitterick has observed, in Carolingian Europe a new more rational, chronological, and linear historiography coincided with

---

[96] The late 600s Iberian "Exhortatio Poenitendi" 147, ed. K. Strecker, *MGH Poetae* 4.2 (Berlin, 1914), 768 nicely expresses the affection cultivators feel for the plots they clear of weeds. Comparative field and garden weeding: van der Veen, "The Materiality," 804–5.

[97] Notker, *Gesta Karoli Magni* 2.12, ed. H. Haefele, *MGHSRG* n.s. 12 (Berlin, 1959), 73 contrasts Pippin the Hunchback and other "seniors" weeding with the "maiora opera" of the youthful.

[98] Adalhard, "Brevis Quem ad Corbeiam Fieri Iussit" 4, ed. J. Semmler, *Corpus Consuetudinum Monasticarum* 1 (Siegburg, 1961), 380: "et postquam tempus venerit quo necessarium fuerit ortos a noxiis purgare herbiis, idest a medio Apreli usque medium Octobrium." Adalhard also thought "aestate" was weeding season (381).

[99] Ibid., 381–2. The gender of these weeders is unclear.

a new more Christian conception of time.[100] The distinctive sense of time that emerged during the eighth century helpfully aligned with the Carolingians' sense that rightful rulers should control Christianized time, its reckoning, and the resulting liturgical events. Their enhanced chronological sensibility explains the persistent interest in calendrical matters and in evaluating exactly the passage of time. The message of Carolingian power was entwined with a distinctive way of measuring time. Knowing the right time, and knowing the proper ways to call time's subdivisions, both defined and conferred authority in Carolingian Europe. And if this applied to the highest echelons of Carolingian society and its political pronouncements, it also applied to the lowest rungs of the social pyramid. For example, beginning in the late eighth century large landowners, like monasteries, expressed their power over rural labor and resources by insisting that peasant dues, including the newly mandatory tithes, be paid on special, religiously charged days, usually the feast days of major saints like St. Martin. The great Carolingian monasteries' growing hegemony over the landscape conferred the ability to order time and create routines without reference to ecology (the time of nature) or agricultural processes (the time of peasants). Thus, from the top to the bottom, Carolingian society experienced political and social power chronologically.[101]

Weeds had their rhythms, too, and the Carolingians respected them. Though the Anglo-Saxon idea of a weed-month seems not to have crossed the Channel, and never won over the Franks, they knew that their crops' competitors sprouted and grew in specific phases of the agricultural cycle. Weeding operations to counter these competitors should be timed to pose the fewest threats to the crops themselves. But Carolingian cultivators (and writers) also knew that weeds were most vulnerable at specific times, mostly when they were young and had not set seed, and were most dangerous at other times, such as when they had grown deep roots and tough stalks, or developed prickly leaves and easily scattered seed pods. If weeds had their rhythms, so did Carolingian weeders.

The bad plants that developed from human failures in Eden and sprang forth with regular cadence from Carolingian soils shaped how

---

[100] R. McKitterick, "*Akkulturation* and the Writing of History in the Early Middle Ages," in *Akkulturation*, ed. D. Hägermann et al. (Berlin, 2004), 382–4.

[101] D. Starostine, "In die festivitatis," Ph.D. dissertation, University of Michigan (Ann Arbor, 2002), 85–216. On tithes, see J. Devroey and A. Nissen, "Early Middle Ages, 500–1000," in *Struggling with the Environment: Land Use and Productivity*, ed. E. Thoen and T. Soens (Turnhout, 2015), 25.

eighth- and ninth-century people thought about the world. Weeds recurring in fields and gardens, season after season, made visible the reality and unavoidable nature of sin. The eternal struggle to contain them, however, also confirmed the potential in humans to cooperate constructively with divine organization. With weeds and with weeders, in God's creation timing was everything.

4   The Worst of Weeds

In Frankish Europe, some "herbs" seemed more consistently evil than others. This is evident in a curious poem in an anonymous collection of lyrics from the ninth century (judging by the sole manuscript's handwriting) that recounts the pleasures and dangers of an incongruous pair, navigation and agriculture. The poem is didactic, so uses a large number of obscure, technical Latin words for the benefit of learners. The botanical vocabulary and lore derive from ancient authorities, like Pliny's *Natural History*. Hence several Mediterranean and Nilotic plants that might have been unfamiliar in northern Francia, in any language, make an appearance in the poet's list of delightful plants that one wants to keep close at hand and be able to pluck: water lilies ("nardi folio"), mandrake, alpine valerian ("colocasia"). Lilies, sweet thyme, and tall poppies were grouped with these exotics because equally pleasing and desirable. But the poet sharply contrasted this group with the most pernicious plants imaginable, which must be kept far from the domesticated darlings. The poet listed the weeds most liable to "harm" the good garden plants: "keep the thorns away, with stringy lolium / let not caltrops nor brambles harm the plants, / nor zizania nor tricky sprouts."[1]

The poem's strict separation of bad and good plants is itself instructive and representative of Carolingian attitudes. But the poet further managed to capture in a pithy list most of the weeds, thorny or duplicitous, that learned Carolingians deemed most abhorrent. Their identity is the subject of this chapter. Since all societies classify plants according to their cultural and agricultural priorities, the characteristics of those plants that most alarmed and horrified eighth- and ninth-century writers are a mirror of the aspirations and fears of Carolingian Europeans; and the greatest botanical enemies of the Carolingians who wrote were certainly not the

---

[1] "Codicis Bernensis CCCLVIII Sylloga" 3.25–32, ed. P. von Winterfeld, *MGH Poetae* 4.1 (Berlin, 1899), 245: "Spine sunto procul, cum lolio filex / Neu ledant tribuli gramina neu rubus/ nec zizania nec reproba germina / Flores ut placitos pollici carpere / Possimus, violas ungue recidere / Cum nardi folio lilia virginum / Et cum dulce thymo tum colocasia / Fructus mandragora, summa papavera."

plants that modern farmers and gardeners might expect, nor what archae-obotany suggests were the preoccupations of Carolingian farmers. Thus, a discussion of the weeds deemed worst in the eighth and ninth centuries reveals something about what mattered most to (literate) people then, just as perusing contemporary weed science literature or gardening magazines can say something about the cultural priorities of modern capitalist socie-ties. In an effort to uncover some deep-rooted structures in Carolingian culture, this chapter aspires to identify the species of plants that Carolingians considered particularly abominable. Unveiling the identities of the worst weeds gives insights into the imprint of scriptural and, to a lesser extent, also of classical erudition on Carolingian weedology.

A Thorny World

Since the Carolingian botanical imaginary was biblically inflected, plants with a bad reputation in the scriptures tended to retain their negative associations in Carolingian writings. Even if, as we saw in the introduc-tion to this book, no one word for weed came to mind, all the Bible's rogue plants *were* weeds to Carolingian readers. And since, in Genesis 3.18, when God condemned a hapless first human to eating "the herbs of the earth" He thereby also condemned him to toiling amidst "thorns and thistles," it seemed the latter two plants, at least, deserved universal disapproval, although the original Hebrew was even less precise than the Vulgate's Latin about what species were involved.[2] Consequently, in Carolingian legal, theological, epistolary, and narrative texts, the Vulgate's "spinas et tribulos" flourished luxuriantly whenever their authors needed a negative vegetable metaphor.[3] The worst weeds were the prickly ones, though their exact botanical nature might be debated.

In some sense, Carolingian Edenic fantasies *required* wastelands where prickly plants grew; these expressed God's indignation over human failings, certainly, but also the potential for a laborious human redemption.[4] By imagining the prickly thickets all around them as the outcome of Adam's transgression, Carolingian authors confirmed the Genesis narrative, reminded themselves of the unmatched softness of the Garden's vegetation (analyzed in Chapter 5), and recalled the possibility to reconstitute it

[2] D. Zohary, *Plants of the Bible* (Cambridge, 1982), 15, 154; M. Alexandre, *Le commence-ment du livre de Genèse I–IV: la version grecque de la Septante et sa reception* (Paris, 1988), 122–32, 321–2.
[3] Eg. "Capitula Pistensis" 1, ed. A. Boretius and V. Krause, MGH Legum Sectio II 2.2 (Hanover, 1893), 304; Alcuin, "Epistolae" 3, ed. E. Dümmler, *MGH Epistolae* 4 (Berlin, 1895), 21; Theodulf of Orléans, "Carmina" 2.123, ed. E. Dümmler, *MGH Poetae* 1 (Berlin, 1881), 445.
[4] V. Di Palma, *Wasteland: A History* (New Haven, 2014), 9–16.

through hard human work. No doubt for this reason they tended to describe the ultimate weeds, the thorn bushes they disliked, growing in uncultivated spaces, far from plowed fields or manicured gardens that imperfectly mimicked God's good garden.[5] This association of "spinae" with places unkempt because of human sloth, or at least lack of human industry, was reinforced by Proverbs 24.30–1, the protagonist of which observed thorns overwhelming the field of the lazy man and the vineyard of the fool. That Jesus himself was on record (Luke 6.44) for pointing out the radical distinction between the fruits of thorn bushes ("spinis" in the Vulgate) and those of cultivated plants no doubt confirmed the orderly Carolingian separation of spaces and associated botanical forms, at least on the written page.

Thorny plants' low status and high literary profile received further confirmation through their role in Jesus' sufferings, particularly in the form of the crown that his guards placed on his head prior to his execution (Matthew 27.29; Mark 15.17; John 19.2). In commenting on the relevant Gospel passages at the beginning of the ninth century, Smaragdus, the exceptionally well-connected abbot of St.-Mihiel, near Verdun in northeastern Francia, duly noted that the thorns in the crown represented sins which prick guilty consciences.[6] Just a few years earlier, with taunting sarcasm Claudius of Turin had asked supporters of the veneration of crosses in churches whether they thought Christians should also venerate thorn bushes, since these too had intimate associations with the crucifixion.[7] He expected his interlocutors to see the irony of assigning any holiness to a kind of plant which, on account of its role in the fundamental Christian narratives, everyone detested. Other Carolingian auteurs thought thorns effective metaphors for lustful thoughts, worldly concerns or anxieties, envy, bad Christians, heretical belief, and sin in general. The suggested remedies included nipping them in the bud, deep plowing to prevent their growth, and a great deal of patience.[8]

[5] Hrabanus Maurus, De Universo 19.6, ed. J. Migne, PL 111 (Paris, 1864), 521 describes "terra inculta in qua sentices spinaeque nascuntur"; Agnellus Ravennatis, Liber Pontificalis Ecclesiae Ravennatis "Prologus," ed. D. Deliyannis (Turnhout, 2006), 146 contrasted thorny with cultivated areas; Einhard, "Passio Marcellini et Petri," ed. E. Dümmler, MGH Poetae 2 (Berlin, 1884), 134 thought "et spinas et vepres" grew far from cultivation.

[6] Smaragdus of St.-Mihiel, "Collectiones in Epistolas et Evangelia," ed. J. Migne, PL 102 (Paris, 1865), 187. The crown-object was little discussed before c. 1200, though crowning with thorns was.

[7] Claudius of Turin, "Epistolae" 12, ed. E. Dümmler, MGH Epistolae 4 (Berlin 1895), 612 (making a point also raised in the Libri Carolini).

[8] Heresy: Opus Caroli Regis Contra Synodum (Libri Carolini) 4.22, ed. A. Freeman, MGH Concilia 2.1 (Hanover, 1998), 543, where heretics swallow "the thorns of error." Lust: Concilium Aquisgranensis 98, ed. A. Werminghoff, MGH Legum Sectio III, 2.1 (Hanover, 1906), 376–7; Hrabanus, De Universo 19.6, 522. Worldly worries: ibid.; Wigbod, "Quaestiones in Octateuchum," ed. J. Migne, PL 96 (Paris, 1862), 1126; Eriugena, Periphyseon 5.5051, ed. E. Jeauneau (Turnhout, 2000), 164. Sin: Smaragdus,

Though Christian thinking prevailed in Carolingian discussions of which weeds seemed worst and why, we should recognize that Frankish feelings about bad plants were sometimes colored by classical agronomical literature, too. Ancient Latin agronomists, some of whose texts Carolingian scribes copied and which were at least occasionally read, had been anxious about spiny plants. Palladius, the Carolingians' favorite agronomist, or the one whose text they most frequently copied, was unimpressed by thorny plants that could not be bent to human purposes, such as reinforcing property claims in fences and hedges.[9] More than three centuries earlier, Virgil complained about the prevalence of tough, thorny plants over tender violets and narcissus, while Pliny suggested that thorny plants were really deformations of unprickly ones, as a result of disease.[10] This classical heritage, especially Virgil, popped up here and there in Carolingian literature, and informed some definitions of really bad plants, such as those in the encyclopedic *Liber Glossarum*.

Like some of the classical landscapes of Virgil, Pliny, or Palladius, pre-Roman Palestine was a place where grazing and over-grazing selected wild species that could avoid herds' browsing, giving them a competitive advantage over more palatable plants of the field.[11] Along with strong flavor and aroma, spinyness was a winning strategy for plants in the Mediterranean regions where the texts that Carolingian scholars admired had arisen. More than on the Latin pastoral tradition, which also reflected the biases of shepherds, the Carolingian classification and interpretation of spiny plants depended on the Bible, which abhorred species that made the life of goatherds and sheep flocks difficult, and not just weeds that disturbed the agriculturalist. Likely because of the economic interests of ancient Palestinian communities, after their starring roles in the creation narrative, plants endowed with thorns received much attention in both Hebrew and Christian scriptures. Carolingian readers of these texts justifiably singled out prickliness as the common denominator of the plants God made to hamper human activities on earth, with the result that, as we

"Collectiones," 187, referring to Jesus' crown; Smaragdus of St.-Mihiel, *Expositio in Regulam S. Benedicti* 1, ed. A. Spannagel and P. Engelbert (Siegburg, 1974), 1, 32. Nipping: Alcuin , "Epistolae" 3, 21. Deep plowing: Theodulf, *Carmina* 28.61–2, 495. Patience: Hrabanus Maurus, "Commentariorum in Matthaeum Libri Octo," ed. J. Migne, *PL* 107 (Paris, 1864), 947.
[9] Palladius, *Opus Agriculturae* 1.34, 3.24, 4.9. See K. Butzer, "The Classical Tradition of Agronomical Science," in *Science in Western and Eastern Civilization in Carolingian Times*, ed. P. Butzer and D. Lohrmann (Basel, 1993), 547–58; J. Gaulin, "Tradition et pratiques de la littérature agronomique pendant le haut Moyen Âge," *Settimane del CISAM* 37 (Spoleto, 1990), 109.
[10] Theodulf, "Carmina" 2.123–6 quoting Virgil, *Eclogues* 5.39; Pliny, *Naturalis Historia* 18.17, ed. C. Mayhoff (Stuttgart, 1967), 184.
[11] H. Allen, *Mediterranean Ecogeography* (Harlow, 2001), 107, 118–19.

have seen, spines became the defining characteristic of their worst weeds.
If the "thorns and thistles" of Genesis had ever been specific species, they
lost this specificity in early medieval readers' minds. These labels
stretched to encompass brambles, cardoons, caltrops, and other plants
endowed with pointy ends, sharp seed casings, or thorns in the same
category. Even the jagged defenses of roses raised some doubts among
Carolingian readers.

Conversely, in Carolingian Europe, plants that had the *physique du rôle*, in
the sense that they conformed to the identikit of the bad plant but did not
appear at all in the Christian scriptures, might avoid being classified among
the worst of weeds. Thus acanthus (*Acanthus mollis*), the large, dark, elegant
green leaf of which develops sharp spines on its ends in maturity, received no
notice from Carolingian weedologists (and none from their late antique
authorities, either). Yet "bear-claw" was well known to classical authors
like Virgil and Pliny for being spiny-leaved, and enjoyed unparalleled celebrity (for a weed) in classical architecture because of its inclusion in the
Corinthian order as ornament: it also featured prominently atop columns
and pillars in Carolingian buildings, beginning with Charlemagne's palace
chapel at Aachen.[12] (See Figure 4.1.) The same indifference surrounded
holly (*Ilex aquifolium*), a noble plant with both sharp-edged leaves and a tiny
footprint in Latin literature, and the wide array of firs and pines the leaves of
which are best described as prickly but, from biblical times onward, were
never disapproved of quite like plants with thorns on their stems.

This might suggest that the prickliness that procured Carolingian writers
the deepest nuisance was of a specific kind, on the stems of plants. In other
words, it might appear that pointy and sharp appendages were not all
created equal, and those growing on branches and stalks seemed worse
than others on the edges of leaves. But since archaeobotanical records show
that Carolingian Europe definitely grew dense stands of blackthorn (*Prunus
spinosa*), an admirable plant but one endowed with long, sharp spurs on its
tough branches, and since no one condemned this shrub for its thorniness,
a second explanation for Carolingian classifications seems preferable: it
was less what might be observed in the field, or botany, and more what
might be read between the covers of books, or theology, that led to certain
thorny plants' inclusion on the lists of very bad plants.[13]

[12] Virgil, *Aeneid* 1.649; *Georgics* 4.123; *Eclogues* 3.45, 4.20; Pliny, *Naturalis Historia* 22.34.76.
See also F. Heber-Suffrin, "L'acanthe dans le décor architectural carolingien," in *L'acanthe
dans la sculpture monumentale de l'antiquité à la Renaissance* (Paris, 1993), 189–210.
[13] W. van Zeist et al., "Plant Husbandry and Vegetation of Early Medieval Douai, Northern
France," *Vegetation History and Archaeobotany* 3 (1994), 199–201; M. Ruas, "Aspects of
Early Medieval Farming from Sites in Mediterranean France," *Vegetation History and
Archaeobotany* 14 (2005), 405, 413.

Figure 4.1 Aachen, palace chapel, bronze railing, detail. (Photo: W. Braunfels, H. Schnitzler, *Karl der Grosse, Lebenswerk und Nachleben* 3 (Düsseldorf, 1965)).

Always, whether informed by classical or scriptural models, the Carolingian sense of which plants were weediest remained anthropocentric, in fact corporeal. Bad plants were defined foremost by their ability to pierce people's skin and visibly hurt them. More than overbearing competitiveness against crops, or sap poisonous enough to kill whatever grazed on their leaves or sucked on their fruits, the sharp appendages on their vegetable frames made some bad plants worse than others. In eighth- and ninth-century Europe nobody seems to have noticed the ability of spiny weeds to dissuade grazers and lower the value of pasture.[14] Worrisome spinyness was aimed at people. The bodily pain it could inflict

---

[14] Only a seventh-century Iberian poet embraced the theme of animals' encounters with prickly fodder: Eugenius of Toledo, "Carmina" 87, ed. F. Vollmer, *MGH Auctores Antiquissimi* 14 (Berlin, 1905), 266.

confirmed God's righteous wrath at humanity. And yet, pernicious as they were, even thorny plants taught useful lessons. Their vigor and truculence confirmed the accuracy of scripture in an immediate way, proving people had been condemned to growing their food amidst a hostile army of sharp-edged plants. The nuisance the Vulgate's "thorns and thistles" created for humans recalled to mind the decisive moment in vegetation history, when plants became less pliant to people's purposes.

Wicked Species

Among thorny weeds, a few species stood out. "Paliurus," "tribulus," "vepres," "sentix," and "ramnus" enjoyed special status in Carolingian weed taxonomy. It is as always very difficult to link with certainty medieval and modern scientific species, but what Carolingian writers called "ramnus" evidently was a member of the buckthorn family (Rhamnaceae).[15] "Sentix," the one thorny plant usually cited in the singular, appears to be wild-brier or one of the many closely related wild roses that grow across Europe. "Vepres," endowed with good classical literary credentials (Cicero, Virgil, Horace, and a series of other Roman writers named them), were brambles and closely related to another thorny bush occasionally noted in Carolingian texts, "rubus": both would today be classified in the vast and variegated *Rubus* genus, and the early medieval botanical authority Isidore of Seville rightly acknowledged the difficulty of distinguishing them, followed in this as in much else by the ninth-century Carolingian encyclopedist Hrabanus Maurus.[16] "Tribulus" instead appears to have been a Mediterranean plant that protects its seeds with a three-pointed casing so hard it can puncture shoes (and now car tires), known in English as caltrop. Its seed was an effective military tool against cavalry, including elephants, which explains why the plant's name is used of antipersonnel equipment still today. Pliny described the caltrop as one of nature's most prickly creatures, while the late eighth-century *Liber Glossarum* noted more telegraphically "it is a type of spiny plant."[17]

First in the Carolingian botanical rogue's gallery was the plant called "paliurus." In Carolingian texts it could be any of several spiny shrubs of

---

[15] Ancient plants' identification: Z. Amar and E. Lev, *Arabian Drugs in Early Medieval Mediterranean Medicine* (Edinburgh, 2017), 71–2; J. Reveal, "What's in a Name: Identifying Plants in Pre-Linnaean Botanical Literature," in *Prospecting for Drugs in Ancient and Medieval Texts*, ed. B. Holland (Amsterdam, 1996), 57–90.

[16] Isidore of Seville, *Etymologiae* 17.7.60, ed. W. Lindsay (Oxford, 1911); Hrabanus, *De Universo* 19.8, 527.

[17] Pliny, *Naturalis Historia* 18.17, 184; 21.15, 411; *Liber Glossarum Digital*, ed. A. Grondeux and F. Cinato (Paris, 2016), http://liber-glossarum.huma-num.fr: "genus herbe spinosae."

the *Paliurus* genus. Gregory the Great considered the "paliurus" the very densest and most entangling of thorny plants, much worse than mere thorns and thistles.[18] To the Carolingian glossators, inspired as so often by Pliny's *Natural History*, it was "a type of bush, a spiny plant that is called 'zura' and 'tugzira,' it is a spiny plant with one curved thorn alternating with another that is erect. It is a most tough and spiny plant." Though the last phrase is drawn from Isidore's *Etymologies* (17.9.56), the *Liber Glossarum*'s entry is botanically informed, if not empirical, and aspires to help Carolingian Latin readers envision what a "paliurus" was.[19] And though the vernacular vocabulary offered to increase readers' understanding merely perpetuated into the ninth century a bit of botanico-linguistic erudition Pliny had picked up eight hundred years earlier from a North African source, the ability to call the "paliurus" by its everyday name *was* relevant to Carolingian audiences, for an Old High German gloss helpfully added that the name of "paliurus" is "hagan."[20]

Prickliness incriminated some other species, too. In Carolingian literature, "spinae" was a rather generic term to indicate spiny plants, various types of brambles, briers, and thistles. But among thistles, "carduus" had a more defined identity. Many thistles, like the wild cardoon (*Cynara cardunculus sylvestris*), are nasty weeds for arable farmers and any who seek to grow pasture, for they are tenacious, able to propagate quickly by several methods, and also very spiny once they become old enough, making them hard to handle, although Mediterranean people also grew domesticated varieties with the thorns reduced or limited to specific parts of the plant structure.[21] Carolingian men of letters may have known these features, or may have reacted to the presence of the wild thistles called "carduus" in their bibles. Several Carolingian exegetes duly referred to 2 Kings 14.9, where the humble "carduus" appears in a story about appropriate social relations. Theodulf of Orléans knew the "carduus" and its spiny appearance, as well

[18] Gregory the Great, *Moralia in Job* 33.4, ed. M. Adriaen (Turnhout, 1979–85), 1678 (impenetrable "paliurus" protects lesser prickly plants growing in association with it).
[19] See Introduction, n. 36 above. Pliny, *Naturalis Historia* 24.71 (115) had said that Africans called paliurus "zura," wisdom the *Liber Glossarum* replicated. On lexical slippage between "zura," "zira," and "tugzira," see J. André, "Notes de lexicographie botanique," *Archivium Latinitatis Medii Aevi* 23 (1953), 122.
[20] *Die althochdeutschen Glossen* 3, ed. E. Steinmeyer and E. Sievers (Berlin, 1895), 466 call "paliurus hagan." Relevant observations on Carolingian "code switching" (mixing languages): E. Roberts, "Boundary Clauses and the Use of the Vernacular in Eastern Frankish Charters, c. 750–c. 900," *Historical Research* 91 (2018), 588, 601–3.
[21] G. Sonnante et al., "The Domestication of Artichoke and Cardoon," *Annals of Botany* 100 (2007), 1096–7; A. Gatto et al., "Population Structure of *Cynara cardunculus* Complex and the Origin of the Conspecific Crops Artichoke and Cardoon," *Annals of Botany* 112 (2013), 855–6. On the garden "cardones" in "Capitulare de Villis" 70, see Chapter 6 below.

as its tendency to become pricklier as it matures, indeed to abandon its harmless herbal nature during its lifecycle and turn into something altogether different and very menacing.[22] It is just possible that the painter of the "labors of the months" in the tenth-century sacramentary now at Berlin had in mind the wild cardoon, or another tall thistle like *Carduus tenuiflorus*, when he depicted June's weeding activities: the targeted weed is tall and spindly, if not quite prickly, and the weeder respectfully avoids touching it with his hands (see this book's cover).[23] The glossaries too described "carduus" and its healthful properties (effective against dandruff), and in the 790s the *Libri Carolini* quoted Virgil (Eclogue 5.38) on this infesting plant to make a theological point against the iconophiles.[24]

Yet many of the most notorious weeds of the Bible were unfamiliar to north European men of letters. For the plants whose prickly leaves, stems, and flowers corresponded to the Carolingian ideal of "bad herb" were mostly exotic in northwestern Europe. "Tribulus" was one of the most famous weeds in the Carolingian empire, considered more dangerous by the *Libri Carolini* than the darnel that, as Jesus had revealed, the devil himself planted in crop fields, and more vicious than brambles, the spineless roots of which proved their essential nature, at least, was not thorny.[25] But its ecological preferences mean few Carolingians can have ever seen a growing *Tribulus terrestris*: even today this plant of arid environments does not grow north of the forty-seventh parallel, and therefore leaves out the Carolingian heartlands from its current range.

In general, the relatively modest presence of eastern Mediterranean spiny weeds within the borders of the Carolingian empire, and especially within sight of the empire's great centers of learning, contrasted with the biblical prominence of plants like caltrop and brambles. This created a tension: the weeds one needed to worry about, because of their importance in biblical narratives, were not the same as the weeds one could observe around oneself. Though hardly scientific empiricists, Carolingian readers responded with curiosity about the physical appearance, as well as the symbolic properties, of the worst plants. Such interest in natural

---

[22] Theodulf of Orléans, "Carmina" 1.112, 447. This was a late antique theme: see above, note 8.

[23] See G. Comet, *Le paysan et son outil* (Rome, 1992), 170.

[24] *Liber Glossarum*: "Cardus ... genus herbae spinose huius natura mordax est; mollis, frigidus, et indigestis; adeo succus eius alopicias curat." *Die althochdeutsche Glossen*, 471, 496, 529, 552, gives four translations. *Opus Caroli Regis* 4.22, 542.

[25] Tribulus: Hrabanus, "De Universo" 19.6, 522. The essential nature of plants was seen in their roots (likely based on an empirical observation by (pseudo-) Augustine, *Quaestiones Veteri et Novi Testamentis CXXVII* 42.1, ed. A. Souter (Vienna, 1908), 69): Walafrid Strabo, "Liber Psalmorum" 57.10, ed. J. Migne, *PL* 113 (Paris, 1879), 928. See also T. Noble, *Images, Iconoclasm, and the Carolingians* (Philadelphia, 2009), 184, 202–3.

things, and plants, surfaced when the *Liber Glossarum* included such
a vivid (and Plinian) verbal evocation of what the "paliurus" looked
like. Similar botanical curiosity underlay the *Libri Carolini*, the
Carolingian text on correct representation in religious art, when its
authors embellished on their late ancient source for the information on
the roots of the prickly shrub "rubus." For whereas Augustine (actually
Ambrosiaster, but Carolingian readers did not distinguish the two) simply
claimed that the shrub "did not have a root armored with thorns" so as to
reveal that it was in its essence thornless and the prickles on its branches
were a choice, just like human sin, the *Libri* added that God appeared to
Moses in the bush "not to make the bush's structure worshippable," but
rather "to demonstrate the thorns of sin. For since rubus does not have
a root armored with thorns, when in its upper branches thorns thicken,
thereby manifestly it is shown that sins are not there by nature."[26] The
790s authors of the *Libri Carolini* contrasted base and superstructure of
the plant vividly, put the plant's nature first, and derived the theological
deduction from it, exactly the opposite of their late ancient source. They
did so on the basis of what they took to be observed, established botanical
facts.

Good Spines

The one partial exception to the general Carolingian aversion to prickly
plants is the rose. Roses lacked a lofty biblical pedigree, and though
they appear occasionally in the Vulgate, this reflects a late antique
rehabilitation of the plant more than any enthusiasm for the Rosaceae
family among scriptural authors.[27] Rare in ancient Palestine, roses
became ritually and commercially significant relatively late, and only
in the Roman world, in effect after the period when most of the scriptural texts were composed. Further, their widespread use in pagan
ceremonies and their association with pagan divinities, especially
Venus, rendered roses suspect to early Christian writers. But the
Church Fathers came around, reflecting in this regard, too, late
Roman taste, and readmitting the rose to botanical respectability. In
late antiquity roses could adorn church altars and symbolize Christian

[26] *Libri Carolini* 3.25, 455: "Non enim ideo in rubo apparuit ut rubi materiam adorandam percenseret, sed ut per eius spinas peccata, pro quibus lex venerate, demonstraret. Qui ergo rubus radicem non habet spinis armatam, cum in superioribus spinis denseretur, in eo evidenter peccata non esse ex natura monstrantur." (Pseudo-)Augustine, *Quaestiones* 42.1, 69: "nam quia et peccata non sunt de natura, sed ex accidenti, rubi, id est spinarum materia non habet radicem spinis armatam."
[27] Most "roses" in Christian bibles seem to have been other species in Hebrew and Greek: W. Walker, *All the Plants of the Bible* (New York, 1957), 176–83.

virtues and role models.[28] As explained in the Chapter 5, they also entered Christian iconographic programs.

For the Fathers, perhaps the greatest asset a rose plant had was the evident contradiction it presented by being at once thorny and endowed with prized, soft, colorful, and aromatic flowers. Roses were particularly "good to think," in other words. Ambrose, who suggested that in Edenic conditions roses had flourished without any thorns, introduced into the Latin canon the idea that the Rosaceae's typical thorniness was punishment for human sin, and therefore acutely instructive.[29] Isidore of Seville, a botanical authority to the Carolingians, agreed that their thorns were a postlapsarian mutation in roses.[30] But the origin of roses' prickliness proved less interesting in Frankish Europe than the theme of the rose amidst thorns, or of desirable and lovely things surrounded by dangerous and hideous ones, which had developed richly in the fifth and sixth centuries, with Augustine among the early adopters.[31] For unlike in Paradise, on earth it seemed that anything pleasant came accompanied by painful reminders of human limitation. A luscious rose, inseparable from its thorns before the modern floricultural industry's hybrids, was therefore an ideologically useful plant to postclassical Christians despite being endowed with that clearest mark of weediness, thorns.

Carolingian writers appreciated the Ambrosian theme of the apparent incongruity between the gorgeous blossom and its spiky stem. Alcuin, for instance, wrote to Arno of Salzburg in 800 that roses might have incomparable color and admirable odor, but their thorns were their most useful attribute, reminding people of God's power and purpose in creation.[32] Other letters, histories, and poems of the ninth century noticed in roses the thorns most of all, not the fragrance, or hues, or even the medical utility. Their writers understood that the unfortunate prickliness was God's reminder to people of all that was wrong in the world, and why. In this sense, the residual weediness of roses, what rendered them imperfect, their most undesirable quality, elevated them above other flowering

---

[28] J. Géczi, *The Rose and Its Symbols in Mediterranean Antiquity* (Veszprém, 2011), 397–433; J. Potter, *The Rose* (London, 2010), 29–39, 75–80; H. Birkhan, *Pflanzen im Mittelalter* (Vienna, 2012), 236–47. See also C. Goodson, *Cultivating the City in Early Medieval Italy* (Cambridge, 2021), 161–4.

[29] Ambrose, "Exameron" 3.11, in *Sancti Ambrosii Opera* 1, ed. C. Schenkl (Vienna, 1896), 91, reproduced in Basil of Caesarea, *Homélies sur l'Hexaéméron* 5.6, ed. S. Giet (Paris, 1949), 300 (and Eustathius, *Ancienne version latine des neuf homélies sur l'Hexaéméron de Basile de Césarée* 6.3, ed. H. Amand de Mendieta and S. Rudberg (Berlin, 1958), 62).

[30] Isidore of Seville, *De Ordine Creaturarum* 10.8, ed. J. Migne, *PL* 83 (Paris, 1862), 940.

[31] N. Henry, "The Lily and the Thorns: Augustine's Refutation of the Donatist Exegesis of the Song of Songs," *Revue des études augustinennes* 42 (1996), 255–66.

[32] Alcuin, "Epistolae" 207, 345.

plants because it was so transparent a sign of God's willingness to communicate with people through the other parts of His creation.[33]

In a poetic dispute between a lily and a rose, written, probably at Liège, around the mid-point of the ninth century by the talented Irish monk-emigré Sedulius, the lily's most trenchant attack on the rose revolved on its "diadem of thorns," and on how communities of roses created briar patches ("spineta") that lacerated any unlucky people who traversed them. The lily contrasted this with its own smooth surfaces and easy cohabitation with other plants. The rose's retort was pedestrian: God had made its thorns, so these instruments of His plan for creation were full of merit. Fortunately, just as the disagreement reached an impasse, Spring and the Poet intervened to settle this dispute between opinionated Carolingian flowers; the arbiters observed the flowers' commonalities and accorded credit to both for symbolizing Christian virtues (virginity and martyrdom). But they also acknowledged the lily's superiority; in the Carolingian hierarchy of plants, it seems, thorns were too great a liability to permit any triumphs. They were divine instruments, as Ambrose maintained, but nevertheless deeply tainted by sin, as their pointed excrescences made manifest.[34]

The Identity of Zizania

The most famous document to have survived from Carolingian Francia is probably the *Capitulare de Villis* that Charlemagne promulgated sometime around 800.[35] It outlines a somewhat idealized, but still quite earthy, view of how royal farms should function. Among its provisions is the injunction for estate managers to ensure that "good seed" be available on each estate. The king ordered that such seed should be purchased or procured elsewhere, betraying perhaps the old belief, well known to premodern agronomical writers, that yields were higher when fields were sown with seed

---

[33] Ninth century: Alcuin, "Epistolae" 207, 345; Anastasius, "Epistolae sive Praefationes" 1, ed. E. Caspar and G. Laehr, *MGH Epistolae* 7 (Berlin, 1928), 398; *Historia Langobardorum Codicis Gothani* 1, ed. G. Pertz, *MGH Scriptores Rerum Langobardicarum* (Hanover, 1878), 8, written c. 810 by a Carolingian-leaning Lombard.

[34] Sedulius Scottus, "Carmina" 14, ed. L. Traube, *MGH Poetae* 3 (Berlin, 1886), 81, 230–1. Sedulius' lily (verse 18) underlined the association of rose thorns with sin: "Quae tibi dant meritas aeterno vulnere poenas." In the 840s, Strabo's "Hortulus" 26, ed. Dümmler, *MGH Poetae* 2 (Berlin, 1884), 348–9 also compared rose and lily, observing (26, 349) that roses are widely loved and honored because they symbolize martyrdom. Early medieval rose symbolism: B. Seaton, "Towards a Semiotics of Literary Flower Personification," *Poetics Today* 10 (1989), 686–7. Sedulius was among the first to string together lilies, roses, Mary, and the Song of Songs: B. Beck, "Jardin monastique, jardin mystique," *Revue d'histoire de la pharmacie* 88 (2000), 382.

[35] "Capitulare de Villis" 32, ed. A. Boretius, *MGH Capitularia Regum Francorum* 1 (Hanover, 1883), 86: "sementem bonum" (see also 51, 89), with J. Devroey, "La céréaliculture dans le monde franc," *Settimane del CISAM* 37 (Spoleto, 1990), 247.

that had not grown "accustomed" to the local soil.[36] And though the formulation in *De Villis* was new to the early Middle Ages, the "good seed" caught on and reverberated through Carolingian literature, in public and less formal documents. Thus Alcuin, who referred to "excellent seed" as well as to "good seed," Lupus of Ferrières, and east Frankish legislators all adopted the notion.[37]

Of course, Charlemagne's preoccupation with "good seed" was not just agronomic; it was also scriptural, for the phrase evokes the biblical concern for "pure" speciation in Genesis 1.12, and echoes the Gospel of Matthew 13.24 ("bonum semen"), as well as the "bad seed" of Isaiah 1.4 ("iniquitate semini"). These were key biblical texts for early medieval weedology, but, as we shall see, Charlemagne's capitulary also reflected a broader concern in Carolingian culture with seeds able to remain "true" to their species and not develop into plants different from those that were sown. For the apparent capacity of some plants to grow from the seeds of other plants disturbed Carolingian writers and lay behind their attention to a weed thought to be a shape-shifter.

Indeed, the weed with the highest literary profile in Carolingian Europe was the mysterious plant Frankish writers called "zizania." This truly awful citizen of the vegetable kingdom dominated the botanical imaginary of the learned because it featured so prominently in the Christian scriptures, where it was the protagonist in the "Parable of the Tares" (Matthew 13.24–30). In this parable a good and wise farmer finds that his wheat field, sown with pure seed, sprouted a terrible weed because an enemy of his sowed the field with "zizania" by night; such hostile sowing may seem improbable to modern, rich-country people, but it was not unknown in the ancient Mediterranean, for the *Digest* of Justinian contains a second-century case where one's neighbor sowed two different kinds of weed in a crop field, creating a legal quandary over whether the damage was too ephemeral to be compensated under the Aquilian Law that protected real property.[38] Regardless, when his laborers sought to eradicate the "zizania" as soon as it germinated, the Gospel's good farmer restrained them,

---

[36] Seed-soil weariness: Comet, *Le paysan*, 143–5; E. Leroy Ladurie, *Les paysans de Languedoc* (Paris, 1966), 54–6; J. Zadoks, *Crop Protection in Medieval Agriculture* (Leiden, 2013), 55; *Geoponika: Farm Work* 2.17.1, 2.19.2, tr. A. Dalby (Totnes, 2011), 83, 85.

[37] Alcuin, "Epistolae" 3 (perhaps the fons et origo) and 311, ed. Dümmler, 20, 480; Lupus, "Epistolae" 29, *MGH Epistolae* 6, ed. E. Perels (Berlin, 1925), 35; "Additamenta ad Capitularia Regum Franciae Orientalis," *MGH Capitularia Regum Francorum* 2, ed. A. Boretius and V. Krause (Hanover, 1897), 210.

[38] *Digesta* 9.2.27.14, in *Corpus Iuris Civilis* 1, ed. T. Mommsen and P. Krueger (Berlin, 1954), 159. Celsus was inclined to think such hostile sowing did not truly alter the field's value.

suggesting instead that they wait until harvest time; then it would be easier to separate the unwanted plant from the wheat and burn it. According to the only Gospel to record it, Jesus' story so baffled his audience that afterward the disciples asked for elucidations, which Jesus duly supplied, in apocalyptic tones (Matthew 13.36–43 suggested the harvest was the Last Judgment). As perplexed as the disciples had been, later Carolingians pondered Matthew's account and thereby contributed to the renown of "zizania."

In attempting to render Jesus' meaning, the Greek text of Matthew had employed a word hitherto unheard in Greek lexica as the name of the weed that the "enemy" had sown in the upstanding farmer's wheat field, and that Jesus considered edifying for any who had "ears to hear." The Greek versions of the Gospel simply recorded the unfamiliar word, now written in Greek characters. When he compiled his Latin version of the parable Jerome confronted equal difficulties. Following the lead of the Vetus Latina, the somewhat amorphous but then-canonical Latin Bible, Jerome sagely left the strange Greek word in, transliterating it into Latin form.[39] Thereafter, Christians who read Jerome's Vulgate found in the Gospel an unfamiliar word of uncertain provenance, yet one Jesus had used to signify a plant of considerable importance.[40] Hence, they quite rightly wondered what weed Jesus had singled out as an instrument of the devilish enemy and representation of "the children of evil."[41]

Uncertainty prevailed throughout late antique times. But already during the lifetime of the first Christian emperor, Constantine, some thinkers had unmasked "zizania" to their own satisfaction. Juvencus, an Iberian aristocrat and priest who wrote one of the many poetic renditions of the scriptures that aimed to improve the Christian texts' palatability to educated Romans, asserted baldly the equivalence of "zizania" and a plant Latin speakers knew as "lolium." Indeed, so confident was his rendition of the term in the Vetus Latina that he did not even mention "zizania."[42] In subsequent decades the uncertainty dissipated a little, and in fact Jerome himself did a great deal to identify Matthew's noxious plant for

---

[39] *Itala. Das neue Testament in altlateinischer Überlieferung* 1, ed. A. Jülicher (Berlin, 1938), 87.

[40] The Syriac Bible (Peshitta), which evidently translated the Gospel from Greek and circulated by the fifth century, also transliterated "zizania." In Coptic, translation from Greek may be earlier, and "zizania" was rendered with a fully different word for plant without negative connotations. Over time, bad connotations accrued to "nteq" because of its use in Matthew. My thanks to Ellen Muehlberger for clarifying these matters.

[41] The etymology of "zizania" is disputed: Zohary, *Plants*, 161; J. André, *Lexique des termes de botanique en Latin* (Paris, 1950), 341.

[42] *Evangeliorum Libri Quattuor* 2.795–830, 3.1–16, ed. J. Huemer (Vienna, 1891), 77, 79. "Lolium" is both "amarum" and (a Vergilian echo) "infelix." This is the earliest claim that "zizania" is "lolium" that I know.

Latin audiences: in his commentary on the Gospel he proposed that "zizania" was the plant that "we call lolium."[43] Equally authoritative, in an aside within his treatment of the botany of creation, Ambrose's "Exameron" noted that the Gospel called "lolium" "zizania."[44] Ambrose's text leant heavily on Basil of Caesarea's sermons on Genesis, which were delivered in the late 370s but circulated in a Latin version from the opening years of the fifth century. Eustathius' translation too unhesitatingly adopted "lolium" for the "adulterated" weed in Matthew 13.24–30.[45] Thus, whether inspired or not, Juvencus' hypothesis slowly insinuated itself among unsure readers of the Gospel, and by the mid-400s even obscure dictionaries of curious Latin terms could proclaim without doubt and without further elaboration, "zizania is lolium."[46]

Naturally, not everyone who read the Gospel in late antiquity was persuaded by the Fathers' identification of "zizania" with a fairly familiar field weed of the ancient Mediterranean: the victory of that identification was contingent, and even later on in the Carolingian age some had doubts. Prudentius, for one, a slightly younger contemporary of Jerome, preferred to think Jesus' least favorite plant was actually wild oats (in Latin "avena"), a notion just as botanically and agronomically plausible as thinking "zizania" was "lolium."[47] Indeed, the *Alphabet of Galen*, a Latin rendition of an ancient Greek herbal that emerged from Dark Age Ravenna, noted that "wild oats are completely like wheat in leaf and ear, but not in seed," a description that matches the evil plant in the "Parable of the Tares" quite perfectly.[48] An influential fifth-century commentary on Virgil, which was copied in ninth-century Francia complete with earlier Irish glosses, represented "zizania" similarly, as wild oats, and the hypereducated Augustine had followed this tradition on occasion, finding that some species "are born looking like wheat," at least in their first leaves, those that emerge soon after germination.[49] The wild oat called "avena" was prolific, quick to grow, and difficult to discern in wheat fields before maturity, so it made good sense to imagine Jesus meant that common cereal weed in his parable.

[43] Jerome, *Commentaire sur S. Matthieu* 2.37, ed. E. Bonnard (Paris, 1977), v. 1, 288, "zizania, quod nos appellamus lolium . . ."
[44] Ambrose, "Exameron" 3.10, 88.   [45] Eustathius, *Ancienne version latine*, 61.
[46] Eucherius of Lyon, "Instuctionum Libri Duo" 2.3, ed. C. Wotke (Vienna, 1894), 147.
[47] "Apotheosis," Praef. 46, in Prudentius, *Aurelii Prudentii Clementis Carmina*, ed. M. Cunningham (Turnhout, 1966), 75. Prudentius knew "lolium" too: "Amartigenia" 216–18, in ibid., 124.
[48] N. Everett, *The Alphabet of Galen* (Toronto, 2012), 168.
[49] Philargyrius, *Explanatio in Bucolica Vergilii* 5.37, in *Servi Grammatici qui Feruntur in Vergilii Carmina Commentarii* 3.2, ed. G. Thilo and H. Hagen (Leipzig, 1902), 97; R. Kaster, *Guardians of Language* (Berkeley, 1988), 284–5; Augustine, "Enarrationes in Psalmos" 74.12, ed. J. Migne, *PL* 36 (Paris, 1865), 784.

The parable's Greek readers seem to have undertaken a similar interpretative journey. Puzzled by the parable's botany, they gradually came to understand that Jesus had meant a plant familiar to them by the name "aira" when he said "zizania." They were no doubt encouraged in this sense by their reading of scientific literature: Theophrastus himself had observed how similar "aira" was to wheat and barley, and also noted how easy it was to confuse the crop with the weed.[50] It may have helped the bilingual readers of scientific writings that Dioscurides (or at least his late antique annotators) recorded the equivalence of "aira" to "lolium" in his great herbal: "aira the Romans call lolium ..."[51] Whether or not the scientific-minded Church Fathers found this useful in their deliberations on "zizania," by the late fourth century it seemed plausible to those who pondered the parable that Jesus' infamous weed was in fact "aira." When Basil of Caesarea threw his weight behind this interpretation of the Gospel's "zizania," it became irresistible. Six hundred years later experts still equated "zizania" with the well-known weed "aira" and found such views unproblematic, obvious: the substantial compilation of ancient and late antique agronomic knowledge called the *Geoponika*, which was dedicated to the Byzantine emperor Constantine Porphyrogenitus (+959), switched between the two words casually, assuming everyone knew it was the same plant.[52]

In gaining an identity over the course of the fourth and fifth centuries, the Gospel's strange weed "zizania" also acquired a history. "Lolium" was a pesky plant in the Latin tradition, at least since the times of Plautus (who was the first to mention it in writing), was canonized as the "unhappy" weed in Virgil's *Georgics* (1.153), and was widespread enough to excite the legal curiosity of Celsus (who wondered, as noted above, whether to apply the Lex Aquilia to it).[53] This background helped literate late Romans accept that "zizania" was the same plant Latin speakers called "lolium" and Greek speakers "aira." As we have seen, the identification was occasionally contested, but by 515 or so, when they discussed "zizania" most Mediterranean

---

[50] Theophrastus, *Enquiry into Plants*, ed. A. Hort, 2 vols. (Cambridge, 1916–26), v. 1, 2.4, 122, v. 2, 8.8, 192; *Les causes des phénomènes végétaux*, ed. S. Amigues, (Paris, 2015), v. 2, 4.4, 69–71 (where Theophrastus allowed that careful inspection would reveal "aira" leaves are brighter, greener, and narrower than wheat's, from their first appearance).

[51] Dioscurides, *De Materia Medica* 2.100, ed. M. Wellman (Berlin, 1907), 174–5. See also R. Gunther, *The Greek Herbal of Dioscurides* (Oxford, 1934), 2.100, 133. This equivalence comforts modern students, who worry about which species to link to ancient plant names. On the text's interpolators, see Pedanius Dioscorides of Anazarbus, *De Materia Medica*, tr. L. Beck (Hildesheim, 2011), xviii–xix. Pliny, *Naturalis Historia* 18.17, 184–5, discusses cereal weeds, including "aera," in ways that suggest it was *not* the same as "lolium": it killed off the wheat it grew with.

[52] *Geoponika*, tr. Dalby, 9–13.

[53] U. Quattrocchi, *CRC World Dictionary of Medicinal and Poisonous Plants* 3 (Boca Raton, 2012), 808 shows the term "lolium" was not native to Latin.

people envisioned the plant called darnel in English, Linnaeus' *Lolium temulentum*. Important evidence for this assertion may be admired in the luxurious manuscript today called the "Vienna Dioscurides," a prestigious counter-gift to Juliana Anicia from some clergymen who were grateful to her, for this daughter and granddaughter of emperors had built a grand basilica in Constantinople for them. The book's illuminators painted a full-page image of darnel next to Dioscurides' text about "aira," which the Greco-Roman doctor had helpfully said was the same plant as that called "lolium" in Latin.[54] (See Figure 4.2.) The painted image is meticulous, naturalistic, and plainly recognizable, unmasking to modern eyes what plant Jesus (probably) had in mind.

Figure 4.2 Vienna Dioscurides, fol. 71v. (Photo: courtesy of Österreichische Nationalbibliothek).

---

[54] Österreichische Nationalbibliothek, Cod. Vindobonensis med. Gr. 1, f. 71v. Gunther, *The Greek Herbal of Dioscurides* 1.22, 133.

The Dangers of Darnel

Its toxicity makes darnel stand out among field weeds, and may have encouraged its identification with the nastiest weed in the Christian scriptures, Matthew's "zizania." Chemicals in the weed's own seeds, and perhaps those in a fungus the seeds are liable to host, can poison hapless darnel eaters. To become lethal, the doses ingested have to be high, yet the nausea, headaches, vomiting, intense gastric distress, weakness, and torpor suffered by people who eat even miniscule amounts of ground-up darnel seeds are certainly sufficient to justify the bad reputation this plant had in many agrarian societies: in first-millennium literature, for instance, people who ate darnel should expect to go blind and suffer from acute headaches.[55] Participants in the Eleusian rituals of Persephone and Demeter, early modern central Italian peasants, nineteenth-century English beer-drinkers, and evidently certain modern Saharan nomads seem to have found some of the effects of controlled, light darnel consumption pleasing, but only in special circumstances, when normal human functions were unnecessary or stupor was desirable.[56] For the most part, darnel was a feared weed because it had deleterious effects on human health, which coincided with the dastardly intentions of the "enemy" in Matthew 13. Generalizing a little, the ninth-century monk Christian of Stavelot warned that darnel caused people to lose their senses, something of which Carolingian readers were expected to disapprove.[57]

Another fearsome characteristic of darnel was its ability to grow every-where. This was a plant equipped to do well in pre-industrial grain fields. It was tough and adaptable, able to cope with quite different environ-ments, from eastern Mediterranean to continental European ones, and to flourish in different kinds of soil, from sandy to clay-rich ones. Beyond its versatility, darnel had further dangerous proclivities. Like many field

---

[55] French "ivraie" replicates the Latin "temulentum" in the scientific name of this plant, thought to produce a kind of drunkenness in consumers. Blindness: Philargyrius, "Explanatio in Bucolica Vergilii" 5.37, 97; *Geoponika* 2.43, tr. Dalby, 97. Headaches: Galen, "On the Powers of Foods" 1, tr. M. Grant, in *Galen on Food and Diet* (London, 2000), 108. The presence of 0.5 percent of darnel in grain produces toxic flour: L. King, *Weeds of the World* (New York, 1966), 91.

[56] H. Thomas et al., "Evolution, Physiology, and Phytochemistry of the Psychotoxic Arable Mimic Weed Darnel (*Lolium temulentum* L.)," *Progress in Botany* 72 (2011), 91; P. Camporesi, *Il pane selvaggio* (Bologna, 1983), 101–2, 151–4; H. Thomas et al., "Remembering Darnel," *Journal of Ethnobiology* 36 (2016), 37–8. Comet, *Le paysan*, 290–1 reports darnel seeds are reserved for special guests in the Sahara.

[57] Christian of Stavelot, *Expositio super Librum Generationis* 13.24, ed. C. Huygens (Turnhout, 2008), 274.

weeds, darnel's main technique of insinuation into human agroecosystems was mimicry, so that darnel germinated and matured at the same
time as such common winter-sown crops as wheat and rye, and the
plant's leaves and seeds closely resembled those of crops in the fields
where it grew. As Hrabanus Maurus said (quoting Jerome), "between
wheat and zizania, which we call darnel ... there is great similarity until
the tip develops the ear, and for discerning them there is either no
difference or one very difficult to observe."[58] Together with the plant's
slender stem and firm rooting, this made it difficult both for cultivators
to find and remove darnel in the field (as envisioned in the "Parable of
the Tares") and for threshers or winnowers to eliminate it from the
harvested crop.[59] Thus, many premodern granaries unwittingly har-
bored the seeds of darnel along with those of the plants people had
grown and stored to eat. Unlike most other weeds, then, which stored
their seeds in the soil while they waited for the next chance to germinate,
darnel stored them amidst humans' seed grain, certain they would be
distributed on to the plowed ground when the sowing season came
because they were so hard to tell apart from the seeds of cultivated
grains. A complex of imitative strategies thus extended darnel's presence in agroecosystems.[60]

Since darnel is a difficult weed to eradicate from grain fields without
modern herbicides and mechanized seed-selection procedures, if the
Gospel's "zizania" really was darnel, Jesus' upstanding farmer was wise
to restrain the would-be weeders of his infested field until the time of
harvest, when they were to burn the more easily recognized weeds. From
late antiquity, commentators on Matthew duly noted that "zizania" was
very difficult to tell apart from wheat until it formed its ears, a botanically
accurate observation that gave Christian readers insight into the meaning
of Jesus' parable, namely the need to tolerate the unworthy within the
community, confident that in the end all would get what they deserved.[61]
Understandably, the parable was very popular in some North African

---

[58] Hrabanus Maurus, "Commentariorum in Matthaeum Libri Octo" 4.13, ed. J. Migne, *PL*
107 (Paris, 1864), 951: "inter triticum et zizania, quod nos appellamus lolium ...
necdum culmus venit at spicam, grandis similitudo est et in discernendo aut nulla aut
perdifficilis distantia." Jerome ("Commentariorum in Evangelium Matthaei Libri
Quattuor," ed. J. Migne, *PL* 26 (Paris, 1845), 94) had said much the same thing.

[59] P. Halstead, *Two Oxen Ahead* (Chichester, 2014), 236 points out how darnel is difficult to
uproot.

[60] Thomas et al., "Evolution," 74–9. Most plants' seed bank is in the soil, so darnel's use of
human silos for its reproduction is unusual (79). An important case study: T. Senda and
T. Tominaga, "Genetic Diversity of Darnel (*Lolium temulentum*) in Malo, Ethiopia,"
Economic Botany 58 (2004), 568–77.

[61] B. Smith, *The Parables of the Synoptic Gospels* (Cambridge, 1937), 197–9; W. Oesterley,
The Gospel Parables in the Light of Their Jewish Background (New York, 1936), 61–2.

circles around AD 400, when Augustine and his peers debated with Donatists about what should be done with sinners found within the Christian community: the parable suggested the righteous should put up with the unrighteous and await God's final selection, rather than, as the Donatists advocated (justified by the more intransigent pronouncement of St. Paul in I Corinthians 5.13), expel them forthwith. Rather more strangely, Anglo-Saxon kings around AD 1000 also eagerly grasped at the parable to justify their religious policies: in particular, the burning of an important church "with its furniture and books" where a group of Danes had taken refuge. For the Danes, who at first appeared just like God-fearing English people, "emerged among the wheat just like pullulating darnel" and thus deserved to be culled and exterminated.[62] Clearly, during the first millennium, Christians of all types could appreciate Matthew's darnel-infused story, as long as they understood darnel's mimetic genius.

But darnel's skill was not just as an impostor able to trick people into thinking it was something other than itself. Darnel is an annual weed with a short generation time, and produces high numbers of offspring with considerable genetic variation between individuals. That meant darnel was genetically very dexterous, able to quickly acquire and disseminate desirable (from the weed's point of view) characteristics. For example, genetic studies suggest that the current annual *Lolium temulentum* evolved from its perennial relative *Lolium perenne*, almost certainly under pressure from early farmers in southwest Asia.[63] Darnel became far more cereal-like than other members of its genus in the last few millennia BC, evolving to survive. Furthermore, it seems that darnel can quickly become indehiscent, meaning that its seeds stay on the ear through the process of harvest, exactly like the seeds of prized crops; and by cross-pollinating among different genotypes, darnel can develop or omit clingy awns around each seed in order to resemble free-threshing or emmer wheats, according to what farmers are favoring in a given place and time. In sum, darnel can evolve as fast as humans change the odds of survival by means of their agrarian practices.[64] It is a singularly mutable plant.

[62] *Codex Diplomaticus Aevi Saxonici* v. 3, 709, ed. J. Kemble (London, 1845), 328: "Dani qui in hac insula velut lolium inter triticum pullulando emerserant." The church of St. Frideswide in Oxford was burned "cum munimenta ac libris."
[63] Thomas et al., "Evolution," 75–7.
[64] Ibid., 78–9, noting that scientists experiment with darnel because its leaves are so like those of grain and fodder crops but grow faster (83–4). Darnel's early evolution: A. Hartmann-Shenkman et al., "Invading a New Niche," *Vegetation History and Archaeobotany* 24 (2015), 12–17. Farming and evolution: E. Russell, *Evolutionary History* (Cambridge, 2011), 40.

A Shape-Shifting Weed

Its malleability reinforced the belief that darnel (or anyways "zizania" and "lolium") was not a distinct species of plant, but a mutation, or rather a perversion of the crops among which it grew.[65] This ancient idea is first attested in the writings of the proto-botanist Theophrastus in the fourth century BC, and Pliny the Elder took it up with enthusiasm four hundred years later when he wrote his *Natural History*.[66] For a shape-shifting potential in plants appeared to explain observed phenomena, namely that one sowed "good seed" but often ended up reaping darnel. Ancient authorities like Cicero asserted that one should reap what one had sowed, a sentiment with which educated folk agreed; in fact, cases to the contrary were perplexing enough to push Roman gentlemen to seek out their causes.[67]

Thus, simplifying Theophrastus, Pliny thought that changes in plants, especially economically useful ones, came about due to the effect of the soil or the climate on seeds before germination, though he also recognized that certain "flawed" seeds were more susceptible to these environmental stimuli than others. Pliny's vocabulary for describing such mutations was negative: the process was a decay, facilitated by a defect ("vitium") in the seed.[68] Likewise, Galen, the great Roman physician of the second century AD, related that his father, once he'd retired and found himself with time on his hands, had sown wheat and barley experimentally to ascertain whether a mutation produced "aira," and determined that indeed the mutation happened when weak grain seeds endured poor conditions (of climate or soil) during the initial phases of growth. Since they had no control over many of the environmental conditions, Galen concluded there was not much farmers could do about the appearance of "aira," save sort their planting seed very scrupulously and eliminate any weak grain seeds liable to turn into darnel (and to produce headaches among unwitting consumers, and also sores in summer). Galen's contemporaries on the other side of the Roman Mediterranean who codified the Mishnah also despaired of being

---

[65] M. Ruas et al., "Vestiges élucidés d'un parasite des céréales," in *Plantes, produits végétaux et ravageurs*, ed. M. Dietsch-Sellami et al. (Bordeaux, 2016), 43, note that until the sixteenth-century invention of microscopes numerous fungal and microbial infections of plants were perplexing and explained by metaphors of corruption.

[66] Theophrastus: *Enquiry into Plants* 2.4, 8.7–8, ed. Hort, v. 1, 122, v. 2, 182, 192; *Les causes des phénomènes végétaux* 4.4–5, ed. S. Amigues, v. 2 (Paris, 2015), 67–73. Theophrastus considered it feasible that deliberate human practices like seed bruising could cause mutations.

[67] Cicero: *De Oratore* 2.65: "ut sementem feceris, ita metes"; echoed by Augustine, "Enarrationes in Psalmos" 74.12, 784. Lucretius too dismissed the possibility that seeds could grow into different plants: *De Rerum Natura* 5.919–25. Evidently it was a pan-Mediterranean idea: B. Shaw, *Bringing in the Sheaves* (Toronto, 2013), 248.

[68] Pliny, *Naturalis Historia* 18.17, 19.10, 183–4, 297.

able to keep wheat and darnel distinct; they classified wheat and darnel as one plant, in this unique case exempting pious Jewish farmers from prohibitions against sowing mixtures.[69] In a similar vein, the late antique *B'reshith Rabba*'s reading of Genesis 6.7 suggested that the confusion brought by the Flood had caused some creatures to go astray and bring forth progeny contrary to their nature, so that when one sowed wheat, darnel sprouted: in effect, that explanation too was the fruit of the justified puzzlement of anyone who saw a properly farmed crop field infested by such an unexpected and successful weed.[70]

Therefore, at the very beginning of the literate botanical tradition in the Mediterranean, Theophrastus had hypothesized that soil and climate could modify plants over the course of some time. This nicely reflected ancient Greek wisdom on the influence of environment over the character of people, but also explained how the quality of plants changed during the course of their lifespans. Theophrastus considered the likeliest changes to be for the worse, a type of "degeneration" that the wrong environment wrought on some plants, including annuals. He also noted that there was a great deal of commerce across the boundary between wild and cultivated species, with some cultivated plants going wild when poorly treated by their cultivators, and some wild ones entering cultivation by modifying their nature slightly. To Theophrastus, in sum, vegetation was not always fixed and stable in its quintessential characteristics.[71]

Darnel was different. Whether one framed the problem scientifically, as Galen did, or legally, as the rabbis had, the growth of weeds, and especially of darnel, among fields sown with carefully winnowed seed deeply troubled ancient Mediterranean people because it happened so often yet really should not happen at all. For Christians the problem was also theological. Late Roman Bible commentators stressed that the darnel in fields was not a mutation of wheat, in effect a new species of plant conjured up by prevailing conditions of soil and atmosphere, but its own distinct kind, the seeds of which had been present all along, even if undetected.[72] The reason for this careful botanical differentiation was

[69] Galen: "On the Powers of Foods" 1, 108, with R. Sallares, *The Ecology of the Ancient Greek World* (London, 1991), 339. Doubts on the relation of darnel to wheat persisted in early medieval Judaism: A. Shemesh, "A Wheat May Change into a *Zunin* and a Male Hyena into a Bat," *Arquivio Maaravi* 11 (2017), 2–4.

[70] Oesterley, *The Gospel Parables*, 61.

[71] Theophrastus, *Enquiry into Plants* v. 1, 2.2, 110–18; 2.3, 120; 2.4, 122; v. 2, 8.8, 190–2; *Les causes des phénomènes végétaux* 1.9, 20–2; 2.13, 97–8; 2.15, 101; 2.16, 104. On the early medieval reception of klimata-theory, see C. Glacken, *Traces on the Rhodian Shore* (Berkeley, 1967), 257–8.

[72] Ambrose, "Exameron" 3.7, 80; Eustathius, *Ancienne version latine* 5.4, 61, based on Basil, *Homélies sur l'Hexaéméron* 5.5, 296–8. In "Exameron" 3.10, 87–8 Ambrose proposed that

that on the third day of creation, when God made vegetation, He also announced that each plant, great or small, would thereafter reproduce "according to its own seed" (Genesis 1.12). Therefore, to suggest there existed a plant, however devious and tainted by devilish frequentations, which developed out of another's seed, was inconsistent with the authoritative account of how the world worked. Such sentiments echoed in the Gospel passages that reinforced crisp and clear lines of botanical filiation, like Luke 6.44–5, which pointed out the absurdity of expecting desirable fruits to grow on the branches of weeds. Summing things up somewhat peremptorily, no less a theological (and, to medieval people, botanical) authority than Augustine said, "whatever is sown, that is what grows."[73]

Carolingian Receptions

Having inherited a rich and complex darnel discourse, the Carolingians zealously grasped at this shape-shifting weed, apparently able to sprout out of the seeds of other species of plant. They diligently replicated the wisdom of the late ancient Fathers on "zizania."[74] Mostly, they accepted that the plant was clearly "lolium," but just as some late ancient Christians had remained skeptical about this fourth-century conviction, also in the ninth century some wondered whether the identification was certain. The anonymous ninth-century poet of "On Navigation and Agriculture," for instance, considered "zizania" and "lolium" distinct species, and though it is possible s/he did so in order to pack into the lyric one more obscure term, there are other signs of Carolingian perplexity.[75] In the early 800s the Irish monk Dungal and, shortly thereafter, the Benedictine one Hrabanus Maurus both kept the two terms and presumably also species separate. Probably they did so because of their attentive reading in the *Etymologies* of Isidore, whose relevant passage on darnel had become garbled by the time they consulted it and facilitated the hypothesis that the bishop of Seville thought "zizania" and "lolium" unalike.[76] Thus, though the extent of their purposefulness is not clear,

inferiority or disease in wheat seed could also produce apparent mutations (but wheat stayed wheat).
[73] Augustine, "Enarrationes in Psalmos" 74.12, 784: "seminatur modo, crescit quo seminatur, erit et messis."
[74] Lolium as zizania: *Liber Glossarum* (following Isidore): "zyzania quam poetae semper infelix lolium dicunt quod sit inutile et infecundum"; Hrabanus, "Commentariorum in Matthaeum Libri Octo" 4.13, 951; Paschasius Radbertus, "Expositio in Mattheum," ed. J. Migne, *PL* 120 (Paris, 1879), 493–4; Walafrid Strabo, "Glossa Ordinaria" 13.30, ed. J. Migne, *PL* 114 (Paris, 1879), 132.
[75] See note 1 above.
[76] Dungal, "Dungali Scotti Epistulae" 9, ed. E. Dümmler, *MGH Epistolae* 4 (Berlin, 1895), 583 suggests the corruption in the relevant section in Isidore's *Etymologies* (17.9.105–6),

a handful of Carolingian writers appear to have entertained the possibility that the gradually developed late antique consensus did not capture the identity of "zizania."

Carolingian exegetes were, however, enthusiastic about the Father's antidote to the pesky weed: it was best treated as Jesus' farmer had, because it was so difficult to tell apart from wheat until it reached maturity and its ears were fully developed. To a man, the Carolingian exegetes espoused interpretations according to which the agricultural activities in the "Parable of the Tares" had ecclesiological meaning: Jesus had advocated not extirpating any weeds from the "field of the Lord" until the proprietor Himself took action.[77] In a long letter of the 850s, the monk of Fulda and Reichenau, and later bishop of Passau, Ermenrich of Ellwangen suggested that Christians must do with the faithless as wheat did with darnel, namely put up with the fetid and bitter rival until the final reckoning. As his teacher at Fulda, Hrabanus Maurus, put it more charitably, some who seemed damnable today might by divine grace turn out to be holy tomorrow, so the pious should recognize their ultimate ignorance and exercise patience with these spiritual "weeds." Their true nature would emerge in due course, predetermined by their seed even if at some stages of their growth it remained opaque to humans.[78]

Still, in Carolingian Francia reading the "Parable of the Tares" opened up the disturbing botanical possibility that good and bad plants were not just indistinguishable, but interchangeable. With annual plants, the selected seed of which was sown every autumn or spring, the problem was more acute than it was with perennial weeds like brambles, the devious mutation of which was easy to track: by digging up the root of "rubus," one could verify that its quintessential weedy characteristic, its thorns, developed with age and was not present underground where it began life.[79] However hideous the switch in nature, from smooth to prickly, it was transparently in accord with the laws of plant life spelled out at the beginning of Genesis, and people could uncover what was going on without too much effort. But with annual plants, over whose germination people exerted more control, it

present when Hrabanus Maurus copied it in *De Universo* (19.8, 529–30), led some to separate the two.

[77] Darnel removal: Hrabanus, "Commentariorum in Matthaeum Libri Octo," 4.13, 947; Christian of Stavelot, *Expositio* 13.30, 275.

[78] Ermenrich of Ellwangen, "Ermenrici Elwangensis Epistola ad Grimaldum Abbatem," ed. E. Dümmler, *MGH Epistolae* 3 (Berlin, 1899), 540 (unique in describing the smell and taste of "lolium"); Hrabanus, "Commentariorum in Matthaeum Libri Octo" 4.13, 951.

[79] See note 23 above.

sometimes seemed that the properties of a species switched in the course of growth, causing a weed like "zizania" to change into excellent wheat.[80]

When such doubts surfaced, there were explanations on hand that soothed attentive readers of the Bible, especially in late antique exegesis, convinced that botanical nature was fixed and no plant could shed its God-given identity. Indeed, the perfect symmetry between the seed a farmer planted and the vegetation it produced was axiomatic to the anonymous poet of the ninth century who rhapsodized that "whoever sows many seeds harvests many crops."[81] Thus, when tackling the final chapter in the Gospel of Luke, several Carolingian exegetes compared doubts about Jesus' resurrection to "bad herbs" and reasserted the age-old Mediterranean agronomic wisdom that "what one plants in a given place, one harvests there," so if one did not plant weeds they would not spring forth, the same applying to doubts.[82] The monk Christian of Stavelot prudently proposed that the problem lay in faulty human perception and the consequent inability of onlookers to tell crop apart from darnel.[83] Like most Carolingian Bible readers, he resisted the notion that "lolium" might be an indistinct species, able to change nature in the middle of its lifecycle, and thereby to disprove the biblical rule according to which plants ineluctably took their qualities from their seed. Even damnable weeds like darnel, so hard for humans to control, could neither mutate nor hybridize and contravene God's established botanical order. They were evil, but subject to the divine plan like any other organism.

Paschasius Radbertus represented the prevalent opinion when he explained that, despite human effort, impurities had become mixed in with the apparently "good seed" farmers sowed, or the sowing seed was "vitiated" by the weed seed: certainly no species slippage had occurred.[84] He echoed Hrabanus Maurus who thought "any uncleanness in a crop is called zizania," and proposed that wheat seed could be soiled, as well as

---

[80] Hrabanus Maurus, "Allegoriae in Universam Sacram Scripturam," ed. J. Migne, *PL* 112 (Paris, 1878), 951: "potest enim fieri ut qui videtur hodie lolium esse, interveniente per Dei gratiam poenitentia, cras fiet triticum."

[81] "Codicis Bernensis CCCLVIII Sylloga" 3.36, 248: "Nam qui plura serit, plura metit sata."

[82] Smaragdus, "Collectiones," 237; Hrabanus Maurus, "Homeliae" 8, ed. J. Migne, *PL* 110 (Paris, 1864), 148. This reasoning derived from Bede, "In Lucae Evangelium Expositio" 24.38, ed. D. Hurst, *Bedae Venerabilis Opera* 2.3 (Turnhout, 1960), 418.

[83] Christian of Stavelot, *Expositio* 13.30, 275: "qui hodie zizania videtur fore, cras potest esse triticum dei."

[84] Paschasius Radbertus, "Expositio in Mattheum," 493: "non quod naturam mutaret tritici, sed quia vitiis infecit eum ... Hoc quippe egit dolis, machinis, fraudibus ut degeneraretur triticum et fieret lolium, non natura, sed per vitium depravatum."

mixed with "alien" seeds.[85] As the *Capitulare de Villis* indicates, Charlemagne himself worried about impure seed and winnowing failures. His legislation does not single out any particular "bad seed," but does reflect Carolingian scholarly debates about weeds and darnel, and how this adaptable plant got into people's carefully farmed fields. Most Franks agreed that no subterranean, invisible, and theologically suspect transformation of crop seeds' intimate nature took place, but humans' failure to purify their sowing seed, in other words their lack of vigilance, made possible the ongoing infestation of cereal fields by the weed about which Jesus told a puzzling parable. Charlemagne hoped his estate managers could sort things out and prevent further contamination of the seeds sown on the king's land.

Conclusion

In his entry for AD 793 the anonymous writer of the *Annales Mosellani*, evidently a contemporary of the events recorded, noted that a famine ("famis") intensified in the Rhineland that year, inducing people to eat unusual foods ("immundicias") and even to cannibalize their relatives. Given the symmetry that the reported anthropophagy established with the perverse and unnatural family relations that allowed Pippin, in 792, to plan rebellion against his father, Charlemagne (whom Pippin intended to murder, along with his brothers), it seems the annalist wanted above all to make clear the direct ties between human sin and hideous chastisements ordained by God: the consequences of disordered royal domesticity were known to reverberate throughout the kingdom.[86] Though echoed in the capitulary issued at Frankfurt in 794, the very odd detail the anonymous writer added to the AD 793 account is unparalleled elsewhere in the Carolingian historical record, so stands out all the more: "That same year there appeared in several places in the kingdom at wintertime a boundless abundance of false

---

[85] Hrabanus, "Commentariorum in Matthaeum Libri Octo," 4.13, 952: "omnis immunditia in segete zizania dicuntur." Paschasius Radbertus, "Expositio in Matthaeum," 494: "ne forte illis dormientibus triticum sordidetur et commiesceatur semini alieno."

[86] "Annales Mosellani" 791 (actually 792) and 792 (actually 793), ed. V. Lappenberg, *MGH Scriptores* 16 (Hanover, 1859), 498. The rebels, including "plures ex nobilissimis iuvenibus seu senioribus Francorum," were variously hanged, beheaded, whipped (all punishments reserved to the unfree), or exiled by the king. Then the famine began. On this episode, see J. Devroey, *La nature et le roi* (Paris, 2019), 229–31, 246–85. Royal households' responsibility: R. Stone, "Kings Are Different," in *Le prince au miroir de la littérature politique de L'antiquité aux Lumières*, ed. F. Lachaud and L. Scordia (Mont-Saint-Aignan, 2007), 74–7. Cannibalism topos: T. Wozniak, *Naturereignisse im frühen Mittelalter* (Berlin, 2020), 731–9.

grain, in fields and woods and swamps, which people could see and touch, but no one could eat."[87]

The Moselle annals recorded a time out of joint, when strange things contrary to the established order happened. The monastic author found the report of a weird crop that deceived people with its appearance particularly apposite in this context. The tricky grain that grew at the wrong time and in the wrong places delivered no nutrition to people who desperately needed some, as a major famine gripped the Rhineland and perhaps some other regions of the empire. Just like darnel, or "lolium," the false grain failed to behave in the expected way. In this case, its distorted botany expressed perfectly the deceptions that had crept into the family and household of Charlemagne with Pippin's scheming, and thus was a perfect signal of divine displeasure with the behavior of the royal family. Though perhaps more pointedly political, the annalist's concern with a natural order that delivered what it promised and whose predictable rhythms and service to humans ought not, normally, fail, is the same concern as that of Carolingian exegetes who contemplated the shape-shifting weed in the "Parable of the Tares."[88] It was utterly unlike the predictable transformations of evil prickly plants like "rhamnum," which started life tender and juicy but in maturity developed the nastiest thorns: their nature was at least regular.[89] Annalist and exegetes strained to see a divine purpose, order, and meaning in the messy, irregular vegetation before their eyes. Of all plants, it was those with an unstable character that deceived people that disturbed them the most. People's attentive scrutiny of vegetation for divine signs was too easily misled by such deceptive plants. Their mistaking of mimicry for mutation risked undermining biblical taxonomy.

Close behind the shape-shifter in the taxonomy of vegetative evil came prickly plants, particularly those that received mention in the scriptures; perhaps more forthright, they were nevertheless bodily

---

[87] "Annales Mosellani" 792: "Ostensa autem eodem anno in ipso regno per diversa loca verno tempore falsa annona per campos et silvas atque paludes innumera multitudine, quam videre et tangere poterant, sed comedere nullus." This "false grain" appears nowhere else in Carolingian literature, but regular "annona" recurs frequently in ninth-century Carolingian diplomas and capitularies: it was "officialese" ("anona" instead occurs in the Salian Law). See Devroey, *La nature*, 116. The Capitulary of Frankfurt 25, ed. A. Werminghof, *MGH Concilia* 2.1 (Hanover, 1906), 168 refers to "vacuas anonas a daemonibus devoratas." Devroey, *La nature*, 263–4 discounts the possibility of intertextuality. He thinks (287–337) the annalist recorded a real phenomenon caused by microparasites (gnats and worms). See Comet, *Le paysan*, 212 on pre-Carolingian "annona."

[88] Devroey, *La nature*, argues that from the mid-700s Carolingian rulers felt responsible for the correct functioning of the Frankish environment.

[89] Walafrid Strabo, "Liber Psalmorum" 57.10, 928.

dangers as well as painful reminders of human fallenness. Where they rivaled the shape-shifting "zizania" was in the textual authority that supported both weeds and worry about them. For Carolingian culture's entanglement with Christianity most decisively oriented the vegetable imaginary of eighth- and ninth-century writers. To these men, far more than weeds pullulating in fields and gardens around them, the most profoundly anxiety-producing weeds were the ones interspersed in the text of the Bible.

5   The Botany of Paradise in Carolingian Rome

In the second half of the eighth century, the bishops of Rome, increasingly anxious about the ideological reliability of their erstwhile allies in Byzantium (iconoclasm had proved more than a flash in the pan), made a pivot toward northwestern Europe. That Byzantine military protection was turning out to be less steely than the Romans might have hoped also encouraged the "evolving separation" from Constantinople.[1] Lombard sieges of Rome in 756 and 773 came to an end only with Frankish armies in northern Italy. In 774 Charlemagne annexed the Lombard kingdom, beginning what turned out to be a century of relative security and stability for central Italy under a new protective umbrella, that of the Carolingian empire.

Rome remained itself, with a distinctive Byzantine-tinged, Mediterranean culture and increasingly self-conscious attachments to its earlier history of Christian martyrs and grand basilicas. Yet, however idiosyncratic a place it was within an empire of which the heartland lay between the rivers Rhine and Rhone, Rome was also an integral part of the Carolingian "discourse community."[2] The Frankish rulers' devotion to Rome's saints, especially Peter, and Charlemagne's enthusiasm for Roman books, buildings, and ecclesiastical standards, made Rome a household word far north of the Aurelian walls.[3] If the Carolingians never quite delivered on their promises to enhance Rome's territorial position, and if they seem to have recognized a separate status for the nascent "papal state," they also consistently treated Rome as integral to their Europe. Their solicitude after the Islamic raid on St. Peter's is a sign of Rome's inclusion in the "Carolingian project" almost a century after Pippin III had first timidly suggested an alliance with Rome's bishop.[4]

Hence Rome is not too eccentric a place to seek out Carolingian representations of heavenly landscapes and their vegetation. Rome was one of

---

[1] J. Osborne, *Rome in the Eighth Century* (Cambridge, 2020), 16.
[2] R. Kramer, *Rethinking Authority in the Carolingian Empire* (Amsterdam, 2019), 22–5, 45–9.
[3] N. Christie, "Charlemagne and the Renewal of Rome," in *Charlemagne, Empire and Society*, ed. J. Story (Manchester, 2005), 167–74.
[4] M. Costambeys et al., *The Carolingian World* (Cambridge, 2011), 430.

the small worlds that made up the Carolingian empire, and contributed to its debates about Christian perfection. Rome's voice had its own timbre and a marked authority, but could be harmonized with others in the pursuit of a coherent understanding of Christian community and culture.[5]

In Chapter 4 we saw how the thorn-infested landscapes that most horrified Carolingian writers did so because they were the antithesis of that ideal place, the divinely curated garden of Eden, with its smooth, soft, and obliging plants. Developing that analysis of the dangers of thorniness, this chapter investigates Carolingian representations of paradisiacal landscapes, and the pointed absence within them of the kinds of bad plants that instead accompanied everyday encounters with vegetation in post-lapsarian conditions. It emerges that the botany of paradise discernible in Carolingian-era artworks, and particularly in Roman mosaics, was a reversal, a diametrical opposite, of the unfortunate prickliness which typified the real world botany with which humans coexisted. Within the selectively historicizing mimicry of Carolingian culture, eighth- and ninth-century artists creatively adapted late antique botanical observations and visual conventions to their weedy needs.[6] In a further ramification, it seems representing the tenderness and lushness of paradise in Carolingian times was not mere ornament but mattered deeply in the context of contemporary theological debates. Like Charlemagne and his adviser Theodulf, popes of the period, from Leo III to Gregory IV, and the craftsmen they patronized, behaved like they knew this.

As this cast of characters suggests, the geographic distribution of the available data on this matter is rather uneven. The vagaries of survival over time mean that today the best places to observe how Carolingian-era patrons and artists imagined perfect landscapes and their vegetation are the areas around the altars of a half dozen basilicas in Rome. As observed above, the lower Tiber valley may have seemed exotic when viewed from Neustria or Austrasia, but Rome nevertheless was part of the cultural world held together by Carolingian patronage. Frankish hegemony facilitated an economic flourish in the Roman periphery of empire that funded numerous construction and restoration projects, and the refurbishing of numerous monumental spaces.[7] In all the most prominent decoration schemes from the decades around AD 800, glass mosaics played a large

---

[5] Kramer, *Rethinking*, 215–25.
[6] L. Nees, "Godescalc's Career and the Problem of 'Influence'," in *Under the Influence*, ed. J. Lowden and A. Bovey (Turnhout, 2007), 31.
[7] P. Delogu, "The Popes and Their Town in the Age of Charlemagne," in *Encounters, Excavations and Argosies*, ed. J. Moreland et al. (Oxford, 2017), 106–15. See also Osborne, *Rome*, 165–9.

role. Through this glass, brightly, we may today best glimpse what paradise looked like to the Carolingians, and what grew there.

To some degree, the prominence assigned to Carolingian Rome's
paradises in this chapter derives from the happenstance that several of
the mosaic programs remain visible, in decent condition today. The
mosaics are not the only Carolingian heavenly landscapes, of course,
and the paradises of ivory carvers or of miniaturists are also important.
But if what is called the Carolingian Renaissance sparked a burst of book-
making across Europe, and introduced vegetable décor into small
churches even in remote corners of the empire like Carinthia, their scale
and brilliance gave the mosaics greater impact: the monumental paradises
in church apses are far bigger, more striking, more public, and more
visible than other eighth- or ninth-century depictions of heavenly landscapes, like book illuminations, and more early medieval viewers saw the
mosaics than ever contemplated the books stored on shelves in silent
Carolingian libraries. Hence a discussion of Rome's eighth- and ninth-
century mosaics establishes parameters applicable more widely to the
Carolingian vegetable imagination.

Parchment Paradises

On a smaller scale than monumental wall-coverings, miniaturists also
depicted the plants of paradise. Several manuscripts from the
Carolingian epoch preserve imaginative reconstructions of paradisiacal
landscapes. In Francia book illuminators developed the theme with considerable horticultural verve, and it is worth considering some of their
creations to gain a sense of how unanimous was Carolingian Europe's
image of the appearance of a proper paradise. In fact, we shall observe that
the page-sized paradises bear more than passing botanical resemblance to
the large-scale grasslands aloft in Roman church apses.

On the illuminated pages of books like the Godescalc Evangelistary,
Carolingian readers might chance upon entrancing recreations of the
botanical circumstances of the heavenly sphere.[8] The Godescalc
Evangelistary (painted c. 781 for Charlemagne and his second wife,
Hildegard, likely to mark the baptism at the Lateran of their son Pippin)
depicts on fol. 3v the paradisiacal Fountain of Life surrounded with
flowers.[9] (See Figure 5.1.) The tranquil grazing of the deer signals the

---

[8] On the identification of Eden and paradise, see J. Rhodes and C. Davidson, "The Garden
of Paradise," in *The Iconography of Paradise*, ed. C. Davidson (Kalamazoo, 1994), 70–3,
78. See also note 20 below.

[9] Paris, BNF nouv. acq. lat. 1203. See B. Reudenbach, *Das Godescalc-Evangelistar* (Frankfurt,
1998); F. Mütherich and J. Gaehde, *Carolingian Painting* (New York, 1976), 34–5.

Figure 5.1 Godescalc Evangelistary (BNF lat. 1203), fol. 3v. (Photo: courtesy of Bibliothèque nationale de France).

plants are not prickly, since thorns are ultimately vegetation's defense against herbivores. The flowers are also subject to avid birds pecking at their petals. Their form faintly resembles flowers we shall find sprouting in the Roman mosaics of the ninth century, but their colors are more muted. The flowers are red and top long sinuous stems, like Carolingian-era mosaic flowers in Rome. Yet the illuminator Godescalc, who signed his work, painted the vegetation around his mystical fountain to look leafier than it does in the mosaic versions of paradise. His stems bear fewer blossoms, too. The Fountain of Life was in any case an unusual topic in early medieval art, and Godescalc had less precedent for this vegetable composition than he did for the opening images in the book, author portraits of Mark and Luke (fols. 1v, 2r), both of whom are shown hard at work on their books in gardens, and for a majestic enthroned Jesus (fol. 3r).[10] At the feet of the Evangelists' cushioned stools there sprout curving, small-leaved plants, with gold leaves and blue stems each holding several round red flowers, while flanking the throne of Christ in Majesty utterly spineless shrubs have red stems bearing red buds, separate from the shrubs' leafy structure. Though they are much smaller relative to the human figures near them, these plants, more than the well-irrigated ones around the paradisiacal Fountain of Life, have botanical characteristics that recall those we shall find in Roman mosaics. They may serve a similar purpose, namely to inform onlookers that the scene they behold took place in special, elevated circumstances, though in the case of the scribbling Evangelists presumably on earth.

Godescalc's illuminated book was an early sign of Charlemagne's commitment to Christian learning and to the revival of religious practice called the Carolingian Renaissance.[11] This revival had many repercussions, but here the pertinent ones are the painterly arts associated with a few central Frankish scriptoria. At Tours during the second quarter of the ninth century, Frankish scribes developed a novel way of illustrating paradise. To accompany the appropriate section of text of Genesis, painters conflated images that in earlier manuscripts (for instance, the sixth-century Vienna Genesis) had been separated. Thereby the Carolingian illuminators in Tours created magnificent full-page compendia of the earliest creation history, down to the expulsion from the

---

[10] Mütherich and Gaehde, *Carolingian Painting*, 34 stress the uniqueness of Godescalc's fountain. P. Underwood, "The Fountain of Life in Manuscripts of the Gospels," *Dumbarton Oaks Papers* 5 (1950), 45–6 lists four Carolingian fountains. All derive from that of Godescalc': Nees, "Godescalc's Career," 27–8, 34. The version in the Gospels of Saint-Médard (Paris, BN lat. 8850, fol. 6v) reduced the plants to tiny swirls of brownish pigment.

[11] F. Mütherich, "Die Erneuerung der Buchmalerei am Hof Karls des Grossen," in *799: Kunst und Kultur der Karolingerzeit*, ed. C. Stiegemann and M. Wernhoff (Mainz, 1999), 560–1.

compliant landscape of Eden.[12] Four such Genesis manuscripts survive, and three, from the Tours scriptorium of the monastery of St. Benedict, depict Eden (the Vivian Bible, the British Library's Moutier-Grandval Bible, and the one now kept at Bamberg); the San Paolo Bible, painted at Rheims around 870 for Charles the Bald and brought by him to Rome as a gift to the pope for his coronation, also shows paradise in detail.[13] Though the four differ in the attention lavished on the botany of paradise (Bamberg, Staatliche Bibliothek, Msc. Bibl. 1 (A.I.5), fol. 7v is the least botanical), they are fairly consistent in showing that trees predominated in the happy circumstances at the beginning of time, while smaller plants prevailed thereafter, when trees had become the raw material for the housing and tools that people found necessary after the Fall.

Among these depictions, the plants in fol. 7v of the Bible of San Paolo bear some resemblance to the leafless, red and white flowering species we shall find the Roman mosaicists inserted in their paradises. (See Figure 5.2.) Though as we shall see they did not disguise what the plants were to Carolingian cognoscenti, such visual affinities are faint and they would not satisfy the identification standards of scientific botanists. Quite aside from the very different ecologies involved, the color and shape of the flowers differ in the two media, and the illuminated stems are red, unlike the yellow-green supports to the mosaic flowers. In the San Paolo Bible paradise, leaves are golden until the Fall, when they appear to evaporate, leaving postlapsarian flowering shrubs, which are far less protected by any overstory, looking skeletal and positively wintry.

Among the surviving ninth-century Genesis illuminations from Tours, that of fol. 5v of the Moutier-Grandval Bible, a fine and harmonious composition, contrasts paradisiacal and post-Edenic plants still more sharply, and indicates that small flowering shrubs with delicate pale blue and faint orange flowers were a fact of life on earth, not in Eden. (See Figure 5.3.) These plants' sooty-colored stems form decorative tangles highlighted by the pale tan ground against which they grow; with their complete lack of any green components, they contribute to the barren aspect of the postlapsarian landscape. Its vegetation is not thorny, but visibly obstructs Adam and Eve's new-found labors just as efficiently as would a bramble patch.

---

[12] H. Kessler, "'Hic Homo Formatur': The Genesis Frontispieces of the Carolingian Bibles," *Art Bulletin* 53 (1971), 143–60.

[13] Thorough description in W. Koehler and F. Mütherich, *Die karolingischen Miniaturen* 6.2 (Berlin, 1999), 109–74.

Figure 5.2 San Paolo Bible, fol. 7v. (Photo: courtesy of Biblioteca Abbazia di San Paolo).

This very brief overview serves to show that, however distant in their styles and maybe also in their models, the Carolingian painters of earliest creation were of one mind: from Godescalc's Fountain of Life onward, the ecological niche of Eden was free of thorns and prickles, and filled with tidy,

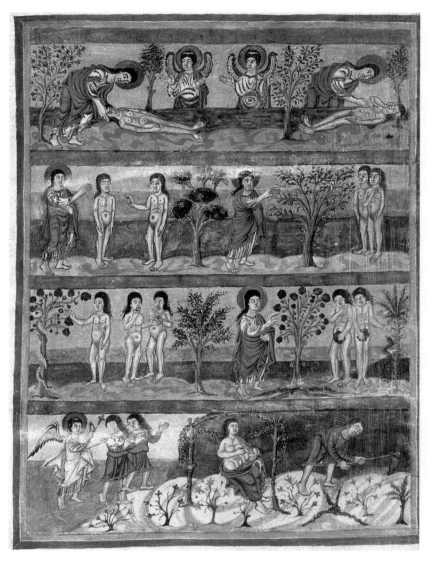

Figure 5.3 Moutier-Grandval Bible (BL Add. MS 10546), fol. 5v. (Photo: Wikimedia Creative Commons public domain).

untroublesome plants; on the other hand, fallen humans wrestled with unruly vegetation.[14] Indeed, in all four Genesis manuscripts of the Carolingian period that depict early creation history in detail, illuminators always show Adam hard at work outside Eden, equipped with (most probably) a weeding hoe.[15] Weeding spindly plants with bent back was the fate of humans beyond the enclosure of paradise. Though the Carolingian innovations in Genesis representation were more compositional than iconographic, and late antique bibles had included most of the elements Frankish painters adopted, from the weeding Adam back to the tree-shaded Eden, the clarity with which surviving Carolingian manuscripts separate fallen from thornless landscapes still reveals a living vegetative ideal.

Paradise in Glass

That today the largest and most splendid collection of paradises dating from Carolingian times is in Rome, on the southern periphery of the empire, is largely a product of chance. Earlier, monument-scale mosaics were known in the Carolingian heartlands, too.[16] A letter of 787 written by Pope Hadrian suggests Charlemagne received shipments of spolia from Ravenna, including marble floor and wall components and mosaics from the imperial palace (though a few decades later Einhard's biography of Charlemagne mentioned only marble columns).[17] Shortly thereafter, most likely in the early ninth century, the palace chapel at Aachen seems to have been decorated with an elaborate and ideologically charged program of mosaic, and around 806 Theodulf of Orléans, apparently impressed by what he saw at Rome in 799–800, and perhaps by

---

[14] Kessler, "Hic Homo Formatur," 144, 152–8 argued for a repertory of Genesis images, related to the late antique Cotton Genesis, circulating in early medieval scriptoria. He suggested (H. Kessler, *The Illustrated Bibles from Tours* (Princeton, 1977), 14, 20–2) that the Bernward Door at Hildesheim, with its bosky paradise and herbaceous postlapsarian world, replicated a now-lost distinct Tours illumination iconography. To my knowledge, early medieval representations of the postlapsarian environment like that of the Bernward Door do not emphasize its prickliness.

[15] A mattock is larger, but scale here is hard to determine. Rather, the unbroken soil signals that the surrounding plants are the main target of the tool.

[16] J. Caillet, *L'art carolingien* (Paris, 2005), 101. Wall mosaics were uncommon in Merovingian Francia: I. Wood, "Art and Architecture," in *New Cambridge Medieval History* 1, ed. P. Fouracre (Cambridge, 2005), 770. L. James, *Mosaics in the Medieval World* (Cambridge, 2017), 296–8 on Charlemagne and mosaics.

[17] *Codex Carolinus* 81, ed. W. Gundlach, *MGH Epistolae* 3 (Berlin, 1892), 614, with commentary in A. Hack, *Codex Carolinus* 2 (Stuttgart, 2007), 840–3; Einhard, *Vita Karoli Magni* 26, ed. G. Pertz et al., *MGH Scriptores Rerum Germanicarum in Usum Scholarum* (Hanover, 1911), 31. On the complex ecclesiastical politics behind this transaction, see J. Nelson, "Charlemagne and Ravenna," in *Ravenna*, ed. J. Herrin and J. Nelson (London, 2016), 239–52.

Charlemagne's Aachen structures as well, commissioned a set of gold-backed mosaics for the church he built at Germigny-des-Prés in the Loire valley, not far from the monastery of St. Benedict of which Theodulf was abbot, and close too to his bishopric at Orléans.[18]

Yet despite the toponym evocative of meadows, there is no real back-drop, vegetable or otherwise, to the surviving mosaics over the Germigny church altar.[19] Since Theodulf took a dim view of frivolous decoration, and the mosaics he sponsored represent the Ark of the Covenant with four angels (cherubim) in attendance, this makes sense.[20] But also at Aachen, apparently, neither plants nor botany played much of a role in the monu-mental program of ecclesiastical wall decoration associated with the Carolingian palace. The mosaics currently in the cupola of the palace chapel (now part of Aachen's cathedral) were manufactured in Murano and installed in the 1880s by Belgian craftsmen. Since the original mosaics had been lost by the nineteenth century, the modern mosaicists were guided by scholarly reconstructions of what had been there in the Middle Ages.[21] The reconstructions were based on a couple of early modern descriptions of what had covered the dome in the 1500s and bolstered by some seventeenth-century drawings, particularly that of Giovanni Ciampini from the 1690s, some twenty years prior to the destruction in 1719 of the originals.[22]

The early medieval mosaics represented the twenty-four Elders rising from their seats to proffer their crowns to the Lord of Heaven, seated demurely on a throne in a rainbow mandorla in the eastern side of the dome.[23] The scene evoked a passage from the Apocalypse of John (4.2–10), and may have

[18] The fraught matter of when the palace chapel received mosaic decoration is lucidly explored by U. Wehling, *Die Mosaiken im Aachener Münster und ihre Vorstufen* (Cologne, 1995).

[19] James, *Mosaics*, 294–5.

[20] A. Freeman and P. Meyvaert, "The Meaning of Theodulf's Apse Mosaic at Germigny-des-Prés," *Gesta* 40 (2001), 125–39.

[21] On the history of the dome's construction and decoration, see F. Pohle, *Die Erforschung der karolingischen Pfalz Aachen* (Darmstadt, 2015), 82–5, and especially Wehling, *Die Mosaiken*, 12–49. Murano: W. Giertz and S. Ristow, "Goldtessellae und Fensterglas," *Antike Welt* 44.5 (2013), 60. The modern history of the chapel's restoration is evoked by L. Konnegen, "Von der Restaurierung zur Konservierung," in *Die karolingische Pfalzkapelle in Aachen*, ed. A. Pufke (Worms, 2012), 63–72.

[22] G. Ciampini, *Vetera Monimenta* 2 (Rome, 1699), 134–6, and fig. 41. A reproduction (p. 362) and imaginative discussion of the chapel's Constantinian-Roman meaning is in J. Fried, *Charlemagne* (Cambridge, MA, 2016), 351–70. See also Caillet, *L'art carolingien*, 20–3.

[23] The chapel, likely unfinished, was consecrated in the summer of 796: J. Fried, "Karl der Grosse, Rom und Aachen," in *Von Kreuzburg nach München*, ed. M. Hartmann and C. Märtl (Cologne, 2013), 99–157. When the mosaics were laid is uncertain (Wehling, *Die Mosaiken*, 39), but as the same tesserae were used at Aachen and Germigny (Giertz and Ristow, "Goldtessellae,") an earlier date for the tiling in Aachen is feasible.

associated the new residence of Charlemagne (and successors), with its new temple and throne, with the heavenly Jerusalem at the end of time wherein peace and justice would prevail.[24]

The legitimating claims of such a mosaic left little room for weeds, or indeed for any plants at all. For in late antiquity Christian efforts to envision the place of bliss where blessed souls awaited definitive judgment separated an urban/architectural tradition from a rustic/pastoral one. In the rural tradition, the first three chapters of Genesis were a pre-eminent inspiration, and the account of Eden's enclosed garden of delights became transposed from the past to the future. Thus, some Christians thought that a celestial place of happy repose after death would resemble in botanical and other particulars the perfect landscape God created during the first six days. In this hope they were comforted by their familiarity with such classical topographies as those surrounding the shady, verdant *locus amoenus*, the Elysian Fields, the Islands of the Blessed, and various Golden Ages.[25] In other words, for late antique Mediterranean people the rewards for virtuous living should include abundant greenery.

When striving to understand what kind of place paradise was, other late ancient Christians instead focused on the end of the Bible rather than its beginning.[26] They derived from Apocalypse 21.9–27 their conviction that blessed souls would inhabit a celestial paradise very much like the square heavenly Jerusalem described by the visionary John, constructed of shiny precious stones and solidly walled. Understandably enough, in such an urbanized, built-up space, vegetation had a negligible role.

Late Roman Christian literature could conflate these urban and rural paradises far more handily than could Christian image-makers. Both the celestial garden and the celestial city existed in Christian iconography of the fifth and sixth centuries, yet they were not brought together into a unified vision of paradise. No perfect garden city, in other words, arose in the centuries after Constantine's conversion, in which blessed souls could confidently await the Last Judgment. Perhaps for this reason, at Aachen in the 800s the mosaic evocation of the heavenly Jerusalem rendered superfluous any populating of the dome's mosaics with

---

[24] So argues D. Rollason, *The Power of Place: Rulers and their Palaces, Landscapes, Cities and Holy Places* (Princeton, 2016), 272–86. Fried, "Karl der Grosse," 143–51 proposes relevant textual evidence.

[25] J. Delumeau, "Que reste-t-il du paradis?" *Rivista di storia e letteratura religiosa* 48 (2012), 222–7; J. Fleischer, "Living Rocks and *Locus Amoenus*: Architectural Representations of Paradise in Early Christianity," in *The Application of Medieval Rituals*, ed. N. Holder Petersen et al. (Turnhout, 2004), 150–5. On meadows and amenity in classical culture, see A. Corbin, *La fraîcheur de l'herbe* (Paris, 2018), 83–4.

[26] Delumeau, "Que reste-t-il du paradis?" is a good guide through this landscape.

appropriate plants. Although Charlemagne's 789 "general admonition" to his subjects had embraced the possibilities of governance leading to the "pastures of eternal life," for the palace chapel the mosaicists chose the more urban, Jerusalem-centered iconography of paradise in order to fortify their patrons' ideological point, the many parallels between earthly Frankish polity and heavenly universal one.[27]

In Carolingian times the palace chapel was probably as botanically bare as Theodulf's church at Germigny-des-Prés, with which the Aachen mosaics shared tesserae, and as bare as the other big mosaic paradise at S. Ambrogio in Milan, much-restored but likely including signs of a major facelift in the first half of the ninth century.[28] This elevates the significance of the large-scale Carolingian-era representations of the botany in paradise found in Rome.

Paradise in Rome: The Native Plants

While the Frankish heartlands manifestly experimented with monumental mural mosaics under the Carolingians, it is on the southernmost fringe of the empire that one can best develop a sense of what a heavenly garden may have looked like to Carolingian people, and what plants were native to that special agroecosystem. At Rome in the last decade of the eighth century and the first decades of the ninth, a series of apse mosaics were installed, all under papal patronage. In various forms they survive at the Lateran, SS. Nereo and Achilleo, S. Prassede, S. Maria in Domnica, S. Cecilia, and S. Marco.[29]

This burst of mosaic-laying activity came after some decades during which Rome saw little such monumental decoration, so its scale and intensity were novel.[30] Yet the Carolingian-era mosaics were also backward-looking, for the eighth- and ninth-century tessera handlers

---

[27] *Capitularia Regum Francorum* 22, praef., ed. A. Boretius, *MGH Legum Sectio* 2.1 (Hanover, 1883), 53: "ad pascua vitae aeternae."

[28] Caillet, *L'art carolingien*, 115–16: Milan's St. Gervasius stands on some indeterminate flowers with red, blue, and yellow stems. At S. Vincenzo al Volturno the crypt of Epiphanius frescos (recently redated to the early 800s by S. Marazzani and F. Gheroldi, "I dipinti murali della cripta," in *Molise medievale cristiano*, ed. F. Marazzi (Cerro al Volturno, 2018), 253–76) include several red flowers under the wings of angels, with slight stylistic affinities to the Roman mosaics.

[29] E. Thunø, *The Apse Mosaic in Early Medieval Rome* (Cambridge, 2015) is a valuable guide. See also U. Nilgen, "Die römischen Apsisprogramme der karolingischen Epoche," in *799: Kunst und Kultur*, ed. Stiegemann and Wernhoff, 542–50. Note that the apsidal wall at S. Maria in Domnica, with a procession of female saints on a paradisiacal meadow, is now hidden by a Renaissance ceiling.

[30] On the hiatus in Roman wall decoration, see M. Luchterhandt, "Rinascita a Roma, nell'Italia carolingia e meridionale," in *Storia dell'architettura italiana* 2, ed. S. de Blaauw (Milan, 2010), 329–30, who argues for the importance of Gregory II's new

interpreted for contemporary purposes the heavenly landscapes created by mosaicists in preceding centuries. This creative engagement with late ancient and Dark Age church decoration could rely on a far larger corpus of material than is visible in Rome (and elsewhere) today, making any reconstruction of the lines of artistic influence even more arduous than it normally is.[31] But whether the mosaicists were resilient Roman survivors of the quarter century (760s–790s) when no commissions were forthcoming, or refugees from iconoclastic Byzantium (which included Sicily and southern Apulia in the eighth century), or came from Lombard southern Italy, where duke-prince Arichis (who ruled 758–87) sponsored a vast construction campaign as part of his effort to revitalize the Lombard polity, there is no doubt that the mosaics placed on walls in Carolingian Rome were deeply affected by centuries-old mosaics that still looked luminous, and embodied a very useful kind of authority. If the Caroligian-era mosaicists did not use stone tesserae, as had been the custom, in the 790s when they took up the task of refurbishing the Lateran complex and redecorating S. Susanna, there was plenty of venerable local material to inspire them.[32]

The intimate relationship between Carolingian-era and late antique apse mosaics in Rome is obvious in S. Prassede's and S. Cecilia's mimicry of the early sixth-century composition of SS. Cosma and Damiano, including of its apocalyptic cloudy sky, but also in the persistent Carolingian-era juxtaposing of image and contextualizing inscription.[33] Most relevant for present purposes is the fact that Roman-Carolingian reconstructions of paradisiacal botany also relied on earlier prototypes then abundantly visible in the city. For example, the choice of species of flower shown blossoming in the celestial sphere for the most part is solidly local, derived from Rome's shimmering treasury of late ancient and Dark Age mural glass. Yet even though we cannot assess everything that was visible to eighth- and ninth-century mosaicists in the city, it is noteworthy how some plants in Rome's Carolingian apses resemble those in sixth-century mosaics further afield,

---

stational liturgy to the restorations of 780–840 (as does C. Goodson, *The Rome of Paschal I* (Cambridge, 2010), 91–2, 101–4).
[31] Thunø, *The Apse Mosaic*, 29–34 gives an idea of what formerly existed.
[32] Roman construction continuities: H. Dey, "Politics, Patronage and the Transmission of Construction Techniques in Early Medieval Rome, c. 650–750," *Papers of the British School at Rome* 87 (2019), 185–6, 193–6, 199; Thunø, *The Apse Mosaic*, 52–8; James, *Mosaics*, 102–4, who doubts iconoclasm drove craftsmen from Constantinople. On Benevento, see H. Dey, *The Afterlife of the Roman City* (Cambridge, 2015), 183–8. Roman mosaic technique: Osborne, *Rome*, 225–6.
[33] The mimicry is well known: Thunø, *The Apse Mosaic*, 13–16, 101–2; Wood, "Art and Architecture," 769–70; James, *Mosaics*, 301. S. Cecilia's mosaic inscription is unique in evoking (figuratively) botanical imagery: "rutilat hic flore iuventus /quae pridem in cryptis pausabant membra beata" (Thunø, *The Apse Mosaic*, 212).

for instance in the conch of the apse at Ravenna's S. Vitale, or S. Apollinare in Classe, or in the contemporary basilica Eufrasiana at Poreç in Croatia. With regards to the botany of paradise, then, the late antique "revival" in Carolingian-Roman art may not have been perfectly local in its models.[34]

Inspired by Roman and maybe other precedents, most of the flowers that bedeck the heavenly landscapes in Carolingian Rome are standardized and conventional in appearance. More various and realistic heavenly vegetation also had late ancient forebears, but at least in the surviving corpus particularizing and lifelike representations appear rarer. Therefore, this discussion of the botany of paradise begins with the more common ones, the anonymous, uniform, unreal plants that predominate around the altars at S. Prassede (c. 818), S. Maria in Domnica and S. Cecilia (both c. 820), and S. Marco (c. 830).[35] (See Figure 5.4.) These flowers resemble each other in size, shape, color, and arrangement. They are heaven's monocrop.

Probably the place in Rome where viewers could (and may still) come closest to these heavenly plants, and observe their unprickly nature most easily without squinting, is the chapel of S. Zeno inside the basilica of

Figure 5.4 S. Cecilia, apse mosaic, detail. (Photo: Sailko/Wikimedia Creative Commons Attribution 3.0).

[34] Thunø, *The Apse Mosaic*, 38–9 explains Krautheimer's influential idea of a Carolingian revival of late antique Roman aesthetics. For a critique of Krautheimer's formalist analysis, see C. Goodson, "Material Memory: Rebuilding the Basilica of S. Cecilia in Trastevere, Rome," *Early Medieval Europe* 15 (2007), 2–6.

[35] The dates are conjectures, based on the *Liber Pontificalis*. See C. Bolgia, "The Mosaics of Gregory IV at S. Marco, Rome," *Speculum* 81 (2006), 2, 11.

Figure 5.5 S. Prassede, triumphal arch mosaic, detail. (Photo: Daderot/
Wikimedia Creative Commons CC0 1.0 Universal Public Domain).

S. Prassede.[36] (See Figure 5.5.) Pope Paschal erected this funerary chapel
within his great creation, the basilica of S. Prassede, to commemorate his
mother, Theodora, who appears in the eastern vault with the square
nimbus of the living amidst three other busts of round-haloed female
saints, including Mary. The splendor of the mosaic surfaces, and the
proximity at which they may be admired in the chapel's small spaces,
may have contributed to the medieval conviction that the S. Zeno chapel
was a "garden of paradise."[37] The effect was certainly reinforced by the
numerous examples in the mosaic of standard, and standardized, flowering plants; their presence certified to onlookers the other-worldly location
in which the lucky figures they were contemplating found themselves.

As customary in Carolingian Rome (and as seen in the triumphal arch of
S. Prassede itself), in the S. Zeno chapel bushes of red-petalled, yellow-
pistilled flowers on spindly pale green stems that seem to sway under the
burden of the blossoms occupy the foreground, contrasting with dark green
meadows on which various holy people stand and walk without casting
shadows or leaving tracks. (See Figure 5.6.) As elsewhere in Carolingian
Rome, though their stems curve, these flowering bushes are very tall, half as

---

[36] Goodson, *The Rome of Paschal*, 168–70.
[37] S. Zeno's medieval name: G. Mackie, "Abstract and Vegetal Design in the San Zeno
Chapel, Rome," *Papers of the British School at Rome* 63 (1995), 160. In medieval Rome,
this epithet also applied to the irrigated garden before Old St. Peter's narthex: Fleischer,
"Living Rocks," 164. Angilbert called the narthex of the abbey church at Centula
a "paradisus," too: M. Driscoll, "Church Architecture and Liturgy," in *A Companion to
the Eucharist in the Middle Ages*, ed. I. Levy et al. (Leiden, 2012), 185.

Figure 5.6 S. Zeno chapel, mosaic, detail. (Photo: Sailko/Wikimedia Creative Commons Share Alike 3.0).

high as the saints, in this case Andrew and James, Peter and Paul, Agnes, Praxedis, and her sister Pudenziana.

Compared with the sinuous acanthus roll in the vault over the chapel altar, S. Zeno's flowers are more firmly linked to botanical reality; unlike other Carolingian flowers of paradise (for instance, in the Godescalc Evangelistary), which instead are always in full bloom, some are just budding.[38] Modern observers would be forgiven for thinking them poppies, carnations, zinnias, or an array of other species unrelated to *Rosa*, but as we shall see, there are good reasons for considering them "roses."[39] For a ninth-century observer would notice their leafless and thorn-free aspect and the vermillion petals, and promptly identify them as the native

---

[38] M. Collins, *Medieval Herbals: The Illustrative Tradition* (London, 2000), 27–8 noted illustrators of botanical manuals faced difficulty showing various stages of development synoptically while remaining true to life.

[39] Zinnias are a Mesoamerican early modern import to Europe. In the late Middle Ages carnations came to stand for the Incarnation (in English their name derives from the theological belief), but their place in first-millennium symbolism is unsure since we ignore their Latin name: J. André, *Lexique des termes de botanique en Latin* (Paris, 1950), 17, 192, 248; C. Hünemörder, "Carnation," in *Brill's New Pauly* 2 (Leiden, 2003), 1115–16. See also S. Kahn, "'Ego sum flos campi': Die Blume als theologisches Konzept im Bild des Mittelalters," *Marburger Jahrbuch für Kunstwissenschaft* 33 (2006), 32–44; P. Cox Miller, "The Little Blue Flower Is Red," *Journal of Early Christian Studies* 8 (2000), 213–36.

vegetation of paradise and symbol of martyrs' blood, red roses.[40] Indeed, since antiquity, in the Mediterranean no flower could grow more appropriately in a funerary garden, suggesting that this was exactly what Paschal built to honor his mother. That the figured presence of several Roman martyrs, whose bones rested in the basilica of which the chapel was part, surrounded Theodora's tomb strengthens the suggestion.[41]

The "roses" have several artistic affinities. They are virtually leafless, a botanical oddity familiar from the foregoing discussion of Carolingian illumination. And unlike the more verisimilar plants at SS. Nereo and Achilleo, to be discussed below, the tall red and yellow "roses" in the churches of popes Paschal I and Leo IV resemble seventh-century prototypes

Figure 5.7 S. Stefano Rotondo, chapel of SS. Primo and Feliciano mosaic. (Photo: author).

[40] C. Stancliffe, "Red, White, and Blue Martyrdom," in *Ireland in Early Medieval Europe*, ed. D. Whitelock et al. (Cambridge, 1982), 26–7, 36–7. Cox Miller, "The Little Blue Flower Is Red," 227–31 analyzes the meaning of red flowers in late ancient martyr cults, especially of female saints.

[41] Mackie, "Abstract," 179–80; F. Cabrol and H. Leclercq, "Fleurs," in *Dictionnaire d'archéologie chrétienne et de liturgie*, 15 vols. (Paris, 1907–53), v. 5, 1693–4 on the garden–burial link in late antique culture.

like those in the chapel of SS. Primo and Feliciano at S. Stefano Rotondo near the Lateran in Rome.[42] (See Figure 5.7.) If they represent members of the rose genus, their rather large yellow pistils make them resemble most of all a dark-hued cultivar of *Rosa gallica*, the rose that Carolingian monks fantasized about; but *Rosa gallica*, which looks quite unlike the roses commercially available in most rich countries today, has slender, straight thorns, unlike the "roses" in S. Zeno's chapel and the other Carolingian mosaics.[43] Though late ancient botanical compilations showed exactly these thorns on *Rosa gallica* stems, in the paradisiacal conditions the mosaics evoked, as in patristic visions of vegetable Eden, roses did not have any thorns.[44] In other words, first-millennium representation of roses depended on context and intended audience, and the same species could have thorns or lack them according to whether they appeared in paradise or elsewhere.

In the apses at S. Cecilia and S. Marco and in the absidal arch at S. Maria in Domnica, along with these curious, long-stemmed round

Figure 5.8 S. Maria in Domnica, apse mosaic. (Photo: author).

---

[42] Thunø, *The Apse Mosaic* argues that early medieval Roman mosaics were an iconographic unit, in conversation with each other during four hundred years of citation and replication.

[43] J. Keppels, *Karl der Grosse: Heilkunde, Heilkräuter, Hospitalitas* (Aachen, 2005), 50 suggests the "rosas" in the Plan of St. Gall are *R. gallica*.

[44] On the postclassical conviction that Edenic roses lacked thorns, see Chapter 4 above. Fol. 282 of the "Vienna Dioscurides" (Vindobon. med. grec. 1 in the Österreichisches Nationalbibliothek), illuminated around 521 at Constantinople, has a lovely painting of "rhodon," reminiscent of the Carolingian mosaic flowers but naturalistic, complete with many small, straight spines. The seventh-century Irish *Liber de Ordine Creaturarum* 10.8, ed. M. Diaz y Diaz (Santiago de Compostela, 1972), 160 represents a minority view: there are thorns in paradise, but they do not prick you.

red and yellow "roses," equally elongated stems hoisting white flowers with almond-shaped petals (in most cases three) and no leaves also cushion the feet of saints and frame mystical lambs. (See Figure 5.8.) Presumably the tall white blossoms represent lilies, a plant dear to Christian theologians since late antiquity and visible in the band that frames the seventh-century mosaic in the apse of the Lateran baptistery chapel of SS. Venanzio and Domnino. These "lilies" are the main botanical innovation of the Carolingian paradise mosaics in Rome; since they do not appear with the same profusion in surviving mosaics of earlier date in the city, but were celebrated by late ancient and Carolingian theologians, they may be a learned introduction into heaven's lofty vegetation, designed like their companion "roses" to convey theological messages.

To botanists it is mainly the color and height of the flower that authorizes the plants' identification as members of the genus *Lilium*, for the petal shape and lack of leaves are un-lilylike, and few real lilies manage as many simultaneous blossoms on the same stem as the Carolingian mosaicists attached to their plants, or hide their stamens quite as perfectly as the mosaics suggest these heavenly "lilies" did.[45] In the end, these beautiful white flowers, like the red "roses" with which they mingle, lack specificity. They serve, as did much of early medieval landscape art, to remind viewers of things they already knew, to ignite mental images that lay dormant until the eye fell upon the represented blossoms. In this way, despite, or perhaps because of, their indeterminacy, the flowers in the mosaics were not at all unspecific or vague: such flawless blooms directed onlookers to the right interpretation of the figures in the scene and their vivid color-code reminded the faithful that lilies and roses were the best and only feasible plant life in paradisiacal settings.[46]

They were also the appropriate vegetation for the altars and immediately surrounding areas in other Carolingian churches. Stylized, thorn-free "roses" and equally schematic "lilies" colonized the carved stone ornamentation inside eighth- and ninth-century churches in Carinthia, for instance, and modern art historians note their affinities with contemporary Roman ecclesiastical décor in various media, including mosaic.[47] It appears, then, that in the holiest portions of Carolingian-era places of Christian worship, even on the rougher eastern edges of empire, the

---

[45] The white lily bushes ringing the bottom of S. Apollinare's conch are quite lifelike. The two closest to St. Apollinaris' feet even have lilies' characteristic protruding stamens.

[46] V. Della Dora, *Landscape, Nature, and the Sacred in Byzantium* (Cambridge, 2016), 35–9, 103–5. See also Thunø, *The Apse Mosaic*, 64; Ü. Sillasoo, "Medieval Plant Depictions as a Source for Archaeobotanical Research," *Vegetation History and Archaeobotany* 16 (2005), 61.

[47] B. Ponta-Zitterer, "Blüten in der karolingischen Flechsteinkunst in Karantanien," *Carinthia I* 207 (2017), 46–52, 56.

botany of paradise was consistent, if rather abstract, and included two
main species of flowering plant. If neither the rose nor the lily known to
modern plant classifiers matches the appearance of the early medieval
representations, still Carolingian viewers knew what they were seeing,
whether carved in stone or laid out in glass.

Onlookers were predisposed to understand these flowers because late
antique commentators on the botany of paradise considered lilies and roses
to be the predominant species of the celestial spheres, and it seems that
western mosaicists, and other artists, followed this insight at least from the
sixth century. The color of both species looked meaningful to Church
Fathers like Ambrose, with the candid white of lilies (which of course
exist in other hues, whatever the Fathers imagined) signifying immaculate
purity and the scarlet of roses (somehow all roses in Christian discourse
were red) alluding to the blood sacrifice of martyrs, as well as of Jesus.[48] In
both cases the color association had a history in the Roman empire, which
Christians inherited and adapted to their cultural purposes in late antiquity. For instance, the ancient Rosalia was a funerary festival set in spring,
involving blood-red flowers, garlands, and petals: death and red blossoms
fit together in the Roman world.[49] Sheer white, a difficult color to achieve
artificially in the age before industrial chemistry and therefore highly
prized, had traditional connections with innocence and cleanness, and
certain flowers that consistently purveyed the candid color enjoyed elevated status in the ancient Mediterranean. Thus, Christian iconographers
in the fifth and sixth centuries did not have to look far when they needed to
populate heavenly landscapes with the right species: by then real flowers
bedecked the naves and altars of churches, and both in themselves and
through their colors conveyed time-hallowed messages.[50]

It was from this deep well of inspiration and association that early medieval monumental art drew, particularly in Rome. The red "roses" and white
"lilies" on the walls of Roman basilicas of the eighth and ninth centuries
today look whimsical and decorative, but in Carolingian Europe they pub-
licized the moral state of the holy people around them, their dedication to
Christian causes, and their immaculate purity.[51] The utter absence on them
of pointy excrescences, sharp stems, or thorns of any kind, which one might

[48] Kahn, "Ego sum flos campi," 44–5; Cox Miller, "The Little Blue Flower Is Red," 227–
30; Mackie, "Abstract," 178. G. Krüssmann, *The Complete Book of Roses* (Portland, OR,
1981), 55–7, 220 points out that the Bible mentions roses only seven times (and may
actually refer to crocuses), and its writers far preferred lilies.
[49] Krüssmann, *The Complete Book of Roses*, 33, 38–9; Cabrol and Leclercq, "Rose," in
Dictionnaire d'archéologie 15, 10–13.
[50] Cabrol and Leclercq, "Fleurs," *Dictionnaire d'archéologie* 5, 1693–9.
[51] P. Kershaw, *Peaceful Kings: Peace, Power and the Early Medieval Political Imagination*
(Oxford, 2011), 231–3 on some Carolingian readings of lily and rose.

expect at least on roses like *Rosa gallica*, positioned the humans (or rather superhumans) who stood over them in Roman apses in paradisiacal perfection, in a Christian place of bliss akin to that Garden where all people were supposed to be but for Adam's blunder, and which only they now enjoyed, on account of their virtue. Through their forms and colors, the plants in the mosaics made purposeful theological pronouncements.

Paradise in Rome: Some Exotics

By far the most biodiverse paradisiacal meadow of the entire Frankish epoch is the earliest one to survive in Rome, laid around 814 under Leo III on the apsidal arch at the small church he rebuilt in honor of the local martyrs Nereo and Achilleo at the beginning of the Appian Way, just down the Caelian hill from the papal residence. (See Figure 5.9.) The protagonist of the composition was Jesus, but Mary, shown seated on the left as she receives from Gabriel the news she is pregnant, and on the right holding Jesus on her lap, flanked by an angel, had an unusually prominent place too.[52] At the pinnacle of the arch a strangely compressed Jesus stands in a bright turquoise

Figure 5.9 SS. Nereo and Achilleo, interior. (Photo: author).

[52] Mary was unusually prominent also in Leo's textile donations to Roman churches: M. Andaloro, "Immagine e immagini nel *Liber Pontificalis* da Adriano I a Pasquale I," *Mededelingen van het Nederlands Instituut te Rome* 60–61 (2001–2), 51–2.

Figure 5.10 SS. Nereo and Achilleo, triumphal arch mosaic, detail. (Photo: author).

mandorla, blessing; his Transfiguration is signaled by three large but prostrate figures at his feet (Peter, John, and James), and two smaller standing ones on either side of him (Moses and Elijah), who seem less surprised by the spectacle they behold.[53] Against a radiant light green surface that climbs the apsidal arch to support Jesus and his companions, numerous flowers sprout, each in full bloom. (See Figure 5.10.) There are also some tiny leafy plants, rendered in yellow, dark green, and brown tesserae, without blossoms, which curators of modern suburban lawns might deem to be weeds, but which clearly in this ecosystem were not: in a place like paradise all plants cooperate in providing perfection, and prelapsarian interspecies harmonies prevail. The flowers have short stems and leaves, quite unlike previous such representations in Rome; they also differ from later Carolingian mosaic renditions in the botanical precision with which they were rendered. Oxeye daisies (*Chrysanthemum leucanthemum*) are easily recognizable, and crocus-like white flowers, as well as orange-red pansy-like flowers, both with blue-grey pistils. More indeterminate are

[53] James, *Mosaics*, 122–4 suggests mosaic was suited to the transfigured Jesus of Tabor, who radiated light.

short-stemmed flowers with petals of a lovely blue, the pistils of which are red and orange.[54]

Even when they share their colors with the flowering vegetation of the later Carolingian churches in Rome, these flowers stand apart stylistically. SS. Nereo and Achilleo's meadow is more varied and naturalistic than the heavenly landscapes shimmering elsewhere in the papal city. It may have resembled the meadow on which stood the twelve apostles in Leo III's triclinium at the Lateran, probably re-laid in 797–8 over Hadrian's program, and maybe the mosaic at S. Susanna which the *Liber Pontificalis* says Leo also had installed, but these mosaics' destruction makes this impossible to know for certain.[55] Thus the effort of botanical observation at SS. Nereo and Achilleo remains unique in Rome, and as far as I know in Carolingian Europe. While its palette of colors reflects that of SS. Cosma and Damiano's apse, its greenery appears tenuously connected to the heavenly meadow's surviving predecessors among early medieval Roman mosaics, such as those in the seventh-century chapels of SS. Venanzio and Domnino in the Lateran baptistery or of SS. Primo and Feliciano in the round church of S. Stefano, both of which have far tidier vegetation, ranked in lines with schematic, unrealistic flowers.[56] Though it, too, lacks prickles and spiny plants, it is more earthy, more intimately connected to observed natural landscapes, and more messy and various than any contemporary paradise.

This late eighth-century Roman paradise, in fact, comes closest to replicating the beautiful and famous heavenly meadow of S. Apollinare in Classe, near Ravenna.[57] It is therefore significant that the *Liber Pontificalis* records Leo III's interest in S. Apollinare, the brilliant mid-sixth-century apse mosaic of which contains perhaps the most lifelike paradise of the entire first millennium, framing the era's most assertive jeweled, triumphant cross.[58] Leo's restoration of that church's roof and (apparently) triumphal arch may have inspired him to include such

---

[54] The Baronian restoration "integrated" the salvageable mosaics with painted plaster (U. Utro, "Una 'falsa testimonianza,'" in *Atti del IX colloquio dell'Associazione italiana per lo studio e la conservazione del mosaico* (Ravenna, 2004), 508), but some of the lowest portions were re-restored in 1832 (U. Nilgen, "Apsismosaik von SS. Nereo ed Achilleo," in *799: Kunst und Kultur*, ed. Stiegemann and Wernhoff, 639). Still, I take the eccentric botany to be original.

[55] *Liber Pontificalis* 2, 98.9, ed. L. Duchesne (Paris, 1892), 3. Goodson, *The Rome of Paschal I*, 21 suggests the triclinium lacked plants.

[56] Nilgen, "Apsismosaik," 640 links the figures' linear drapery to seventh-century Roman models.

[57] H. Belting, "Die beiden Palastaulen Leos III. im Lateran und die Entstehung einer päpstlichen Programmkunst," *Frühmittelalterliche Studien* 12 (1978), 70 suggested that Leo III was primarily interested in the mosaic that Leo I installed at S. Paolo outside the walls, with affinities to S. Apollinare.

[58] *Liber Pontificalis* 2, 98.106, 31–2. See R. Wisskirchen, "Leo III und die Mosaikprogramme von S. Apollinare in Classe in Ravenna und SS. Nereo ed Achilleo

a worldly botany at SS. Nereo and Achilleo, where the topic of Jesus'
divinization was tackled frontally, including with a great mosaic cross in
the apse conch that is now lost, and which scholars reconstruct on the
basis of a much-manipulated painting made around 1600, when Cardinal
Baronius overhauled the church.[59] For, unlike other possible models –
the great cross from around AD 400 in the apse of the Roman church of
S. Pudenziana, which towers over a deeply urban landscape, or the
apocalyptic landscape at Jesus' feet in the apse of nearby SS. Cosma
and Damiano (from AD 530–6), which is barren and stony – the
Ravennan mosaic includes numerous non-flowering, leafy plants and
shrubs in its paradise, behind the church's titular saint and below the
radiant cross contained in a starry orb flanked by Moses and Elijah (with
three sheep presumably standing for the three apostles who accompanied
Jesus on his excursion to the "high mount" – the Vulgate's "montem
excelsum" in Matthew 17.1 – where the Transfiguration transpired). Like
that of SS. Nereo and Achilleo, S. Apollinare's idiosyncratic composition
is a modified Transfiguration. Beyond the deployment of this rare subject
for early medieval art, and the favor of Pope Leo III, the two churches
share other affinities.[60] Aside from the allusion to the extraordinary events
just prior to Jesus' death on what most commentators identified as Mount
Tabor, many botanical details also coincide. In both churches, credible
red and white flowers play starring roles, and among surviving early
medieval paradise representations, only these two basilicas allow such
a proliferation of flowerless plants; even the apse vault of S. Vitale in
downtown Ravenna, contemporary with S. Apollinare's mosaics and
similar in style, exclusively depicts blooming plants, while in Rome's
SS. Cosma and Damiano, the overgrazed pasture under Jesus, which

in Rom," *Jahrbuch für Antike und Christentum* 34 (1991), 139–51; James, *Mosaics*, 240–2;
D. Deliyannis, *Ravenna in Late Antiquity* (Cambridge, 2010), 267–9; F. Deichmann,
Ravenna, Hauptstadt des spätantiken Abendlandes 2.2 (Wiesbaden, 1976), 246–64, 269.
Andaloro, "Immagine," 53 notes similar iconography in the cloths Leo donated to both
churches.

[59] R. Krautheimer, *Corpus Basilicarum Christianarum Romae* 3 (Vatican City, 1971), 143,
150. As Leo first visited Ravenna in early 805 and restored S. Apollinare about a decade
later, Belting, "Die beiden Palatstaulen," 71–2 proposed a connection with the SS. Nereo
and Achilleo mosaics. On the Ravennan apse restoration, see Andaloro, "Immagine," 53.
Utro, "Una 'falsa testimonianza,'" 508–15 argued that the Vatican Library painting of
SS. Nereo and Achilleo's apse, with the jeweled cross, is a forgery from the nineteenth
century.

[60] After the sixth century, there are few Transfigurations in Europe before the late Middle
Ages: E. Saxon, "Art and the Eucharist," in *A Companion to the Eucharist*, ed. Levy et al.,
141. The niche over the altar in the S. Zeno chapel may have had a Transfiguration before
the high Middle Ages: James, *Mosaics*, 303. Carolingian-era popes otherwise eschewed
the subject, and indeed most scriptural themes in monumental art: Andaloro,
"Immagine," 59–60.

displays a few spindly small-leafed but unspecific shrubs sprouting from fifteen outcrops, lacks flowers.[61]

Admittedly there are also some botanical differences between the Roman and Ravennan mosaics: most obviously, SS. Nereo and Achilleo's lacks the evergreen trees (holm oak, cypress, pine, olive) that shade the flowering undergrowth at S. Apollinare in Classe. But in any case, since the context in which the Roman church arose is little known, it is rash to assign the untraditional botanical elements on the absidal wall of SS. Nereo and Achilleo simply to observation and imitation of the mosaics laid in Ravenna's port cathedral 250 years earlier, when the ancient tradition of naturalistic representation of plants retained its vigor, and masterpieces of close botanical observation like the "Vienna Dioscurides" received their illustrations.[62]

The green tesserae that constitute the base on which the absidal wall scene unfolds at SS. Nereo and Achilleo offer a solid ground on which the Transfiguration may take place. That they rim the apse conch, and therefore climb the slope up to the central figure of Jesus, confers on this meadow the appearance of a mount. It is in fact a hill with a peculiarly even, rounded shape, exactly as Carolingian exegetes described Mount Tabor: "a mountain in Galilee, rounded and lofty and that ends equal on all sides."[63] This suggestion of the context where, according to the synoptic Gospels, two major ancient prophets appeared alongside him and God addressed Jesus as His son, should not be geographical: the Evangelists did not specify which high mountain Jesus and companions climbed before being engulfed in a luminous talking cloud. Yet medieval Christians believed Mount Tabor was the very place where Jesus' special relationship with God became public and where the glory of Christ became manifest in the natural world to mortal men. The event happened on earth, on a real mountain that early medieval travelers classified as

---

[61] *Liber Pontificalis* 2, 98.106, 32 claims Leo donated an iconographically elaborate tapestry to hang over S. Apollinare's altar, decorated with roses. Such "roseate" cloths were common in papal donations of the eighth and ninth centuries: Cabrol and Leclercq, "Rose," in *Dictionnaire d'archéologie* 15, 13–14; for an AD 772–824 catalogue, see Andaloro, "Immagine," 48. For SS. Cosma and Damiano, see Thunø, *The Apse Mosaic*, 13–16.

[62] The "Vienna Dioscurides" (see note 44 above) is considered the last gasp of botanically accurate representation in books; though several other manuscripts of Dioscurides' herbal were painted in the Middle Ages, their images do not help to identify the plants discussed in the text: see Collins, *Medieval Herbals*, 25–6, 184–6.

[63] In this they followed Jerome's lead. See Hrabanus Maurus, *Commentaria in Libris Regum* 10, *PL* 109 (Paris, 1859), 37: "Thabor mons est in medio Galilaeae, campo mirae rotunditudinis sublimis"; Haymo, *Enarratio in Duodecim prophetas minores* 5, *PL* 117 (Paris, 1852), 39: "Tabor ... mons est situs in campestris Galilaeae, rotundus atque sublimis et ex onmi parte aequaliter finitur."

outstanding because it was "very grassy and full of flowers."[64] The unusual verisimilar lawn at SS. Nereo and Achilleo could therefore be a subtle Roman insertion of theological truth into the basilica's liturgical space. The meadow looked like a genuine Mediterranean alpine meadow might look on a good day in spring because that way it contributed to prove Jesus' divine-and-human nature, as a Transfiguration required. The botanical realism confirmed early medieval Latin interpretations of the Gospel accounts and of their representability.

Conclusion

In the great centers of learning of northwestern Europe, illuminators of Carolingian bibles used vegetation to confrm Christian truths. In the provinces of empire, carvers of stone chancels for rural churches did the same. Troublesome plants existed in the context of sin, of everyday human existence, while lovely, cooperative plans grew in places where divine grace shone warmly. In their glassy medium, and on a heroic scale, Rome's mosaicists participated in this "discourse community." They did so, as we have seen, in two distinct modes.

The heavenly pasture on the absidal wall of SS. Nereo and Achilleo was Carolingian Rome's most naturalistic, but it was also an outlier. For the rest, as we have seen, much more stylized "roses" and "lilies" prevailed in Carolingian paradises. Yet these heavenly meadows were not the only place in the Carolingian compositions where significant plants sprouted forth. The magnificent vegetable garlands that frame the eighth- and ninth-century scenes at S. Maria in Domnica, S. Prassede, S. Cecilia, and S. Marco derive from the botanically more accurate ones in earlier Roman churches, especially the seventh-century S. Agnese. These involve geometrically interwoven branches of recognizable conifers, of quince, of pomegranate, of laurel and oak, and of a few other less determinate flowering species reminiscent of the "roses" and "lilies" in the heavenly pastures of the conches and absidal walls.[65] All are at the peak of maturity and in perfect condition, like most plants of paradise. But though they may replicate concepts and patterns, and even species,

---

[64] Adomnan, *De Locis Sanctis* 2.27, *PL* 88 (Paris, 1864), 804: "Mons Thabor in Galilea tribus millibus a locus Chenerath distat mira rotunditate ex omni parte collectus, a parte boreali respiciens supradictum stagnum, herbosus valde et floridus." The 1912 *Catholic Encyclopedia* agreed that "remarkable vegetation which covers its sides of calcareous rock" distinguishes Mount Tabor.

[65] Since Tertullian, learned Christians linked the process by which flowers became fruits to the conception and birth of Jesus, so the mixture of flowering and fruit-bearing plants in the Carolingian framing garlands may have theological meaning. See Kahn, "Ego sum flos campi," 37, 51.

from the seventh century, the concerted effort of the Carolingian-era artists was to show that, like the paradisiacal meadows they circled and highlighted, these plants were utterly thorn-free, without any of the burrs, needles, prickles, and spines that characterized postlapsarian vegetation and landscapes, and real specimens of the species evoked. The garlands were pruned of any pointed propagules and potentially offending branches, and the stems of species that tend in actuality to be spiny appear unthreatening, tame, symmetrical, reduced to cushiony verdure in imitation of the grasslands within the apses that framed and supported the holy interactions on which onlookers' attention should focus.

Indeed, in early medieval culture, paradise was "the paradigmatic place of earthly tranquility and order."[66] Therefore Edenic fields and gardens should be lush and fertile, with all species simultaneously at the pinnacle of their vegetative development, but also orderly and compliant, posing no threats to the other members of the ecosystem. They should require no maintenance, no weeding. The poised and dignified postures of the holy inhabitants were echoed by the plants they stood upon, without trampling. In effect the perfection of saints and holy figures was reflected botanically: all were staid and tidy, physically intact, completely self-contained. Hence no prickly plants sprouted in the Roman apses of the Carolingian period, including the most realistic among them, because they did not in the places of whose nature they reminded spectators.

Carolingian-era Edenic landscapes in Rome were therefore more than statements of self-conscious conservatism, a Krautheimerian resuscitation of late antique décor in the city of empire. They were self-conscious evocations of a past the utility of which was contemporary. In fact, the representation of celestial plants in the Roman apses could be understood as polemic, and set in the context of early medieval theology, whether in the debates around Jesus' humanity derived from Iberia (Adoptionism), or in those ignited by iconoclasm and enmeshed in the continuous ideological sparring of the decades around 800 between eastern and western Christian polities.[67] During that period, popes like Leo III, Paschal I, and Gregory IV sponsored mosaics that vigorously reasserted the legitimacy of representing the supernatural as natural and heavenly landscapes with a recognizable, more-or-less earthly vegetation. Since at the time the mosaic medium most closely associated with imperial Byzantine art was

[66] Kershaw, *Peaceful Kings*, 9.
[67] See Andaloro, "Immagine," 63. F. Alto Bauer, "Die Bau- und Stiftungspolitik der Päpste Hadrian I. (772–795) und Leo III. (795–816)," in *799: Kunst und Kultur*, ed. Stiegemann and Wernhoff, 525 argues the mosaics at SS. Nereo and Achilleo were not theologically informed.

not being used in this way at Constantinople or in the lands under its sway, the vast mosaic programs of 795–840 gained special poignancy.[68]

One of the effects of iconoclasm on eastern Christian art and iconography, even after the reinstatement of imperial support for icons in 843, was to reduce the representation of plants (and animals) in religious contexts, and particularly of verisimilar landscapes. As Maguire has argued, iconoclasm rendered awkward for patrons and artists the depiction of vegetation that previously had adorned church pavements and walls to teach Christians about the harmony, beauty, and variety of God's creation, and to situate the martyred saints standing amidst them squarely in that most *amoenus* of loci, paradise.[69] For the iconoclasts, the pagan and magical connotations of nature-derived imagery were too strong, and their iconophile opponents in Byzantium evidently saw their point. After the 720s, on both sides of the icon divide, springtime meadows full of flowers seemed too easy to misunderstand, able to induce people to imagine the plants themselves had some kind of spiritual power. A result was landscapes of "boiled sweets" in later Byzantine mosaics, as in the Ascension in the dome of Haghia Sophia in Thessalonica.[70] Precisely for this reason, as Byzantine art turned its back on naturalistic representations, in early ninth-century Rome placing luxuriant, plausibly rendered meadows at the feet of holy people (and their papal patrons) signified the popes' commitment to the iconographic status quo ante, and to the Carolingians.[71] More than that, the paradisiacal vegetation allowed the Roman bishops to flex their political muscle and act in a truly imperial manner, a fitting complement to their new residence, a Constantinople-inspired palace at the Lateran equipped with ample reception spaces.

One context for the Carolingian–Roman botany of paradise, then, was eastern and Mediterranean: in the decades around AD 800, a botanically plausible paradise could serve as visual reminder of papal autonomy from Byzantium, whatever the particulars of Byzantine policy at any given moment (Leo V reinstituted iconoclasm in 815). Citing as it does the real world of Mediterranean vegetation, the surviving mosaic of SS. Nereo and Achilleo asserts papal attachment to the theological truths of old-style iconophile art, even if it was botanically detached from any known Roman predecessors. But, of course, this need not have been the mosaic's sole purpose: if the now

---

[68] C. Wickham, *The Inheritance of Rome* (London, 2009), 241.

[69] H. Maguire, *Nectar and Illusion: Nature in Byzantine Art and Culture* (Oxford, 2012).

[70] James, *Mosaics*, 327. The composition dates to c. 885.

[71] F. Svizzeretto, "Il mosaico absidale, manifesto iconodulo," in *Caelius* 1, ed. A. Englen (Rome, 2003), 241–56. On the politics of papal mosaics, see also James, *Mosaics*, 308–13.

lost apse conch in Pope Leo's new basilica contained a triumphant cross, with the Transfiguration scene above it the arrangement became a vigorous rejoinder to the Adoptionist devaluation of Jesus' divinity that worried Carolingian theologians throughout the 790s and occupied the attention of the Roman church at a council held in 798, in the opening years of Leo's pontificate.[72] In this, the highly visible placement of Mary, doubly as recipient of divine revelation and as mother of God, high in either corner of the absidal wall, also had an important function.[73] Thus, another context for understanding Rome's heavenly meadows was decidedly western and continental, related to Iberian and Frankish Christians' most urgent concerns at the turn of the ninth century.

In one visual idiom at SS. Nereo and Achilleo, and in another at S. Prassede, S. Maria in Domnica, S. Marco, and S. Cecilia (and surely at other, now lost sites like Leo III's S. Susanna), pious onlookers of the ninth century gazed at the ongoing commingling of natural vegetation with otherworldly landscapes that advertised the pope's attachment to the Europe of the Franks. That all these paradisiacal landscapes were free of the prickly weeds that evoked Adam's Fall and showed vegetable nature as God had originally intended it to be only sharpened the Roman bishops' polemical point. So did massive, more-than-life-size garlands along the apses' rims, framing the compositions with triumphal wreaths that evoked the crowns of victory worn by elders and martyrs in the nearby scenes, and especially by the hand of God at the apex of the compositions in S. Marco and S. Prassede.[74] Representing, at huge scale, the lush and weed-free vegetation of heaven festooned by its own ornamental roping of plants was an assertive act in the decades around 800. Building on late ancient and Dark Age iconographic tradition, mosaicists in Carolingian Rome recreated a silky vegetable world in the perfect landscape of heavenly bliss, one utterly without the thorns and thistles people knew all too well to expect in their earthly circumstances.

---

[72] D. Giunta, "I mosaici dell'arco absidale della basilica dei SS Nereo ed Achilleo e l'eresia Adozionista del secolo VIII," in *Roma e l'età carolingia* (Rome, 1976), 195–7. See also H. Belting, "Die Einhardsbogen," *Zeitschrift für Kunstgeschichte* 36 (1973), 100–4.

[73] Delogu, "The Popes," 112, 115 stresses Leo's personal devotion to Mary.

[74] Thunø, *The Apse Mosaic*, figs. 50, 62.

6   The Uses of Weeds

Sometimes, weeds became good. In the biography of the holy man Gall, much elaborated in Carolingian times, the Dark Age Irish ascetic is said to have chosen a site for his spiritual striving with the help of some notorious weeds. One evening, when his companions were preparing a fish they had caught in a short tributary of Lake Constance, Gall moved away in order to pray. But whereas the earliest version of the *Vita* and a later one by Ekkehard IV (+1056 c.) emphasize the holy clumsiness of Gall by reporting that he sprinted too quickly, and so stumbled and fell into the brambles, Walafrid Strabo instead claimed Gall had moved at a dignified pace "into the thick growth of brambles," inevitably becoming entangled and only then losing his balance.[1] In this way Walafrid drew a parallel between Gall and Carolingian Francia's most famous ascetic and monk, namely St. Benedict of Nursia. For the biography of Benedict included in Gregory the Great's *Dialogues* mentioned Benedict's body-mortifying use of a bramble patch next to his favorite cave at Subiaco, in which he carried out prayers and activities, much impressing the local shepherds by his indifference to human conventions.[2]

In all these accounts, bushes of brambles, those classic bad plants of early medieval imaginary, participated actively in the spiritual life of holy men, and contributed to fixing in place the ephemeral bodily presence of the divinely inspired. According to Walafrid, once he had picked himself up and dusted himself off, Gall decided to build a chapel where the brambles had detained him. Later hagiographers like Ekkehard reveled in identifying the very place and its authenticating vegetation.[3]

---

[1] Wettinus, "Vita Galli," ed. B. Krusch, *MGHSRM* 4 (Hanover, 1902), 263; Walafrid Strabo, "Vita Galli" 1.11, in ibid., 292–3; Ekkehard IV, "Casus S. Galli," ed. G. Pertz, *MGH Scriptores* 2 (Hanover, 1829), 135, where a tree replaced the brambles to shade the chapel.

[2] Gregory the Great, *Gregorii Magni Dialogi* 2.1, ed. U. Moricca (Rome, 1924), 78 describes the shepherds' bemusement on discovering Benedict, clad in skins "inter frutecta."

[3] At Subiaco's Sacro Speco today, a rose bush marks the spot where the brambles grew.

Along with their prickliness, the most infamous Carolingian weed species shared some other botanical features that suited them to Christians' moralizing purposes. For instance, the literary popularity of "ramnus" depended on its potential, when properly observed, to signify something else. The growth cycle of buckthorn (and several other prickly weeds, in fact), with its increasing prickliness over time, rendered it metaphorically irresistible to Christian moralists. Branches and leaves that were tender in youth toughened in maturity, developing sharp and dangerous spines. Like thistles, "ramnus" was thus a perfect admonishment against sin, which grows into habit over time, and which the Carolingians knew at first appears harmless, even pleasant, but soon hardens into intractable nastiness.[4]

This meant that weeds' thorns were not pure evil, even beyond hagiographical heroics. First Ambrose, then Augustine more explicitly and with greater verbal virtuosity, had noted the useful assonance between the Latin words for pricking (related to the verb "pungere") and that salutary feeling of guilt called compunction.[5] Exactly like the biting back of remorse, compunction happened when the pious felt pricks to their conscience; it was a desirable feeling, and partly rehabilitated thorns. The late antique Church Fathers had played with the botanical backdrop to this Christian virtue and pointed out that the "very thick thorns" of the blackthorn are able to torment flesh, producing both pain and compunction. The seemingly "sterile" thorns, hardened into a veritable menace by the sun as the plant matured, therefore were a good thing, stimulating desirable sensations and behaviors in their victims and offering all excellent ecological material to ponder.[6]

Carolingian theologies of guilt were somewhat less botanically inclined. Only Hincmar of Reims, writing in 860, seems to have appreciated the rich possibilities for moral improvement that thorniness created: in his treatise about the *Divorce of King Lothar and Queen Theutberga*, Hincmar allowed that clergymen like himself should always have about themselves the sharp goad of compunction to stimulate good behavior.[7] Other Carolingian writings abound in references to compunction, and Carolingian rulers often claimed to be "pricked by divine love," but no

[4] Hrabanus Maurus, "De Universo" 19.6, ed. J. Migne, *PL* 111 (Paris, 1864), 521–2 gives a run-down of prickly plants ("rhamnus" is in second place); Walafrid Strabo, "Liber Psalmorum" 57.10, ed. J. Migne, *PL* 113 (Paris, 1879), 928.
[5] Ambrose, "Exameron" 3.11, in *Sancti Ambrosii Opera* 1, ed. C. Schenkl (Vienna, 1896), 91; Augustine, *Enarrationes in Psalmos* 57, ed. H. Müller (Vienna, 2004), 306–8.
[6] This idea was popular among Carolingian writers, e.g. Hrabanus, *De Universo* 19.6, 521.
[7] Hincmar of Reims, "De Divortio Lotharii Regis" resp. 14, ed. L. Böhringer, *MGH Concilia* 4.1 (Hanover, 1992), 191: "ut videlicet ad reprehendentes nosmetipsos semper accincti acutum circa nos stimulum compunctionis habeamus."

one seems to have admired Augustine's spiny pun, grounded as it was in botanical facts, though everyone appreciated the potential for goodness that all creation, even a thorny bush, might have.[8] Thus, when meditating on "real remorse" a sophisticated theologian like Hrabanus Maurus altogether overlooked compunction and what stimulated it.[9] Given the importance in ninth-century Frankish politics of the theme of repentance this was a real missed opportunity.[10] It suggests that Carolingian thinkers were slightly less ecumenical in their contemplation of bad plants than had been the earlier Mediterranean Fathers.

Regardless, Carolingian-era weeds were on occasion liable to rehabilitation, and if the surviving literature overwhelmingly locates examples of such upward phytosocial mobility in the sphere of the miraculous, a reflection of the charisma of holy people, it also surfaces in theology and exegesis. Ultimately it derived from the fundamental early medieval conviction that all plants had originally been created good, and might in the right circumstances show their quintessence again. Especially exceptional, gifted humans could be expected to reveal or unlock the vegetational potential that remained obscure to ordinary mortals.

This chapter explores some of the circumstances when bad plants turned out to be not so bad after all. It shows that the very same weeds that were routinely condemned for their antisocial behavior, or their scriptural associations, were sometimes very valuable to Carolingian people. At the very least, the worst weeds could, in the right hands, prove themselves excellent enhancements to meritorious asceticism, cures for various ailments, or sources of income.

Stinging Nettles

In the early Middle Ages stinging nettles, in Latin "urticae," were the homey weed "everyone knows," as they were labeled in the enduringly popular late ancient herbal, or list of medical remedies derived from vegetable (and some other) sources, called *The Alphabet of Galen*.[11] In the late seventh century, stinging nettles, though of course they were not named outright, were famous enough to enter Aldhelm's list of one hundred riddles, the only small plant to be so honored.[12] And in fact

---

[8] Louis the German, his son Carloman, and his son Arnulf issued legislation that presented them as "divino amore compuncti."

[9] Hrabanus Maurus, "Paenitentiale ad Heribaldum" 10, ed. J. Migne, *PL* 110 (Paris, 1864), 475.

[10] See M. de Jong, *The Penitential State* (Cambridge, 2009).

[11] "Urtica est omnibus nota": N. Everett, *The Alphabet of Galen* (Toronto, 2012), 368.

[12] Aldhelm, "De Metribus et Enigmatibus ac Pedum Regulis" 46, ed. R. Ehwald, *MGH Auctores Antiquissimi* 15 (Berlin, 1919), 117: "Torqueo torquentes, sed nullum torqueo

various kinds of *Urtica* are well adapted to Mediterranean and continental climate conditions, and flourish profusely on "disturbed" soils, especially those where humans have left traces of their activity in the form of heightened nitrogen content.[13] Nettles were hence so familiar in Carolingian Europe that, in what is by far the most famous Carolingian text dealing with plants, getting rid of them was seen as any observant cultivator's first priority. For in Walafrid Strabo's poem "about the cultivation of gardens," the elimination of "urticae" is the first step a good gardener must take on the path to a verdant and pleasing garden. The attentive poet-gardener further reminded readers that some really excellent and helpful plants such as catmint, which he called "nepeta," had leaves that looked very much like those of noxious nettles, though they smelled different and should of course be treated differently.[14]

Yet even well-known nettles reserved some surprises, as Walafrid himself privately acknowledged.[15] The most unusual characteristic of *Urtica dioica*, and of several other species of the *Urtica* genus, is that their leaves and stems are covered with tiny hair-like trichomes, many of which are hollow and so brittle that the slightest touch breaks them in two, virtually turning them into injecting needles. Several chemicals may flow through the broken trichome; in the case of human skin touching them, it is especially the histamine that proves irritating and produces a stinging sensation as well as temporary inflammation.[16] That unpleasant characteristic was surely why "everyone knows" stinging nettles, as the *Alphabet of Galen* said.

Still, *Urtica* reserved surprises, and at the beginning of the first millennium Pliny the Elder had recognized this, after observing that nothing is

---

sponto / Laedere nec quemquam volo, ni prius ipse reatum / Contrahat et viridem studeat decerpere caulem. / Fervida mox hominis turgescunt membra nocentis: / Vindico sic noxam stimulisque ulciscor acutis." Though based on an earlier riddle about onions, Aldhelm's was an original composition (A. Juster, *Saint Aldhelm's Riddles* (Toronto, 2015), 114). Apple, fig, and palm tree round out the vegetable part of the riddle list.

[13] L. Holm et al., *World Weeds: Natural Histories and Distribution* (New York, 1997), 889–94.

[14] Walafrid Strabo, "Liber de Cultura Hortorum" 2, ed. E. Duemmler, *MGH Poetae* 2 (Berlin, 1884), 336, and (on catmint) 24, 348. See F. Guizard-Duchamp, *Les terres du sauvage dans le monde franc (IVe–IX siècle)* (Rennes, 2009), 57 on how Hrabanus, *De Universo* 19.6, 521–2, has nettles stand for vice, suggesting Strabo's weeding (and distinguishing good from bad plants) may be symbolic.

[15] Walafrid's notebook (Stiftsbibliothek Cod. Sang. 878) mentioned nettles' pharmacological virtue: N. Everett, "The Manuscript Evidence for Pharmacy in the Early Middle Ages," in *Writing the Early Middle Ages*, ed. E. Screen and C. West (Cambridge, 2018), 125.

[16] H. Yi-Fu et al., "Identification of Oxalic Acid and Tartaric Acid as Major Persistent Pain-Inducing Toxins in the Stinging Hairs of the Nettle *Urtica thumbergiana*," *Annals of Botany* 98 (2006), 57–66.

less pleasant than nettles, by cataloguing some of the qualities to be found in such plants: nettles were good tenderizers for tough foods, had prophylactic powers against illness, and when young made tasty food.[17] Yet in the early Middle Ages it was other features of *Urtica* that people prized. For by external application stinging nettles could help ascetics master sexual desire. Carolingian Europe's model monk, St. Benedict, had experimented with this chemistry. According to Gregory the Great, one day Benedict was sorely tempted to abandon his ascetic ways by the memory of a woman he had once seen. As her form returned to his mind's eye, he was turned on, and the "flame of love" burned in his heart. Mercifully divine grace intervened and Benedict regained control of himself enough to notice bushes of stinging nettles and brambles nearby; having removed his clothes, he rolled naked "in those sharp thorns and burning nettles" for a long time. When he emerged, his skin was covered with wounds, but these healed the graver wound that the memory had opened in his steely determination.[18]

Gregory's account of Benedict's urtication, as the willing application of stinging nettles to one's body is known, was grounded in a refined understanding of late Roman medical theory, wherein certain plants by their nature had certain qualities, suited to re-establishing balance among the body's humors when these got out of whack. It was also grounded in the established medical idea that one could cure like with like, and diseases caused by an excess of heat were remedied by administering substances that by their nature were fiery. Benedict's lapse into sexual temptation was a humoral imbalance, an excess of bodily heat typical of youthful males.[19] The best medicine was the fiery weed *Urtica*.

Early medieval readers took note of Benedict's urtication. Although the cult of Benedict, and the popularity of the *Dialogues*, flourished mightily in Carolingian Europe, the best evidence for spiritual use of the weed nettles comes from other phases of the postclassical period. Around 940

---

[17] Pliny, *Naturalis Historia* 25.15, ed. C. Mayhoff (Stuttgart, 1967), 411 (22.13, 449: "urtica quid esse invisius potest?"). Modern scientists agree that nettles are good to eat, and have diuretic as well as antirheumatic properties: Holm, *World Weeds*, 893.

[18] Gregory, *Dialogi* 2.2, 78–9: "quandam namque aliquando feminam viderat, quam malignus spiritus ante eius mentis oculos reduxit; tantoque igne servi Dei animum in specie illius accendit, ut in eius pectore amoris flamma vix caperit, et iam paene deserere heremum voluptate victus deliberaret. Cum subito superna gratia respectus, ad semetipsum reversus est, adque orticarum et vebrium iuxta densa subcrescere frutecta conspiciens, exutus indumento, nudum se in illis spinarum aculeis et orticarum incendiis proiecit: ibique diu volutatus, toto ex eis corpore vulneratus exiit, et per cutis vulnera eduxit a corpore vulnus mentis, quia voluptatis traxit in dolorem."

[19] Ibid. 2.2, 79: "quod in iuventute carnis temptatio ferveat; ab anno quinquagesimo calor corporis frigescat." Gregory the Great, *Moralia in Job* 18.20, ed. M. Adriaen (Turnhout, 1979–85), 907: "urtica vero igneae omnino naturae est."

Flodoard of Reims invoked the episode of Benedict's self-administered cure for sexual ardor. Flodoard claimed that the young Umbrian ascetic had extinguished "venereal fire" by romping through stinging nettles.[20] As Flodoard's story modifies Gregory's version and omits its thorns, his interpretation is particularly meaningful. Flodoard expected his readers to understand the chemistry and the symbolism of rolling unclothed in stinging nettles, and to know the qualities of this plant, though it is almost absent from the scriptures and required the reinforcement of thorns for real efficacy in the *Dialogues*. Thus, Flodoard's retelling of the episode reflects a growing estimation, in ascetical circles, of the controlled and premeditated use of the unique botanical qualities of *Urtica*. By the tenth century the sympathetic medicine of "fiery" nettles curing the burn of lust made perfect sense.

In early medieval Europe urtication was best established among the masters of penitential piety in Ireland. The *Table of Commutations* is an eighth-century Old Irish text that calculated "arrea," or substitute penalties for those who sought to shorten the period of discipline, generally a fast.[21] Both female and male repentants who were unable to fast could compensate for their abbreviation of foodless periods by spending the night (separately) on a bed of nettles. This practice, like sleeping on nuts, in water, or with a cadaver, was thought to mortify the flesh and ensure people would stay awake, praying through the night. Vigils in uncomfortable positions, including recumbent on a pile of stinging nettles, were as good as the longer but blander "agonies of expiation" that fasting procured. They too were a form of urtication.

Early medieval Ireland seems to have been a major center for the religious use of nettles. The Irish St. Kevin (+618), founder of the monastery of Glendalough, was thought to have escaped the sexual advances of a local woman by dashing to a thick bed of nettles he knew of and, after rolling himself utterly naked in the vegetation, beating her with a bundle of the same plant. Understandably enough this experience changed the mind of the would-be seductress: she renounced her amorous pursuits and herself became a nun.[22] Though some of the details this narrative includes seem to be late medieval, it sheds light on the widespread acceptance of the notion that even a well-known weed with nasty

---

[20] Flodoard of Reims, "De Triumphis Christi" 13.8, ed. J. Migne, *PL* 135 (Paris, 1879), 838: "igne urticarum Veneris depellitur ignis." Gregory credited both the "sharp thorns" and the "burning nettles" for curing Benedict's "voluptas." But as his body emerged covered in "wounds" from the thicket, Gregory assigned to thorn punctures a greater role (*Urtica* seldom does more than irritate skin for a few hours).

[21] J. McNeill and H. Gamer, *Medieval Handbooks of Penance* (New York, 1990), 142, 144.

[22] "Vita Sancti Coemgeni" 4, ed. C. Plummer, *Vitae Sanctorum Hiberniae* 1 (Oxford, 1910), 235–6: "et cum illa esset lacerata urtica, extincta est voluptas amoris sui."

characteristics had physical and spiritual utility, in particular for extinguishing desire. Whether voluntary (as in the case of the saint) or involuntary (the seductress), urtication worked. Rubbed on one's skin, stinging nettles were an excellent antidote to the enduring human problem of uncontrolled sexuality.[23]

Though such "urtication" as prevailed among early medieval Irish ascetics may not have been as common in Europe as the nettles themselves were (and are), the association of wild plants and sex was well known to Carolingian writers. Hincmar of Reims' scathing reference to "various herbs" that people administered with incantations to restore conjugal relations is an example.[24] And an uplifting mortification similar to urtication could be obtained from "thorns and thistles" in the Carolingian provinces. Charlemagne, who disliked the fancy attire of Carolingian aristocrats in northern Italy, invited them on a hunt where the prickly plants reduced the inappropriate clothes of the too-elegant hunters to tatters. Suitably humbled by the plants, the aristocrats understood the wisdom of Charlemagne's homespun dress code: the emperor alone had returned home warm and unaffected by the brambles and prickly bushes he had traversed in pursuit of the quarry.[25] His sheepskin outfit was down to earth and practical, but especially impermeable to thorns. Charlemagne's superior moral stature received botanical confirmation in Notker's story, with the prickly plants leaving no marks on the king-emperor's body or clothes; the foppish aristocrats, instead, proved their vanity by dressing inappropriately. They ended up miserable and humiliated because of their preceding moral condition. It required botanical correction. Weedy, wild, and apparently useless plants came to their aid and set them on the path of repentance.

Stinging nettles and other prickly plants were definitely weeds in early medieval Europe. However, they had qualities that experts, whether wise rulers or divinely inspired men, perceived and could use to excellent effect. Their weediness could occasionally be suspended. When it was, usually irritating vegetation became cooperative, beneficial, and useful to people, especially in the spiritual and moral realms.

Medical Weeds

The early ninth-century Plan of St. Gall, drawn at Reichenau in the 820s for abbot Gorbert of St. Gall and now preserved in that Swiss monastery,

---

[23] Thus, Aldhelm's riddle (note 12 above) may be part of his ongoing polemic against Irish religious practices.

[24] Hincmar, "De Divortio Lotharii Regis" resp. 15, 206.

[25] Notker, *Gesta Karoli Magni* 2.17, ed. H. Haefele, *MGH Scriptores Rerum Germanicarum* n. s. 12 (Berlin, 1959), 86–7.

depicts an ideal abbey in which human and vegetable spaces commingle. Aside from the monks' final place of rest, shaded by fruit trees of various species, the Plan also included two gardens, beyond the two cloisters where vegetation likely found a place too, and an orchard. Next to the gardener's quarters lay a plot for seedlings ("seminaria olerum"), quite rationally close to the vegetable garden that is labeled "hortus" on the Plan. This garden was distinct from the smaller herb garden ("herbularis"), which specialized in medicinal plants. The latter was situated next to the infirmary and was subject to a different administration from the vegetable garden: the residence of St. Gall's doctors, including that of the chief physician, loomed over it.[26]

The interpenetration of built-up and open spaces in the Plan depended on the presence of different kinds of garden, with different purposes. If we follow the labels inserted on the small square that represents it, in the vegetable garden monks grew onions, garlic, leeks, shallots, celery, parsley, coriander, chervil, dill, lettuce, poppy, summer savory, radishes, parsnips, something called "magones," cabbages, chards, and "gitto" (likely black caraway). Fifteen different plants grew instead in the medical herb garden, with only a sixteenth ("sataregia" or summer savory) in common.[27] Thus, the Plan's designer envisioned stark botanical separation between gardens set a few dozen meters apart. Consequently, to the monks who toiled in the herbal garden growing plants of which the medical properties were prized, the appearance in their soil beds of plants their colleagues tended in the vegetable gardens would have been inappropriate, and chards there would have seemed invasive weeds. Similarly, a volunteer stalk of mint that sprouted in the vegetable garden would have been ruthlessly rooted out as a weed. Within one monastic community – in other words, in the very same place – the human purposes for plants could differ so much that utterly disparate evaluations of which plants were bad, to be extirpated, and which good, to be fostered, coexisted.

Quite aside from the purposes for growing plants in circumscribed, specialized plots, some vegetation that people generally disparaged and disliked wherever it grew might seem precious in medical contexts. We have already seen that some of the worst weeds known to Carolingian people could, if properly manipulated, produce morally uplifting outcomes, so it makes sense that Carolingian pharmacology also sought virtue in several weedy plants. Isidore of Seville, who seems to have been the first Latin writer to use the term "dinamidia" for the active

[26] W. Horn and E. Born, *The Plan of St. Gall* 2 (Berkeley, 1979), 181–4, 203–9. The fine UCLA website www.stgallplan.org/index.html also offers access to the Plan.
[27] M. Goullet, "L'imaginaire du jardin monastique," *Pris-Ma* 26 (2010), 49 traces this list back to the "De Villis" capitulary.

principles to be found in medical herbs, found it entirely natural that plants should have such potency.[28] It was up to people to figure out what the "dinamis" of a plant was, and to apply it intelligently to cure disease. Though Alcuin sometimes despaired of ever reaching the bottom of that immense task, his mention of the possibility shows that Carolingian thinkers tried, because they expected *all* plants to contain a useful, curative power.[29]

This was in any case a venerable medical tradition. Ancient "herbals" advertised the benefits to humans of the regulated consumption of some weeds. The leaves of stinging nettles, for instance, which Pliny thought effective against sixty-one maladies, were known to Dioscurides to stymie bleeding and in a decoction to soothe sore throats; the seeds instead were efficacious against gangrene, pleurisy, and infertility.[30] Several copies of his *De Materia Medica* in Latin translation survive from Carolingian times.[31] Quintus Serenus, a Roman medical writer well known to Carolingian readers and used by the compiler of a medicine book for Charlemagne, more modestly suggested that the boiled seeds of *Urtica* alleviated the chills, and Carolingian handbooks transmitted some of this wisdom.[32] For instance, the early ninth-century *Liber Glossarum* reported that "there are two kinds of nettles, male and female. The male one if touched burns you, the female one does not," a piece of information that may reflect empirical investigation (some *Urtica* species do not sting) but also replicates and interprets an early medieval medical text which was less certain about the uselessness of female *Urtica* and far more detailed about the physiological benefits to be derived from nettles. For the Carolingian glossators also dolefully noted that "chopped up with salt, nettles do not

---

[28] Isidore of Seville, *Etymologiae* 4.10.3, ed. W. Lindsay (Oxford, 1911), with Everett, "The Manuscript Evidence," 122–4. Later writers used the term more broadly, not just of plants.

[29] Alcuin, "Epistolae" 155, ed. E. Dümmler, *MGH Epistolae* 4 (Berlin, 1895), 250. In epistle 213 (356–7) Alcuin defines doctors as those who identify, collect, and mix herbs that cure people. See P. Dendle, "Plants in the Early Medieval Cosmos," in *Health and Healing from the Medieval Garden*, ed. P. Dendle and A. Touwaide (Woodbridge, 2008), 49–50.

[30] Pedanius Dioscorides of Anazarbus, *De Materia Medica* 4.93, tr. L. Beck (Hildesheim, 2011), 290. Pliny, *Naturalis Historia* 22.13, 449–51 lists more remedies from *urtica* than from any other plant, while considering it the worst weed of all.

[31] K. Butzer, "The Classical Tradition of Agronomic Science," in *Science in Western and Eastern Civilization in Carolingian Times*, ed. P. Butzer and D. Lohrmann (Basel, 1993), 575–9 synthesizes well. See also J. Riddle, "Theory and Practice in Medieval Medicine," *Viator* 5 (1974), 163; M. Niederer, *Der St. Galler "Botanicus": Ein frühmittlelaterliches Herbar* (Bern, 2005), 10–11.

[32] Serenus, *Liber Medicinalis* 9, ed. R. Pépin (Paris, 1950), 12, with xxiii–xxiv on the Carolingian fortunes of this text. On the status of medicine in Carolingian culture, see M. Leja, "The Sacred Art," *Viator* 47 (2016), 1–34.

help against dog bites," correcting thereby both their predecessors and the assumption that such a plant must have medical efficacy.[33]

Even those formidable spiny plants "carduus" and "tribulus," protagonists in Chapter 4 above, when used appropriately, mitigated fevers, bad breath, kidney stones, and viper bites.[34] To the authors of the *Liber Glossarum* "cardus" was a formidable cure for dandruff.[35] But if plucked at dawn under the right astral influences, a leaf of "carduus silvaticus" carried on one's person kept *all* ills at bay, according to the herbal of Pseudo-Apuleius, another text with a wide ninth-century dissemination, and one Walafrid Strabo consulted when composing his poem on gardening.[36] Indeed, an updated and adapted copy was made in ninth-century Lombardy and soon shelved in the monastic library at St. Gall (it is still there as St. Gall. Stiftsbibliothek, 217); in its pages pious readers might also learn that crabgrass, if cooked in water and placed on the spleen, relieves pain in that organ, and as a potion in wine "does wonders."[37]

The medical reputation of spiny "cardus" might explain the appearance of "cardones" in "Capitulare de Villis," that great statement of Charlemagne's best botanical intentions.[38] They are certainly a cultivated garden crop, not the same as the other "cardones" in that capitulary, which are wool carding combs. This appears to be the earliest medieval European mention of cardoons as a crop. They are proof that a plant with a negative image in the scriptures and in Christian literature could enjoy upward phytosocial mobility in the cultivations of the Carolingian era, and indeed on some of the model farms of that time. The likeliest cause of this good fortune is the domestication of the wild thistle, its agronomical

---

[33] *Liber Glossarum Digital*, ed. A. Grondeaux and F. Cinato (Paris, 2016), http://liber-glos sarum.huma-num.fr: "Vrticae genera sunt duo, masculis et femina; masculis si tangatur ustulat, femina non. Vrtica cum sale triti morsu canis non succurrit" (in liber-glossarum.huma.num.fr). The *Dynamidia* 2.93, ed. A. Mai, *Classicorum Auctorum e Vaticanis Codicibus Editorum* 7 (Rome, 1835), 450 says: "Cindii, hoc est urticae, genera sunt duo. Masculus ustulat; femina cum sale trita morsui canino, ulceribus nigris, cancromatibus, furunculis, parotidibus succurrit" and goes on to advise on the salutary effects of nettle seed too. It is based on Dioscurides: see Pedanius Dioscorides, *De Materia Medica* 4.93, 290.

[34] "Carduus" and "tribulus": H. Kästner, "Pseudo-Dioscurides *De Herbis Femininis*," *Hermes* 3 (1896), 607 with Riddle, "Theory and Practice," 163 on the medieval dissemination of this adaptation of Dioscurides.

[35] See liber-glossarum.huma-num.fr.

[36] "Pseudoapulei Herbarius" 110, ed. E. Howald and H. Sigerist, *Corpus Medicorum Latinorum* 4 (Leipzig, 1927), 195, with H. Sigerist, "Zum Herbarius Pseudo-Apulei," *Sudhoffs Archiv für Geschichte der Medizin* 23 (1930), 197–209 and G. Maggiulli and M. Buffa Giolito, *L'altro Apuleio* (Naples, 1996), 36, 85 on this text's medieval reception. See also Pliny, *Naturalis Historia* 20.23, 379.

[37] Niederer, *Der St. Galler "Botanicus"*, 32, and 118, on "erba gramen" which "mire facit."

[38] "Capitulare de Villis" 70, ed. A. Boretius, *MGH Capitularia Regum Francorum* 1 (Hanover, 1883), 90.

improvement for human purposes, and the emergence of the edible cardoon in post-biblical times, in either the Roman empire or the early caliphate, and its adaptation to northern European conditions thereafter. The rehabilitation of this spiny bad plant in Carolingian culture seems linked to its medical utility.[39]

The medical recalibration of how to interpret these weeds might surprise readers of Carolingian exegesis, accustomed to that genre's dour evaluations of prickly and deceitful plants that grew despite people's best efforts. But the more optimistic view of weeds reflected the classicizing tendencies of Carolingian culture, for Pliny's *Natural History*, much consulted in Frankish libraries, noted that all plants existed either for human health or for human pleasure, so none were useless.[40] Indeed, Pliny thought no plant grows without a (human) purpose. Although they also recognized that sometimes plant ecology had less human-centered objectives, Carolingian literati replicated this anthropocentric conception of botany, which dovetailed nicely with their own ideas of how God had arranged the world. Indeed, they even applied it to bad plants with low scriptural status.[41] A good example is darnel, a weed with a redoubtable reputation in Christian literature (see Chapter 4). Numerous medical manuals on Carolingian bookshelves identified darnel, or "zizania," or "lolium," as a fine cure for festering sores, and allowed that its consumption alleviated pain of the sciatic nerve and facilitated conception.[42]

In evaluating bad plants positively, as healthful for humans, Carolingian writers had more to go on than classical opinion. Late ancient patristic thinking also offered an important precedent and ideas to follow.[43] Ambrose of Milan, for example, had opined that people were too quick to judge plants negatively, and observed that even vegetation everyone deemed toxic, like hellebore (*Helleborus viridis*), was excellent medicine if administered properly.[44] Thus, in the last years of the eighth

[39] G. Sonnante et al., "The Domestication of Artichoke and Cardoon," *Annals of Botany* 100 (2007), 1095–1100; A. Gatto et al., "Population Structure of *Cynara cardunculus* Complex and the Origin of the Conspecific Crops Artichoke and Cardoon," *Annals of Botany* 112 (2013), 855–65. Carding combs: "Capitulare de Villis" 43, p. 87. Pliny (*Naturalis Historia* 19.8, 290) considered cultivated "carduos" absurd, a monstrosity since even quadrupeds shunned them.

[40] A. Borst, *Das Buch der Naturgeschichte: Plinius und seine Leser im Zeitalter des Pergaments* (Heidelberg, 1994), 9–12.

[41] Pliny: *Naturalis Historia* 18.1, 141; 22.1, 440. Borst, *Das Buch der Naturgeschichte*, 121–93 traces an aspect of Pliny's Carolingian reception. For Leja, "The Sacred Art," 3–4, Carolingian "correctio" motivated the dissemination of medical texts.

[42] For instance, Pedanius Dioscorides, *De Materia Medica* 2.100, 134.

[43] H. Birkhan, *Pflanzen im Mittelalter* (Vienna, 2012), ch. 3.

[44] Ambrose, "Exameron" 3.9, 84–6. Ambrose followed Basil of Caesarea, *Homélies sur l'Hexaéméron* 5.4, ed. S. Giet (Paris, 1949), 294.

century, at the beginning of the Carolingian exegetical trajectory, when the herculean effort to compile and transcribe the patristic corpus was being launched, Wigbod already knew that apparently useless plants often produced cures, or helped people in other ways. A couple of decades later, Claudius of Turin recognized that even poisonous plants contain health-giving substances, and the late Carolingian monk Remigius of Auxerre proposed that no plant is truly fruitless, since all have some use. At Luxeuil, his contemporary, Angelomus, likewise postulated all plants have hidden value, often medicinal.[45]

In other words, a potent inducement in Carolingian culture for some hesitation before consigning weeds to the category of evil and uselessness was their innate medical potential. Monasteries like St. Gall, even if they never built themselves separate gardens full of medicinal herbs, were sites where men pondered the utility of plants in human health, and in the process re-evaluated the weedy destiny of plants like nettles, or darnel, or hellebore. Thinking clinically, Carolingian writers abandoned the ordinary taxonomies of vegetation. In consequence, theirs was an inclusive botany.

The Weed Economy

Even in the most intensively cultivated areas, weeding was actually not always worth the trouble. In certain cases, when the weeds were ineffective competitors of the crops, because they germinated late, or could not keep up with the crops' growth cycle, or would not interfere with harvesting operations, weeding could safely be neglected. Then the benefit was double: not only did one labor less, but one also gained an asset. For after humans had removed their crop from the ground, the surviving weeds might feed people's domesticated animals, and then be plowed in to become an ingredient in the topsoil that nurtured next year's crops. Anthropologists have recorded just this kind of careful calculus of labor-cost-to-weeded-field-benefit in small farms in central Mexico.[46] There, it

---

[45] Wigbod, "Quaestiones in Octoteuchum," ed. J. Migne, *PL* 96 (Paris, 1862), 1126. Claudius of Turin, "Commentarii in Genesim" 1.1.10, ed. J. Migne, *PL* 50 (Paris, 1846), 898. Remigius, *Expositio super Genesim* 3.17, ed. B. Van Name Edwards (Turnhout, 1999), 63. Angelomus, "Commentarius in Genesin" 1.11–13, ed. J. Migne, *PL* 115 (Paris, 1881), 120.

[46] In the Toluca valley east of Mexico City, farmers accept seventy-four species of weed in their maize fields as fodder or "green manure" or erosion limitation, and only labor availability limits weed use: L. Vieyra-Odilon and H. Vibrans, "Weeds as Crops: The Value of Maize Field Weeds in the Valley of Toluca, Mexico," *Economic Botany* 55 (2001), 426–43 (for some European parallels, see R. Mabey, *Weeds* (London, 2012), 130–1; G. Comet, *Le paysan et son outil* (Rome, 1992), 170).

seems, peasants leave certain species of infesting plants in their maize fields because the work needed to extirpate them is not justified by the damage the weeds do. The tolerated species are those that germinate well after the crop, so do not compete with it during the vital phase of early growth, and do not much obstruct harvesters' movements. Once harvests are in, these weeds can be fed to cattle, plowed into the soil, or left standing to help limit topsoil erosion with their roots.

Resources came from less manicured territories, as well. In many traditional societies, gathering wild foods is an accepted, even expected practice, and most of what gets gathered is vegetable.[47] In the rich countries of Europe, during the hard times of the mid-1900s, people routinely turned to gathering plants they normally avoided, like nettles and chicory, which became food and fiber.[48] Even in advanced economies, in the twenty-first century, foraging food from uncultivated lands persists, either as a means of fighting back against capitalist commercialism, in pursuit of better health, or as a pastime. In an agrarian economy like the Carolingian one, with almost everyone living in rural sites, for most people access to the hedgerows, woodlands, and wastelands where plants grew spontaneously was easy. Though Roman writers, too, were sensitive to the bounty that uncultivated areas (*saltus*) offered humans, the great innovation of the early medieval economic system was the fuller, deeper integration of uncultivated, or less cultivated, with more humanized and agricultural spaces.[49] Thus, early medieval legislators could acknowledge that some prickly brambles ("rubus"), which otherwise figured on lists of abhorrent plants that grew spontaneously, were fruitful and sometimes became an economic asset worthy of legal protection.[50] Early medieval reliance on the vegetable bounty of untended nature had religious sanction, too: St. Ambrose had approved of it as the most appropriate (vegetarian) way for people to feed themselves.[51] Hence the settlement and economic patterns, as well as the cultural orientation prevalent in Carolingian Europe, induced people to consider, know, and use wild plants on a regular basis.

---

[47] M. Leonti et al., "Wild Gathered Food Plants in the European Mediterranean," *Economic Botany* 60 (2006), 130–42.

[48] C. Griffin-Kremer, "Humble Plants," in *Plants and People: Choices and Diversity through Time*, ed. A. Chevalier et al. (Oxford, 2014), 273; E. Salisbury, *Weeds and Aliens* (London, 1961), 270–1.

[49] This was the fundamental insight of Italian early medievalists, like M. Montanari, *L'alimentazione contadina nell'alto medioevo* (Naples, 1979). See J. Devroey, *Économie rurale et société dans l'Europe franque (VIe–IXe siècles)* (Paris, 2003), 26–7, 81–2.

[50] *Lex Baiwariorum* 22.2, ed. E. von Schwind, *MGH Legum Sectio I*, 5.2 (Hanover, 1926), 469.

[51] Ambrose, "Exameron," 3.8, 84.

Most wild plants were considered weeds when they grew in farmers' fields. As Helmut Birkham wisely observed, in the wilderness really there are no weeds, because the concept of weediness requires agriculture.[52] But a large number of the plants people gathered in uncultivated spaces, mostly as food for themselves or their domesticated animals, were the very same species that they would attempt to root out if they grew elsewhere. A good instance is the by now familiar stinging nettle, which was (and is) an alternative food, most popular in times of scarcity: since it is an early spring grower, and since its leaves are tender and sweetest tasting (and full of calcium, potassium, and vitamin A) at the beginning of its growth cycle, which happens to coincide with the season when people's harvested stores might run thin and new crops had not yet matured, eating *Urtica* was not uncommon. A story about St. Columba bears this out: encountering an old woman who gathered nettles, and learning from her that she was eating them daily in a broth while she waited for her cow to give birth (at which point presumably her diet would vary), the hyper-aristocratic Irish holy man decided to imitate her humility. But stinging nettles carried some social (and gender?) stigma, and his cook was horrified, enough that he secretly added butter to the nettle soup on which Columba lived for years, until the holy man discovered the culinary trick.[53] Nettles, the famine food of the poor, could become the prestigious food of ascetic abasement precisely because of their marginal status. Regardless, the weed became an asset and, in special circumstances, entered early medieval economic systems.

During Lent Charlemagne himself hoped his estates would supply him with "little dried herbs or green ones," quite likely some of the wild plants that on other occasions were just weeds. Less austere than an Irish saint, the Frankish ruler assumed these should be supplied with various forms of animal-based fat, like cheese and butter. In the earliest spring, when the Lenten season tended to fall, one contented oneself with eating plants that at other times of the year one perhaps abhorred.[54]

But well beyond the meager season before Easter, weeds continued to be of service in the Carolingian economy. For, once dried, nettles lose their pungency and make an excellent, nutritious fodder for domestic animals. And it is as feed for sheep, goats, and cows that Carolingian weeds did their greatest service to people and, from a human point of view, redeemed

---

[52] Birkhan, *Pflanzen*, 49–50.

[53] The eleventh-century narrative is in *Félire Óengusso Céli Dé*, ed. W. Stokes (London, 1905), 146–7. How the cook procured nettles (an annual, frost-sensitive plant) over twelve months is not specified, but dried nettles lose their sting and are good fodder: Salisbury, *Weeds*, 271. See also F. Kelly, *Early Irish Farming* (Dublin, 2000), 354.

[54] Charlemagne punctiliously exacted "herbulas siccas vel virides" from his dependents: "Capitulare de Villis" 44, p. 87.

themselves. Much more than as human food, weeds mattered to the Carolingian economy as feed for domestic animals; indeed, they were essential to that delicate balance between cereal farming and animal husbandry that, we are told, made northwestern Europe different and set it on a historical "special path" distinct from Byzantium's, the caliphate's, and Song China's.[55] In effect weeds' photosynthetic prowess made available to people, through the mediation of the herbivores that ate them, solar energy that was otherwise unattainable, or had assumed a form people found unpalatable.

Pasture land was (and still is) quite difficult to tell apart from weed patch or wasteland, not least because the intestinal tracts and fur of animals that graze on both are vectors for plant seeds and burrs; the animals' movement reduces the botanical differences between the two forms of land use designated by people.[56] In part for this reason, the prominent Soviet botanist Nikolai Vavilov invented the category of "secondary domesticate" to describe those plants that were variably weedy, depending on whether they grew in farmed fields or in areas set aside for other types of use.[57] For often enough waste and pasture lands are botanically the same thing, with the very plants that people disapprove of in their gardens or crop fields allowed to flourish in pastures and grazing fields, or among the stubble after the harvest. But economically a plot of land where domestic animals can ruminate is anything but a waste. This changes the status of its botanical community. It is, as noted above (Chapter 3), a matter of timing, of when a plant grows where it grows.

In the pastures in and around Carolingian-era villages where sizeable numbers of sheep and cattle found their sustenance, in the fallow fields that continued to be the principal means of soil fertility maintenance even as three-field rotations became somewhat more prevalent during the 800s, and in the meadows that farmers mowed in summer so as to store for winter hay that would keep their animals alive, communities of plants grew with minimal human interference.[58] Areas set aside for grazing

[55] M. Mitterauer, *Why Europe? The Medieval Origins of Its Special Path* (Chicago, 2010), 5–6, 15–6, 21. T. Kjaergaard, "A Plant that Changed the World," *Landscape Research* 28 (2003), 45–6 made the same point, without using the loaded word *Sonderweg*.
[56] M. Ruas, "Prés, prairies, pâtures: éclairages archéobotaniques," in *Prés et pâtures en Europe occidentale*, ed. F. Brumont (Toulouse, 2008), 16–21 carefully distinguishes types of grazing land. See also Corbin, *La fraîcheur de l'herbe*, 65, 136. Grazers as vectors: S. Karg, "Plant Diversity in the Late Medieval Cornfields of Northern Switzerland," *Vegetation History and Archaeobotany* 4 (1995), 49; R. Probst, *Wolladventivflora Mitteleuropas* (Solothurn, 1949); R. Zimdahl, *Fundamentals of Weed Science* (Amsterdam, 2013), 89–90.
[57] D. Rindos, *The Origins of Agriculture* (Orlando, FL, 1984), 123–5.
[58] On the spread of three-field rotation, see Y. Morimoto, "L'assolement triennial au haut Moyen Âge," in *Économie rurale et économie urbaine au Moyen Âge*, ed. J. Devroey and

expanded from about AD 750 on large estates around Orléans in the Loire valley, judging from the palynological evidence.[59] At Villiers-le-Sec in the Île-de-France, pollen remains also suggest that circa 800, alongside the usual grain fields, there were pastures where fescue (*Festuca pratensis*), meadow grass (*Poa annua*), chicory, dandelion, nettles, silverweed (*Potentilla anserina*), cockspur grass (*Echinochloa crus-galli*), and knotweed (*Polygonum* genus) all flourished.[60] A large array of ruderal weeds characterized the pollens of contemporary rural settlements in the Indre valley south of Tours, in the Eifel hills south of Aachen, in the Burgundian Morvan, and the plain north of Rennes, too.[61] At Sermersheim on the Rhine, seeds in the fill at the bottom of a well represent a similar variety of weeds, with a preponderance of nettles, knotgrass (*Polygonum aviculare*), and sandwort (*Arenaria serpyfolia*) datable to the eighth to tenth century.[62] And given the preponderance of cultivated grains in the archaeological record at Huy, in the Meuse valley, near Liège, the conspicuous presence of seeds and other carbonized remains of uncultivated grassland vegetation from a period of roughly two centuries between AD 700 and 900 seems significant, and probably indicates land set aside for grazing.[63]

Y. Morimoto (Ghent, 1994), 91–125; J. Devroey and A. Nissen, "Early Middle Ages, 500–1000," in *Struggling with the Environment: Land Use and Productivity*, ed. E. Thoen and T. Soens (Turnhout, 2015), 43–4. Animal husbandry: ibid., 48; C. Loveluck, *Northwest Europe in the Early Middle Ages, c. AD 600–1150* (Cambridge, 2013), 54, 67, 93; E. Peytremann, *Archéologie de l'habitat rural dans le nord de la France du IVe au XIIe siècle* (Saint-Germain-en-Laye, 2003), 342–3; R. Hodges, *Dark Age Economics* (London, 2012), 54–61.

[59] S. Jesset, "Les formes de l'exploitation rurale du IXe au XIe siècle," in *Lumières de l'an mil en Orléanais* (Turnhout, 2004), 91.

[60] P. Guilbert, "Étude des pollens prélevés dans les couches archéologiques de Villiers-le-Sec," in *Un village au temps de Charlemagne* (Paris, 1988), 197; M. Ruas, "Alimentation végétale, pratiques agricoles et environnement du VIIe au Xe siècle," in ibid., 209; and Ruas "Prés, prairies, pâtures," 38.

[61] Indre: A. Querrien et al., "Évolution et exploitation du paysage végétale au Moyen Âge," in *Trente ans d'archéologie médiévale en France*, ed. J. Chapelot (Caen, 2010), 42–3 (without microscope analysis only genus was identified). Eifel: C. Herbig and F. Sirocko, "Palaeobotanical Evidence of Agricultural Activities in the Eifel Region during the Holocene," *Vegetation History and Palaeobotany* 22 (2013), 459. Morvan: I. Jouffroy-Bapicot et al., "7000 Years of Vegetation History and Land Use Changes in the Morvan Mountains (France)," *The Holocene* 23.12 (2013), 1897. Rennes: M. Ruas and B. Pradat, "Les semences découvertes," in *Les habitats carolingiens de Montours et La Chapelle-Saint-Aubert*, ed. I. Catteddu (Paris, 2001), 75.

[62] Sermersheim: E. Peytremann and S. Wiethold, "L'apport de la carpologie à l'étude du site du premier Moyen Âge (VIe–XIIe siècle) de Sermersheim (Bas-Rhin)," in *Des hommes aux champs*, ed. V. Carpentier and C. Marcigny (Rennes, 2012), 205–9.

[63] S. Preiss et al., "Approche des pratiques agricoles durant le haut Moyen Âge en Hesbaye," in *Plantes, produits végéteaux et ravageurs*, ed. M. Dietsch-Sellami et al., (Bordeaux, 2016), 166–7, 174.

Such spontaneously occurring plants were not, of course, the same everywhere. Soil chemistry, climate, and relief modulated the phytosociology as much as the tastes of four-legged browsers and, to some extent, the choices of farmers (the absence of prickly plants in the Villiers-le-Sec pollens may be a trace of human interference or of attempts to limit plants that browsing animals do not like; and in Carolingian Tuscany cultivators eschewed raising cattle, and therefore also plants for grazing, a situation which somewhat more surprisingly seems also to have prevailed at Nogara, on the plain of Verona).[64] But all weeds, whether ruderal, facultative, or obligate, adapted and responded to the various stimuli that human economic activities provided, not least to the teeth and hooves of ruminants and the blades of scythes, even if no one plowed or manured the soil for them or sowed their seeds (in fact, when these pastures *were* plowed, the purpose was to destroy them).[65] Though no one went after them with weedhooks or hoes, either, still these were communities of weeds in the sense that they were not cared for by people, though certainly they were tolerated by them during specified periods of the year.[66] Those periods usually ended after less than eight months in early medieval European rotation cycles: Wandalbert of Prüm suggested that at Cologne around 850, one let stabled animals out to graze in April, and kept them outdoors until the autumn sowing, variably between September and December, depending on the crop. At the end of the grazing season, farmers would extract one last service from the weeds, converting their biomass into green manure by plowing them into the soil.[67]

The weedy profusion within and around Carolingian settlements was permitted and even to some extent fostered because it made agrarian life possible. The "salvage accumulation" of Carolingian farmers focused on

[64] M. Buonincontri et al., "Multiproxy Approach to the Study of Medieval Food Habits in Tuscany," *Archaeological and Anthropological Sciences* 9 (2017), 665. Verona (ninth- to tenth-century plant remains): E. Castiglioni and M. Rottoli, "Nogara, l'abitato di Molino di Sotto," in *Nogara*, ed. F. Saggioro (Rome, 2011), 135–9.

[65] Carolingian scythes: P. Reigniez, "Histoire et techniques: l'outil agricole dans la periode du haut Moyen Âge," in *The Making of Feudal Agricultures?*, ed. M. Barceló and F. Sigaut (Leiden, 2004), 96; P. Anderson and F. Sigaut, "Reasons for Variability in Harvesting Techniques and Tools," in *Explaining and Exploring Diversity in Agricultural Technology*, ed. A. van Gijn et al. (Oxford, 2014), 91–2. On the impact of such tools on phytosociology, see above, p. 43–5, 54–7. Weeds' response to browsing: J. Zadoks, *Crop Protection in Medieval Agriculture* (Leiden, 2013), 132–3; Salisbury, *Weeds*, 197–9.

[66] J. Harlan, *Crops and Man* (Madison, 1992), 89 measures farmers' varying acceptance of plants. On Carolingian-era "prata" and weeding, see F. Sigaut, "L'evolution des techniques," in *The Making of Feudal Agricultures?*, ed. Barceló and Sigaut, 23.

[67] F. Sigaut, "Le labour, qu'est-ce que c'est?" in *Nous labourons* (Nantes, 2007), 23–6; Butzer, "The Classical Tradition," 587. Wandalbert of Prüm, "De mensium XII nominibus, signis, culturis," ed. E. Dümmler, *MGH Poetae* 2 (Berlin, 1884), 607. Charlemagne's calendar juxtaposed pasture-month and fallow-month (May and June).

the economic exploitation of weeds growing on the margins of the cultivated area as much as on the completely uncultivated woodlands, swamps,
and heaths of the empire. By extracting nutrients from the "disturbance-
based ecologies" that were a side-effect of rural life, cultivators took advantage of resources they incompletely controlled.[68] Weeds from such spaces
ultimately undergirded the animal husbandry that provided Charlemagne
with the butter, cheese, meat, skins, and beasts of burden that sustained
him and his armies.[69] It furthermore contributed helpful nutrients to fallow
fields when they were returned to cultivation by weed-fed Carolingian plow
teams, though if the weeds were mature it also returned their seeds to the
ground. All told, the fallow fields, roadsides, and meadows of rural Europe
under the Carolingians sprouted weeds with an important role to play in
the economy, and therefore in the politics of the empire. The formerly
useless, bad plants, on their own, with little interference from cultivators,
sustained rural communities and the ancillary activities of aristocracies and
states simply by going about their usual business of sprouting leaves and
setting seeds with unmatched efficiency.

Conclusion

Agreeing with Remigius of Auxerre that all plants have a use, Carolingian
people set out to discover the spiritual potency of nettles, the medical
efficacy of hellebore, and the nutritional potential of wasteland plant
communities. This unanimity derived from the prevailing Carolingian
conception of weeds. As we have seen, all vegetation was ambiguous, its
status to some extent unstable. As ever, phytosocial mobility prevailed.
So, while weeds ranked lowest among plants, this status was not irreme-
diable. Their relationship with humanity was fluid, and in the right
circumstances they might produce unexpected religious, physiological,
or economic benefits for people who understood them. For ascetics the
trick was to use them without enjoying them excessively, never to permit
their inferior materiality to become a distraction. But if most Carolingian
people probably agreed that one should never love weeds, the most
obnoxious of plants had several saving graces for those men and
women, of high and low social status, who perceived them rightly.

---

[68] A. L. Tsing, *The Mushroom at the End of the World* (Princeton, 2017), 5, on making a living
in "disturbed" ecosystems, and 55–71 on postindustrial "salvage accumulation."
[69] "Capitulare de Villis" 13–15, p. 84 (horses); 23, p. 85 (cattle and their flesh); 30, p. 85
(cartloads for the army); 34, p. 86, 44, p. 87 ("formaticum, butirum"); 35, p. 86 (fat
sheep and oxen); 62, p. 89 (skins and horns); 64, p. 89 (waterproof skins for army carts).

7 The Politics of Weeding in the Carolingian Empire

To adequately celebrate his illustrious predecessor's 1165 canonization, which he orchestrated, Frederick Barbarossa commissioned the composition of new liturgical chants for St. Charlemagne.[1] Among Charlemagne's numerous excellent rulerly qualities that one chant enumerated, his skill as a weeder gives pause. In the toolkit of medieval sovereigns, and maybe especially of early medieval ones, we expect to find the ability to squelch aristocratic rivals, to direct the activities of uppity churchmen, to lead armies, to wisely legislate, and to equitably dispense charity; but his ability as a farmer, and particularly his adept disposal of unwanted plants, is seldom included on the curriculum vitae of the model early medieval king and emperor. Yet the cantors at Aachen in 1165 belted out the claim that Charlemagne "cleanses the soil of darnel / and with his sword cuts out / the tares from the harvest. / This is the great emperor / good sower of good produce / and prudent farmer."[2]

Though there are few attestations of the royal farmer motif in Carolingian literature, kings that knew how to farm well were an ideal of Frankish political culture. For the saintly Merovingian king Dagobert II (+679) was said by his hagiographers (who apparently wrote at the very end of the ninth century) to have been a skillful sower of grain: indeed, his peasant subjects once stopped him near Reims with the request that he sow their fields. The result was a magnificent harvest.[3] The well-known capitulary *De Villis* no doubt informed Hohenstaufen propaganda and the idea that Charlemagne, at least, was a "prudent farmer." It is feasible that the twelfth-century chant's evocation of sowing "good produce" (*boni fructus*) might echo the capitulary's request that royal estates stock good seed (*sementem bonum*), which

---

[1] M. McGrade, "O Rex Mundi Triumphator," *Early Music History* 17 (1998), 183–219.

[2] "De Sancto Karolo" 4–5, in Einhard, *Vita Karoli Magni* 26, ed. G. Pertz et al., *MGH Scriptores Rerum Germanicarum in Usum Scholarum* (Hanover, 1911), 51: "Terram purgat lolio / atque metit gladio / ex messe zizania. / Hic est magnus imperator, / boni fructus sator / et prudens agricola."

[3] "Vita Dagoberti III Regis Francorum," ed. B. Krusch, *MGH Scriptores Rerum Merovingicarum* 2 (Hanover, 1888), 515. Date: C. Carozzi, "La vie de saint Dagobert de Stenay," *Revue belge de philologie et d'histoire* 62 (1984), 243–6.

meant seed duly winnowed and purified of the intrusive seeds of mimic weeds, and which perhaps also evoked seed of Edenic purity.[4] So, although muted, compared with the sonority of the Hohenstaufen liturgies, the theme of the good ruler as good weeder, as someone who understood bad plants and how to eliminate them, was present in Carolingian political rhetoric. Specifically, it seems Charlemagne, whom Gibbon would mock for his agricultural zeal, was the Carolingian most closely associated with separating out good and bad plants.[5]

Yet the tool assigned by the liturgists to Charlemagne the weeder is fully royal, and his appropriate weeding is martial. Charlemagne cut the darnel out (*metit*, in the sense of "mete out punishment") using a sword, presumably the same instrument that was in his hand a few verses before, when he mowed down thousands of insubordinate dukes and, as a "strong soldier of Christ," led unconquerable armies.[6] However effective musically and politically, Charlemagne's technique was agronomically unsound, for though weeding *is* violence, and forcefully imposes human priorities by destroying the natural vegetation of a given area, Carolingian farmers seldom did it with military equipment. Even Carolingian theologians may have found such weeding by sword a contradiction of the patience advocated by Jesus in the "Parable of the Tares."

The tension between the figure of ruler as military hero and that of ruler as steward of agricultural fertility is nicely resolved in the twelfth-century text. Charlemagne's surgical strikes against vegetable enemies in the field are the high medieval solution. Eighth- and ninth-century texts are far less explicit about any link between martial prowess and weeding, but as this chapter elucidates there *was* a specifically Carolingian politics of weeding among the Frankish elite. It was intimately related to the strong current of political thought that made Carolingian kings and emperors personally responsible for the smooth functioning of nature, God's creation, or anyway, for that northwestern European corner of it the Franks knew and cared about the most.

---

[4] "Capitulare de Villis" 32, ed. A. Boretius, *MGH Capitularia Regum Francorum* 1 (Hanover, 1883), 86 (see also Chapter 4, n. 35 above). Avitus of Vienne, *Histoire spirituelle* 3.158–9, ed. N. Hecquet-Noti (Paris, 1999), v. 1, 278, thought postlapsarian crop seed was necessarily mixed, different from the "puro semine" of the Garden. On the capitulary, see D. Campbell, "The 'Capitulare de Villis,' the 'Brevium Exempla,' and the Carolingian Court at Aachen," *Early Medieval Europe* 18 (2010), 243–64.

[5] Edward Gibbon, *Decline and Fall of the Roman Empire* (New York, 1901), 142 on how petty was Charlemagne's legislation, descending to "the economy of his farms, the care of his poultry, and even the sale of his eggs."

[6] "De Sancto Karolo" 4, 51: "Hic est Christi miles fortis / hic invicte dux cohortis / ducum sternit milia."

The Moral Ecology of Weeds: A Genealogy

As noted at the outset of this book, official Carolingian pronouncements, like capitularies, sometimes evoked vivid metaphors of weeding and weeds. Ecclesiastical councils, themselves intimately associated with the production and transmission of capitularies, also favored such metaphors.[7] Carolingian literate culture operated around a set of shared assumptions, within a "discourse community."[8] Thus the verbs "extirpate," "uproot," and "cast out" (often "from the roots") were a normal part of Carolingian political rhetoric, and bishops, priests, kings, and emperors were represented as armed with hoes, or more rarely sickles, as they tackled the thorns, or darnel, or "harmful shoots" of sin, incest, evil, and doctrinal error.[9] The record of Paulinus of Aquileia's intervention at the council held at Cividale in 796 or 797 is emblematic: the archbishop and long-time member of Charlemagne's court asked the gathered clergy to redouble its efforts in the field of the Lord, and to cast out "the pestiferous shoots ... from their roots," a bit incongruously using sickles, so they might rot away, leaving their leafless stems to choke on their own poison, while making it easier to "utterly overturn" the whole plant, an operation which the imminence of war (against the Avars) in the region made more urgent. The targeted plant was described as pullulating, thorny, able to mix with wheat, and thriving in dark, umbrageous places. It was, however, not a botanical nuisance of which he spoke, but a theological one, namely Paulinus' old bugbear, the Iberian heresy called Adoptionism.[10]

The efficacy of such rhetoric depended on audiences whose vegetable imaginations had been nurtured on biblical readings and who knew, for example, what to expect from darnel. But for maximum impact Carolingian weed discourse also relied on an understanding of how proper and acceptable authority should be wielded, whether in fields and gardens by upstanding cultivators, in pastures by responsible shepherds, or in the socio-political arena by good administrators. These roles were connected, for Carolingian moralists reputed the behavior of the sovereign to have direct repercussions on the fertility of the realm's

---

[7] W. Hartmann, *Die Synoden der Karolingerzeit im Frankreich und in Italien* (Paderborn, 1989), 12–13.

[8] R. Kramer, *Rethinking Authority in the Carolingian Empire* (Amsterdam, 2019).

[9] The verbs "extirpare," "eradicare," and "evellere": *MGH Concilia* 4, ed. W. Hartmann (Hanover, 1998), 10; *MGH Concilia* 3, ed. W. Hartmann (Hanover, 1984), 81; *MGH Capitularia* 2.1, ed. V. Krause (Hanover, 1890), 38, 124. Both "radicitus" and "funditus" qualify the action of weeding: *MGH Concilia* 4, 10; *MGH Capitularia* 2.1, 38. The "sarculus" is invoked in ibid., 52; *MGH Concilia* 2, suppl. 2, ed. H. Willjung (Hanover, 1998), 303.

[10] *MGH Concilia* 1.1, ed. A. Werminghoff (Hanover, 1906), 179–180, including the "pestifero ... virgulto" whose woody roots clergy must "funditus evellere."

ecosystems, on the size and quality of harvests, on weather, and on the regular procession of the annual seasonal cycle.[11]

This was not the same as the fairly traditional (also biblically based) belief that the inadequacies of the people would receive condign ecological punishment from God. In late antiquity, for example, as the authority of the rabbis waxed, eastern Jewish communities had embraced this notion, even though some Talmudic tractates were uncertain that virtue always obtained favorable weather, or that the pious would always understand the message in unusually trying climatic events.[12] The view that God chastised people ecologically was known in Francia, too. A morose Nithard expressed it in 841–2, right after an unseasonable snowfall, in the very last section of his *Histories*.[13] And at the grand gathering Charles the Bald organized at Pîtres in 862, this idea was preferred to others, and the sins of the collectivity, rather than those of Charles, were singled out as the root cause of Frankish tribulations in the preceding few years.[14] Instead, from the middle of the eighth century, when Pippin the Short determined to adopt special measures to deal with what today might be called natural disasters in his realm, Carolingian governments developed an ideology that ascribed to the personal morality of the ruler great relevance for the smooth working of the universe. The frigid winter of 763–4, which wrought havoc on southern Francia's agriculture, persuaded Charlemagne's father to deploy a barrage of liturgies, some fasts, and careful charity to restore nature's previous abundance. His measures, duly tweaked for the circumstances (also shaped by natural disasters) of 779, 792–4, 805–7, 814–30, and of the 860s, were readopted by his successors. They rested on a moral ecology that presumed divine interventions lay behind the interruptions of the normal routines of nature. Such interruptions were therefore always possible and justified.[15] The likeliest justification was the king's recent misbehavior.[16]

---

[11] R. Stone, "Kings Are Different," in *Le prince au miroir de la literature politique de l'Antiquité aux Lumières*, ed. F. Lachaud and L. Scordia (Mont-Saint-Aignan, 2007), 69–86.

[12] J. Belser, *Power, Ethics, and Ecology in Jewish Late Antiquity* (Cambridge, 2015), 11–21, 85–95, 116–17, 377–9.

[13] Nithard, "Historiarum Libri IIII" 4.7, ed. E. Müller, *MGH Scriptores Rerum Germanicarum in Usum Scholarum* (Hanover, 1907), 49–50. See M. de Jong, *The Penitential State* (Cambridge, 2009), 101.

[14] J. Devroey, *La nature et le roi* (Paris, 2019), 231.

[15] M. Cândido da Silva, "L'économie morale carolingienne," *Médiévales* 66 (2014), 159–78; Devroey, *La nature*, 183–7, 197–201, 223–9, 284–5, 408–23 and his "La politique annonaire carolingienne comme question économique, religieuse, et morale," in *Settimane del CISAM* 63 (Spoleto, 2016)," 324–32; P. Delogu, "L'ambiente altomedievale come tema storiografico," in *Agricoltura e ambiente attraverso l'età romana e l'alto medioevo*, ed. P. Nanni (Florence, 2012), 96–8; de Jong, *The Penitential State*, 116–17, 151–5.

[16] G. van Bavel et al., *Disasters and History* (Cambridge, 2020), 89–99 discuss the political fall-out of natural disasters in the second millennium AD, when the nature of regimes was consistently associated with ecological vulnerability.

Mid-eighth-century Carolingian rulers and their entourages did not invent the notion themselves, though the clarity of their vision and the persistence of the ensuing ideology do make this Carolingian political theology stand out in the medieval record. In the midst of the crises of the third century, pagan Roman emperors had given some currency to the idea that the ruler's upright behavior shaped the meteorological and agricultural fortunes of the empire. Christian writers in the apocalyptic vein joined in the chorus, eagerly adapting to their ends the classical concept of an aging world, increasingly erratic and unable to sustain fertility: like the pagans, they too plumbed natural phenomena, including "catastrophic" ones, for religious meaning, only that to them the meaning was the beginning of the end. Whatever their exegetical inclination, however, emperors, their apologists, and their critics all agreed that virtuous behavior and rule produced ecological effects, in particular natural constancy, predictability, and fecundity. The ruler's *clementia* mirrored that of nature. The opposite was true too, of course. The harmonious natural order could easily melt into deluges, droughts, failed crops, and human misery. All depended on the quality of the emperor, on his moral performance of his rulerly ministry. His misbehavior, his misrule, subverted nature.[17]

That rulers' morality mattered to the orderly advancement of the seasons and rendered the traditional human adaptations to it a little easier was, as we have seen, not just a Roman imperial idea: it existed in several earlier monarchical cultures, with the Hellenistic one particularly influential in imperial Rome.[18] Attentive Carolingian readers of the Hebrew scriptures could also find inspiration for the notion in the received accounts of the doings of certain early kings of Judea, especially David and his dynasty. David was one of Charlemagne's nominal models, and an important mediator of the shepherd-king motif that colored Carolingian royal ideology, just as the weeder-king did. In fact, to Smaragdus of St.-Mihiel, a good shepherd went to work equipped with a weeding hook, ready to root out noxious plants from his flock's pasture.[19]

---

[17] J. Haas, *Die Umweltkrise der 3. Jahrhundert n. Chr. im nordwesten des Imperium Romanum* (Stuttgart, 2006), 25–37, 42–6, 53–64. See also C. Glacken, *Traces on the Rhodian Shore* (Berkeley, 1967), 151–4. Also in "early medieval" China emeprors were expected to control natural hazards: N. Rothschild, "Sovereignty, Virtue, and Disaster Management," *Environmental History* 17 (2012), 783–812, esp. 784–8.

[18] Devroey, *La nature*, 229; L. Totelin, "Botanizing Rulers and their Herbal Subjects," *Phoenix* 66 (2012), 122–44.

[19] O. Murray, "The Idea of the Shepherd King from Cyrus to Charlemagne," in *Latin Poetry and the Classical Tradition*, ed. P. Godman and O. Murray (Oxford, 1990), 10–14; Smaragdus of St.-Mihiel, "Epistula de Processione Spiritus Sancti," ed. H. Willjung, in *MGH Concilia* 2, suppl. 2 (Hanover, 1998), 303. The text was written around 809 in the context of debates on the "filioque clause."

Though Davidic models of leadership helpfully exalted the ruler, who had a privileged (if occasionally strained) relationship with God, they also brought heavy moral burdens and stringent demands. Such kings could hide nothing from their severe sponsor, and their mis-steps were not a private affair pertinent only to their souls or their own relationship with God. On the contrary, divine retribution for the king's moral deficiencies would fall disastrously upon the environment, affecting the whole realm and people. Carolingian vision literature therefore is full of recently deceased kings' souls suffering torments in the afterlife: it was easy to keep track of their failings by observing environmental patterns in their realms.[20]

In the eighth century, Insular culture helped to reinforce the point that a kingdom's ecology reflected its king's moral stature. The anonymous seventh-century Irish treatise about "The Twelve Abuses of the World," which, ascribed to the North African Church Father Cyprian, circulated widely in Carolingian Europe, and listed unjust kings as the ninth abuse liable to subvert the social and natural order.[21] In particular, morally inadequate kings brought famine and ruin on their kingdoms ("the fruitfulness of the land diminishes") and "with tempests of the skies, and perturbed atmospheres they [bad kings] impede the fertility of the lands and the fruitfulness of the seas, and frequent lightning strikes will destroy the crops and the flowers and shoots of the trees." Such a truculent view of the consequences of royal inadequacy was reiterated in Cathwulf's letter to Charlemagne of about 775, in which the Anglo-Saxon clergyman advised the Frankish king that "the fecundity of the land and sea and everything that grows there" depended on him being an upright ruler; if he stumbled, Charlemagne could expect "famines of the people, pestilence, the land's infertility, and the fruits of the land and sea prostrated by many storms."[22] As well as texts, people, often Anglo-Saxon clergymen, also brought to the attention of the Franks the scripturally inflected moral ecology according to which kings were personally responsible for their realms' environments. Alcuin, who became one of Charlemagne's closest

---

[20] Stone, "Kings Are Different," 85–6.

[21] Ps.-Cyprianus, *De XII Abusivis Saeculi*, ed. S. Hellmann (Leipzig, 1909), 51–3: "terrarum quoque fructus diminuuntur" and "tempestates aeris et hiemisperia turbata terrarum fecunditatem et maris ministeria prohibent et aliquando fulminum ictus segetes et arborem flores et pampinos exurunt." On the Carolingian reception, see R. Meens, "Politics, Mirrors for Princes and the Bible," *Early Medieval Europe* 7 (1999), 345–57; C. Wickham, *The Inheritance of Rome* (London, 2009), 407–8.

[22] *MGH Epistolae* 2, ed. E. Dümmler (Berlin, 1895), 503: "terre marisque cum omnibus in eis nascentibus fecunditas ... populorum fames, pestilentia, infecunditas terrae, maris quoque tempestatibus fructus terrarum diversis percussis."

advisers at the end of the 780s and determined a "clericalization" of that king's inner circle during the 790s, was familiar with the idea.[23]

Natural Perfections

Alcuin thought that not just kings, but also their great allies, the bishops of the realm, should be "good at amputating from the roots up the sprouting thorns, with a hoe like good farmers."[24] Indeed, the metaphorical mixture of land and soul stewardship that he adopted fit into a broader commingling of political and spiritual authority within Carolingian Europe. Though this heightened awareness of the peculiar, hybrid "ministerium" that the powerful wielded in society may have reached its apogee under Charlemagne, it did not evaporate after the emperor's death in 814. The "penitential state" of Louis the Pious and his sons ultimately was founded on rulers whose special status and authority, but also heavier burdens of responsibility, derived from their special connection to God.[25] The conviction that a good Carolingian ruler should bring tranquility to his subjects and their lands extended to the regulations of natural processes, meteorological, zoological, and botanical. In other words, successful agriculture in the realm was such kings' purview.

Most of all the "good farmer" and ruler should produce stability. Early Christian exegesis of Genesis extolled the marvelous constancy of nature, its regular, predictable, repeated delivery of bounty usable by people. Although the passages in Genesis (8.21, 9.8–11) wherein the creator announced to the survivors of the Flood a new arrangement in which nature would no longer be disordered or dangerous were seldom cited in Carolingian literature, the Pentateuch was the Franks' favorite part of the Old Testament (save the Psalms), Charlemagne was unusual in his enthusiasm for exegesis of the first books in the Bible, and Genesis was read out loud and expounded in Frankish churches every year, during the week leading up to Lent.[26] Thus Carolingian people, and certainly the learned ones who knew Genesis well, expected natural cycles to repeat themselves benignly, without interruption.

---

[23] Devroey, La nature, 223–7. Clericalization/Anglicization: I. Garipzanov, The Symbolic Language of Authority in the Carolingian World (Leiden, 2008), 269–86; M. Garrison, "The Franks as the New Israel?" in The Uses of the Past in the Early Middle Ages, ed. Y. Hen and M. Innes (Cambridge, 2000), 145–50.

[24] Alcuin, "Epistolae" 3, ed. E. Dümmler, MGH Epistolae 2 (Berlin, 1895), 21: "ut sicut boni agricultores sarculo nascentes spinas … radicitus amputare valeant."

[25] De Jong, The Penitential State, 3–4, 40.

[26] J. Contreni, "The Patristic Legacy to c. 1000, in New Cambridge History of the Bible 2, ed. R. Marsden and E. A. Matter (Cambridge, 2012), 507. Readings: D. Ganz, "Carolingian Bibles," in ibid., 327; J. Nelson, King and Emperor (Berkeley, 2019), 251. See also S. Shimahara, "Charlemagne, premier souverain chrétien commendataire d'exegèse biblique?" in Charlemagne, ed. R. Grosse, M. Sot (Turnhout, 2018), 101–17.

The well-structured order of nature reflected its creator. John Scottus Eriugena (+877) perceived in the lifecycle of plants, specifically, a proof of how orderly, harmonious, logical, and beneficent was the God who devised the cycle and could be expected to sustain it.[27]

Genesis also supplied evidence that God intended humans to watch over and manage the benign environment He created. Since at least the time of Augustine, Latin readers had noticed that before the Fall, God had set Adam and Eve to work, gardening to maintain the excellence of Eden. This work was not at all comparable to postlapsarian toil (among other things it was gender neutral). In Eden it had been joyous, recreational human participation in the perfection of paradisiacal botany.[28] Such sinless stewardship of nature was itself a kind of "ministerium," and though everyday farming after expulsion from Eden was different, Augustine recognized in the pleasure farmers got from farming well a remote trace of that first "tending" of Edenic plants.[29] The "good farmer" of Carolingian times could thus aspire to recreate some of the divine botanical order and fecundity that had prevailed in the beginning.[30]

The most accountable administrator of the Carolingian landscape was, as we have seen, the ruler. In the social contract between God and him, and by extension his subordinates, moral lapses were failures of his ministry, and could cost his realm dear.[31] Perturbations of the "ordinary" workings of nature, which meant those that people considered advantageous or at worst neutral to themselves, and therefore usually were stable and predictable workings, served as warnings or punishments for such transgressions. Reestablishing the expected, "familiar" bounty of nature, and then maintaining the polity on an even-keeled course that would permit the correct ecological order to prevail, depended on the king, recipient of God's favor and "ministerium," but also potential lightning rod for God's wrath, effective conductor of it into that nature where people lived and could experience its devastating might.

---

[27] *De Divisione Naturae* 5.3, ed. J. Migne, *PL* 122 (Paris, 1865), 866 (=*Periphyseon. Liber Quintus*, ed. E. Jeauneau (Turnhout, 2003), 11). With his usual prescience Glacken, *Traces*, 210, understood the significance of regular natural cycles to the Carolingians.

[28] M. Lauwers, "Le 'travail' sans la domination?" in *Penser la paysannerie médiévale, un défi impossible?*, ed. A. Dierkens et al. (Paris, 2017), 321–2.

[29] The Vulgate translated as "operaretur" and "custodiret" the Hebrew "avad" of Genesis 2.15, which probably implied a kind of worship, within a sacred enclosure: see Chapter 3, note 41 above.

[30] Revealing the immense versatility of the Genesis story, in the very different circumstances of Russia in the 1780s, similar enthusiasm for the labor that would recreate an imperial Eden in Crimea filled Catherine the Great's court: A. Schönle, "Garden of the Empire: Catherine's Appropriation of the Crimea," *Slavic Review* 60 (2001), 16–17.

[31] De Jong, *The Penitential State*, 116–17, 133, points out that social and religious "contract" were coterminous in Carolingian Europe.

A ruler responsible to God for the proper Christian behavior of his person, his household, and his subordinates did, of course, obtain a powerful justification for his policies.[32] He also was open to constant examination, particularly by the learned, clerical experts in the interpretation of moral and natural phenomena. Charlemagne might respond to cold, rainy weather that hampered agriculture in northwestern Europe by instituting realm-wide, universal tithing to "repay" the creator (and his other agents, the bishops) for creating nature's abundance, thereby reciprocating for the divine gift, re-establishing balance, and, hopefully, restoring passable meteorological conditions.[33] Louis the Pious, also confronting a series of unfortunate meteorological events, could twice voluntarily abase himself in public penitential liturgies in hopes of regaining divine approval and bringing the environment back to its prior, fecund modus operandi.[34]

Combined with the belief that nature was inherently stable and beneficent, Carolingian monarchical ideology created immense expectations of Carolingian sovereigns. They were like lynchpins in the cosmos, practically able to make, and unmake, the good weather that caused grain to grow, fruit to ripen, cows to calve, and agroecosystems to function in the ways that humans found most congenial. The continued predictable playing out of the ecological conditions within which people flourished depended on them.

Devroey has suggested that the heightened responsibility of Carolingian sovereigns for taking care of their subjects' wants, and particularly of food and caloric intake, had two mainsprings. Invoking both Weber and Foucault, Devroey connected the new Carolingian duty toward God and toward the ruled people, on the one hand, to a Christian pastoral obligation in which good shepherds pasture their flocks on verdant meadows, and, on the other hand, to a "deep" patriarchal obligation for providing sustenance to the members of the household. Both ideologies made provisions and feeding a central aspect of monarchical power. Good rulers ensured adequate supplies and caloric intake for their subjects. Conversely, bad rulers proved unable to feed their followers.[35]

There were political benefits to the pastoral-patriarchal and scriptural models of kingship that Carolingian rulers adopted after about AD 750. All political regimes require justifying ideologies in order to obtain and keep their subjects' support and consent; the ideal Carolingian provisioning king who guaranteed favorable environmental conditions to the realm

---

[32] M. Costambeys et al., *The Carolingian World* (Cambridge, 2011), 186, 213.
[33] Cândido da Silva, "L'économie morale," 163, 178; Devroey, *La nature*, 186–7, 204–9.
[34] De Jong, *The Penitential State*, 240–7, 263–7.
[35] Devroey, "La politique," 324–7, 330; Devroey, *La nature*, 27–8, 133, 148–54.

and its inhabitants was a considerably more persuasive justification for power than mere victory over enemies or the consensus of some faithful followers. But, as already observed, the model's downside was that environmental conditions sometimes were obviously adverse, that storms sometimes raged, temperatures occasionally dropped or peaked at inconvenient times, and that harvests failed. In such conditions the moral ecology of the Carolingians authorized people (at least knowledgeable people) to hold their ruler accountable. An ecology manifestly out of joint reflected poorly on the performance of God's special agent on earth.

Within this Carolingian moral ecology weeds occupied an ambiguous place. Since late antiquity they were reminders to Christians of human sin: ultimately, weeds taught people of their limitations. Like storms, weeds were difficult to control, an aspect of nature that had a legitimate place in the created world, and could even be useful, but could also become devastating to human agricultural interests. Hence the good ruler should strive to control them, demonstrating by his successful performance in this regard the proper functioning of the arrangement that bound together God, sovereign, and subjects.

As noted earlier, the capitulary *De Villis* does not explicitly mention weeds, weeding, or the equipment needed for the latter task. Yet through this silence, this "moralized" set of agricultural directives for royal estate managers – a document closely connected to learned clerical musings on the nature of justice – conjures up a weedless ideal.[36] Charlemagne's ambition was farmland without weeds, and with prelapsarian purity of sowing seed. In the eighth and ninth centuries, the "royal landscapes" (*Königslandschaften*) around kings' favorite residences and estates, especially in the valleys of the Oise, Aisne, Meuse, and middle Rhine, and around Regensburg further east, were meticulously tended so as to project Carolingian power, and in some sense realize the ideal laid out in the *De Villis* capitulary of orderly, agriculturally productive spaces reflecting the solid bond between good king, generous nature, and God. We could consider the "royal landscapes" early examples of that "miniaturization" by which "high modern" states intensify their manipulation of small-scale ecologies, fashioning in miniature the kinds of orderly spaces they are unable to impose throughout their territories but which represent perfectly their aspirations of territorial sovereignty.[37] Real Carolingian "royal

---

[36] For Wickham, *The Inheritance*, 537, *De Villis* expressed a "highly moralized royal political practice." Nelson, *King and Emperor*, 366 points out how the capitulary echoes Theodulf's poem "Against Judges" of 798.

[37] The concept is developed in J. Scott, *Seeing Like a State* (New Haven, 1998); its application to postclassical Europe was suggested in P. Squatriti, "Digging Ditches in Early Medieval Europe," *Past and Present* 176 (2002), 18. It resembles N. Elias' idea

landscapes" were definitely not free of weeds, for no agroecosystem ever is. But Charlemagne's capitulary about his estates can represent to us how he wanted to imagine his landscapes of power.[38] Such places were cleared of pesky plants the disorderly dynamism of which reminded everyone of human powerlessness, and of that of the ruler in particular.

More than in the tidy fields of Carolingian "royal landscapes" or of the *De Villis* capitulary, it is in Carolingian rhetoric that the performance of royal "ministerium" as weeding becomes clearest. If weeds were a scourge, an ongoing chastisement for human inadequacy, good admin- istration and wise "tending" should rein them in. The persistent deploy- ment of the image of weeding in documents of the eighth and ninth centuries associated with the higher echelons of government, the depic- tions of the wielders of God's "ministerium" also wielding weeding hoes, the insistence on uprooting thistles, wild oats, nettles, and other notorious weeds in Carolingian literature, all betray the longing for a more perfect world. But in the current imperfect, weed-infested one, Carolingian moral ecology made kings and emperors the weeders-in-chief.

Throughout the Carolingian dynasty's ascendancy, then, among the burdens of a ruler's "ministerium," weed control figured prominently. Charlemagne often declared his aim to root out heretical belief, using technical weeding terms: "it pleases us most glorious king Charles that the vices which have grown up in the holy church of God during our times be eradicated and overturned."[39] Around 819, Louis the Pious acknowl- edged he must "by daily efforts cultivate with a weeding hoe, since harmful plants always flourish in the good field of the church, so by continuous labor and zeal the noxious weeds may be eradicated, and useful plants be planted."[40] At Ulm, in 854, Louis the German settled a dispute over property between rival churches by invoking the need to "extirpate" such dissension within the community.[41] A diploma written at Ravenna in 882 advertised that Charles the Fat would not tolerate

(*The Court Society* (New York, 1983), 227–8) of absolute kings' gardens as "more perfect approximation" of the social control they aspired to.

[38] Numerous works use the phrase "landscape of power," but the most pertinent here (because of its monarchical focus) is D. Rollason, *The Power of Place: Rulers and their Palaces, Landscapes, Cities and Holy Places* (Princeton, 2016).

[39] The preface of the capitulary of Mantua (AD 781) recites "Placuit nobis Karolo glor- iossimi regis ut vitiis que nostris temporibus in sancti Dei ecclesia emerserant eradicentur et evellantur": *MGH Legum Sectio* 2.1, 92, ed. A. Boretius (Hanover, 1888), 194. See also the preface to the synod of Frankfurt (June 794), in ibid., 73.

[40] *MGH Legum Sectio* 2.1, 274: "cotidianis exercitiis adhibitis sarculo bone operationis est excolenda ut sicut semper nociva in ea in bono agro emergent, ita semper laboris bonique studii eradicentur noxis, plantentur utilia."

[41] *MGH Diplomata Regum Germaniae ex Stirpe Karolinorum* 1, 69, ed. P. Kehr (Berlin, 1934), 98: "hoc malum dissensionis poenitus per futura tempora extirpandum."

further oppression of peasants: "from this day forward," he declared, such abuses must be abolished and "torn up by the roots."[42]

A well-ordered king ran a well-ordered kingdom and presided over a pleasant (to humans) environment. Such environments had as few weeds as humanly possible, and none at all when rhetoric intervened. Kingdoms overrun with weeds were ominous. They suggested and made public the failings of the king, his inability to maintain favorable relations with the creator and to manage thereby the ecosystem. But unlike the positive notion of the king as good farmer who nurtured nature and the human populations in the realm through his upstanding morals, the ruler as weeder was authorized to exercise a negative, purgative or purifying role. Weeding was sound stewardship and participated in the construction of appropriate ecological relations; indeed it reinstituted a pallid replica of those perfect ones that had prevailed at the very beginning of the human adventure on earth. The good king who weeded the landscape of ominous presences removed danger to the community and cleansed the realm of filth.[43] While weeding failures were always possible, and visible in the same way that bad weather or poor harvests were, the metaphors that justified a king's vegetational purification augmented his sphere of influence among his subordinates beyond what the proponents of the king-as-guarantor-of-abundance proposed. Weeds, and their legitimate removal, licensed a considerable enhancement of the ruler's place in the Carolingian moral ecology.

Conclusion

In the early twenty-first century, when the United States' government decided to launch a "war on terror," it scrambled to find staff for the domestic part of the task. In particular, as it sought simultaneously to better control access to the country and maintain the steady functioning of transportation and communications, providing greater security at points of entry (and exit) became a priority. Among the somewhat ramshackle resulting set of solutions to the perceived porousness of US borders was the invention in late 2002 of a new governmental agency, the Department of Homeland Security, responsible among other things for vigilance over the flow of people and goods across the boundaries of the nation. The new department, with extensive powers over domestic security, was constituted out of more than twenty extant US government

---

[42] *MGH Diplomata Regum Germaniae ex Stirpe Karolinorum* 2, 49, ed. P. Kehr (Berlin, 1937), 82: "ab hodierne die et deinceps abolendas et extirpanda radicitus."
[43] Notker is unusual in speaking of weeds as filth (*recrementum*: see Introduction, n. 9), but weeding and purity often went together in Carolingian weedology.

agencies, surprisingly few of which were previously engaged in police or military matters. In fact, a significant portion of the staff for the nascent Department of Homeland Security was recruited from the former Animal and Plant Health Inspection Service of the Department of Agriculture, as well as the Immigration and Naturalization Service of the Department of Justice.[44] It seems, then, that personnel able to surveil and control plants and their movements had know-how useful to a modern state's pursuit of greater territorial sovereignty, as well as order among its human populations. Such contemporary conflation of botanical with social purity rather surprisingly evokes early medieval patterns of thought, like those that this chapter has reconstructed in the Carolingian empire.[45]

Neither Charlemagne nor the newborn Department of Homeland Security monopolized the notion that controlling vegetation and controlling people were related exercises. Hellenistic kings in Asia Minor and Egypt were expected to be model gardeners, able to prune, plant, clear beds of infesting competitors, and so on: their courtiers, and maybe their subjects, considered these skills excellent signs of governmental competence, of the ability to rule people properly.[46] In the high Middle Ages, Scottish king Alexander II, a contemporary of the emperor Frederick II of Hohenstaufen, worried enough about the presence of the corn marigold (*Glebionis segetum*) in Scotland's grain fields that he ordered people who allowed this rather cheerful-looking weed to grow on their land to be punished as traitors and rebels.[47] Weeds, in other words, have long been political, and the Carolingians merely developed with their usual diligence the tradition according to which controlling plants is part of good rulers' duty to regulate the conditions of life for their subjects.

Perhaps because people imagine plants to be "sessile" and passive, and therefore exceptionally stable, vegetable dynamism alarms. Modern governments often react to what they see as too-mutable plant behavior with attempts to control the unwanted presence of plants in their territories, and such attempts naturally tend to reflect their ideological paradigms. Just as rulers of the contemporary European Union, USA, or UK address

---

[44] F. Pearce, *The New Wild* (London, 2015), 142.

[45] When the presidents of France and the USA carefully choreographed for maximum media effect their joint planting of a sapling in the White House garden in April 2018, they, too, assumed that their image as good stewards of plants and people should intertwine.

[46] Totelin, "Botanizing Rulers."

[47] *The Acts of the Parliaments of Scotland* 1.2, ed. C. Innes and T. Thomson (Edinburgh, 1844), 386–7. On the authenticity of the provision, see H. MacQueen, "Canon Law, Custom, and Legislation: Law in the Reign of Alexander II," in *The Reign of Alexander II, 1214–49*, ed. R. Oram (Leiden, 2005), 239–40. R. Oram (personal communication) thinks the law related to later thirteenth-century ones of King John Balliol.

the "invasion" of their homelands by "exotic" plants by appealing to a kind of nativism with roots that extend far beyond scientific botany, so too Carolingian authorities contemplated weeds in their own culturally inflected way, within a Christian and imperial framework.[48] In particular, the Carolingian desire for divinely sanctioned order, regularity, and stability put Frankish rulers at loggerheads with those destabilizing agents, anarchic weeds. They alone could keep vegetable chaos at bay, by being good, and by being good at weeding.[49]

Order was a transcendent value to the Carolingians, and to most medieval people.[50] Authors as unalike as the Saxon Poet and Nithard lionized the "most righteous order" of the Carolingian empire.[51] Carolingian dynasts tended to agree with the men of letters: establishing and sustaining order justified and legitimated their supremacy. Such order extended beyond their personal life, the morality of their courts, and justice in their institutions; it also involved nature. As Dutton noted, a Carolingian's sovereignty rested on "control ... of the natural world."[52] Under Charlemagne, especially, but also under his son Louis and grandson Charles the Bald, the longing to discern Edenic order in the realm's often insubordinate landscapes had proved irresistible.

For when good rulers ruled the realm well, the creator's satisfaction became legible in the predictable functioning of ecosystems. When instead rivers flooded, wolves besieged villagers, or harvests withered, these expressions of God's displeasure meant that the social contract between God, Carolingian rulers, and their subjects had been breached. Unruly nature, in sum, reflected poorly on the political status quo. In such a moral ecology the failings of a ruler were the easiest explanation for famines and other unexpected outcomes from natural processes over which people were supposed to have some control.

[48] Contemporary policies: P. Coates, *American Perceptions of Immigrant and Invasive Species* (Berkeley, 2007), 6–26; Pearce, *The New Wild*, 142–9, 160–1; R. Mabey, *Weeds* (London, 2012), 122–4.
[49] P. Dendle, "Plants in the Early Medieval Cosmos," in *Health and Healing from the Medieval Garden*, ed. P. Dendle and A. Touwaide (Woodbridge, 2008), 59.
[50] Carolingian order-obsession: Costambeys et al., *The Carolingian World*, 189, 192; P. Depreux, "Ambitions et limites des réformes culturelles à l'époque carolingienne," *Revue historique* 623 (2002), 735–6. In the *Libri Carolini*, a definition of the order only Frankish kings are capable of sustaining covers respect for tradition, comprehension of grammatical rules, and keeping lay and ecclesiastical things separate: T. Noble, *Images, Iconoclasm, and the Carolingians* (Philadelphia, 2009), 209.
[51] "Rectissimus ordo": Poeta Saxo, "Annales" 4, ll. 318–20, ed. P. von Winterfeld, *MGH Poetae* 4.1 (Hanover, 1899), 53; Nithard, "Historiarum Libri IIII" 1.3, 4.
[52] P. Dutton, *Charlemagne's Mustache and Other Cultural Clusters of a Dark Age* (New York, 2004), 54.

Sprouting up against human wishes, depriving cultivators of the fruit of their labor, bringing instability to yields (and so to tithes), freely crossing the property boundaries that were the foundation of Carolingian agriculture (not to mention society), and demanding much back-breaking toil, weeds were the quintessence of anti-imperial disorder. As such weeds were political, and rulerly discipline aimed to re-establish order in the "fields" of the empire. For this reason, in official documents from the Carolingian empire the rhetoric of "uprooting" error and of deploying hoes and weed-hooks against the wayward was common. Fear of "pullulating" weeds that could "suffocate" desirable plants prompted much Carolingian legislative action.

The resulting norms were only indirectly related to real weeds in real places, and had more to do with the appropriate Christian ordering of relations among people. We saw in Chapter 2 that *Lolium temulentum*, the bad "herb" that garnered the most attention from literary weeders, is so far inconspicuous in the early medieval archaeobotanical record; likewise, although the runners up in the Carolingian championship of botanical wickedness – thistles, brambles, and stinging nettles – look and behave unlike the crops people favor, and so are easy to winnow out both in the field and in crop processing, they too have left a slight impression in the archaeological record, including that from pollen banks.

The vegetational worries of literate Carolingian commentators were more tenuously connected with rustic realities than one might expect of people in an "organic economy," all of the members of which depended intimately for their subsistence on local agrarian activities, with which they were necessarily familiar. What happened in Carolingian gardens or fields – and this book at least shows that a lot happened – seemed to contemporary writers less urgent than what happened in their scriptoria. There biblical botany, supported by classical scientific and agronomical knowledge, reigned supreme.[53]

But such botany was practical. It informed politics and its manifestation in power. As Greenblatt acutely reasoned, "one of the highest achievements of power is to impose fictions upon the world and one of its supreme pleasures is to enforce the acceptance of fictions that are known to be fictions."[54] The Carolingian fictions of weedlessness, of swarming darnel, and of weeding reconstructed here were a demonstration of authority. That literate elites wrote and maybe even worried deeply about weeds that did not exist on the ground, and tended to overlook those that did, proved their participation in the prevailing "discourse community," reinforced their

---

[53] On the relationship of Carolingian literati to biblical narratives, see M. de Jong, "Carolingian Political Discourse and the Biblical Past," in *The Resources of the Past in Early Medieval Europe*, ed. C. Gantner et al. (Cambridge, 2015), 87–91.

[54] S. Greenblatt, *Renaissance Self-Fashioning* (Chicago, 1980), 140–1.

connections with the centers of power, and advertised their membership in the networks of the powerful. The Carolingians' shared fictions of dangerous weeds, based on shared knowledge of biblical botany, were a political discourse. Discussions of bad plants and their eviction "from the roots" explained how an upright, truly Christian society ought to function. At its center, and responsible for all environmental relations, sat the Carolingian rulers whose moral performance made the world go around properly.

Epilogue: Sorting Weeds Out

Ancient, medieval, and modern political cultures seem in accord about the close relationship between legitimate rulership and appropriate dealing with good and bad plants. But since the categorization of plants as weeds to be cast out or as desirable domesticates is contingent, the general agreement does not extend to the species involved. Dandelions, that bugbear of modern lawn-cultivators, seem to have bothered no one in Carolingian Europe, while caltrops seldom figure on modern lists of invasive species, and contemporary wheat farmers do not dread darnel above all.[1] What unites efforts to put plants in their place is the urge to categorize, to sort plants out into good and bad kinds.

The relationship among nature, classification systems, and power has of course attracted a good amount of exegesis. At the beginning of *The Order of Things* (1966), for instance, Michel Foucault placed a Borgesian image that playfully evoked the relativity in human taxonomies of nature, in how people arrange and classify phenomena that they perceive in the world around them. Thus, it presented a supposedly Chinese division of all animals into groups such as animals owned by the emperor, embalmed animals, tame animals, sucking pigs, sirens, fabulous animals, stray dogs, "et cetera."[2]

Foucault aimed to emphasize the arbitrary nature of all human classifications that encompass physical reality, to show how rooted they are in the specifics of the culture that produced them. As one would expect, he was neither the first nor the last to ponder classificatory systems. In the European tradition, Aristotle's *Categories* is an early monument to curiosity about how humans can make sense of the world by subdividing it into groupings of things based on perceived affinities and distinctions. It had profound influence on subsequent taxonomies, not least because of its

---

[1] On the contingencies of modern plant classification, see T. Steinberg, *American Green* (New York, 2006).
[2] M. Foucault, *The Order of Things* (New York, 1970), xv.

absorption into late antique Christian considerations on the ordering of natural phenomena.[3]

Hence one reason why so many Carolingian authors cared about weeds and where they fit in the grand scheme of things is that classifying is one of humanity's most deep-seated preoccupations. All people, in other words, assiduously separate the realities they observe into categories. It is one of their most effective strategies for making sense of their physical circumstances, and it probably improves their chances of survival in the world. Precisely how this urge to divide similar and dissimilar things into groupings evolved, in the eons of prehistory, must remain obscure, but the urge developed, becoming instinctive. When humans began to domesticate other organisms some ten thousand years ago, to live in settled communities, and to tend fixed fields, they already knew how to impart some order on things through taxonomies.[4] Still, as it became prevalent, Neolithic farming sparked a conceptual transition: people reconsidered their relationship with flora. When they assigned to specific plants the role of competitor, they invented weeds.[5]

As in classifying crops and weeds, so in other things: categories were not everywhere and always the same, which was Foucault's point. Environment and culture – in a word, history – gave different meanings to the same things. In different situations, various groups of people squeezed identical things into different categories. For this reason, plants that seemed harmless or even beneficial to some communities, or at some times, seemed positively scary or harmful to other people in other conditions.

As classifying nature, and other things, is never a neutral process based on universal, objective criteria, it can become a window into the specifics of the classifying society. Pioneering researches in the twentieth century established that organizing natural phenomena depends on prevailing social structure, economic system, and cultural patterns. In 1903, the French sociologists Émile Durkheim and Marcel Mauss teamed up to study the connections between systems of classification and social hierarchies in different cultures.[6] They postulated that intimate ties bind

[3] The classic treatment is A. Lovejoy, *The Great Chain of Being: A Study of the History of an Idea* (Cambridge, MA, 1957), 56–67.

[4] J. Scott, *Against the Grain* (New Haven, 2017), 66–75, 90–4, 110–13; E. Weiss et al., "Autonomous Cultivation before Domestication," *Science* 312 (June 16, 2006), 1608–10.

[5] N. Clayton, "Weeds, People and Contested Places," *Environment and History* 9 (2003), 321. As noted in Chapter 1, pre-agricultural people had weeded, too. But their targets were not consistently the same plants.

[6] É. Durkheim and M. Mauss, "De quelques formes primitives de classification," *L'année sociologique* 6 (1903), 1–72.

taxonomies and societies. Though their analysis of aboriginal Australian ways of classifying nature proved to be flawed, their insight was still deep enough to inform numerous later studies of humans' lust for classification. Foucault is just one example. Even cutting-edge, contemporary "biopolitical" work, such as that of Bruno Latour, found inspiration in Mauss and Durkheim's observation that classification always reflects the classifiers' cultural and social norms at least as much as it does qualities in observed reality. To take another influential example, eighteenth-century Europeans imposed social categories on nature, like families of plants, only to reimport them as natural into politics: botanical affinities "proved" how natural were the kinds of associations Europeans preferred.[7] The Linnaean nomenclature that now prevails in most botanical discourses (with some competition, since Linnaeus' speciation often has to be corrected to match current genetic culture) reveals a system of thought so thoroughly assimilated that it is embedded, naturalized. But such orderings of the natural world were first common sense in hierarchical societies with specific cultural and social systems, like that of eighteenth-century Europe. They became globalized in the equally specific circumstances of the colonial and industrial power relations that existed for roughly two centuries after 1750.[8]

Both Enlightenment and Romantic theological and political convictions shaped modern scientific systems of biological classification. David Bloor demonstrated that theories of social contract elaborated in the preceding century forged the Darwinian ideas of nature and relations among its various components that came, however laboriously, to predominate in Europe by 1900 or so.[9] Even twenty-first-century classifications of weeds show their intellectual genealogy when they begin with scientifically observed characteristics such as leaf width and shape, speed of growth, or method of propagation, and end with calculations of the monetary damage they do to agriculture: they reflect modern western culture's prioritization of empirical science and economic gain. They do that also by omitting references to the ecology or cosmology, or even the labor practices, into which the weeds fit.[10]

Following Aristotle, high medieval categorizers divided plants into six kinds, based on their form. They also ranked them by size, with trees

---

[7] G. Bowker and S. Star, *Sorting Things Out* (Cambridge, MA, 1999), 60.

[8] J. Reveal, "What's in a Name? Identifying Plants in Pre-Linnaean Botanical Literature," in *Prospecting for Drugs in Ancient and Medieval European Texts*, ed. B. Holland (Amsterdam, 1996), 57, 81–4.

[9] D. Bloor, *Knowledge and Social Imagery* (London, 1976), 60–2, 66; see also his "Durkheim and Mauss Revisited," *Studies in the History and Philosophy of Science* 13.4 (1982), 267–97; M. Douglas, *Purity and Danger* (London, 1985), 113, 161.

[10] G. Zanin et al., "Definizione e classificazione delle malerbe," in *Malerbologia*, ed. P. Catizone and G. Zanin (Bologna, 2001), 25–34.

highest and grasses lowest on the list, and proclaimed that each plant's size correlated to its complexity, as well as its excellence. Such vertical hierarchy ultimately depended on proximity to God, but it affected terrestrial considerations like digestibility: the fruits of trees were better human food than the seeds of grasses, which, however, surpassed plants like turnips because of their location in the hierarchy and closeness to the soil. In the "scala naturae," or "Great Chain of Being," high medieval ideas of social and moral nobility thus intertwined with botanical ones. The vegetable rungs on this ladder were solidly fixed, and phytosocial mobility was difficult to countenance.[11]

During the early Middle Ages, Aristotelian categories were less influential, but writers continued to consider that the natural world, however flawed, could be analyzed in terms of how closely it resembled the perfections of the supernatural world.[12] Thus the most popular early medieval European classifier, Isidore of Seville, located plants in book 17 of his encyclopedia, *The Etymologies*, far behind "God, angels, and saints" (book 7), "animals" (book 12), and even after "stones and metals" (book 16), signaling their lowly place in his "ladder of nature." Among plants Isidore classified grains first, then legumes, grape vines, trees (the longest section), aromatic plants, garden vegetables, and finally aromatic garden plants. Unsurprisingly, in light of this book's discussions, weeds were not a distinct category to the bishop of Seville, though individual bad plants did find a place here and there throughout book 17 of his compilation. But, like other categorizers, how he arranged plants reveals his priorities and assumptions. In leaving wild plants out, the groupings in *The Etymologies* reflect Isidore's literary, and perhaps his agricultural, milieu. Even an Iberian pastoralist who shared the Sevillan's anthropocentric, agrarian sense of botany would find disorienting the absence in the great compendium of common meadow vegetation.[13]

A similar but adjusted and updated taxonomy of vegetable life emerges in the pages of Hrabanus Maurus' equally vast *De Universo*, written in the 840s.[14] This encyclopedia can be taken as a summation of Carolingian

---

[11] A. Grieco, "The Social Politics of Pre-Linnaean Botanical Classification," *I Tatti Studies* 4 (1991), 131–49.
[12] Lovejoy, *The Great Chain*, 51–8.
[13] Isidore of Seville, *Etymologiae* 17, ed. W. Lindsay (Oxford, 1911) followed Pliny, *Naturalis Historia* 12–27 in some details, but not in the organization of natural phenomena or plants. For instance, Pliny's geology comes after his sixteen chapters dedicated to botany, which are still more anthropocentric than Isidore's.
[14] Hrabanus Maurus, *De Universo*, ed. J. Migne, *PL* 111 (Paris, 1864), 9–613. In book 22 (on implements) Hrabanus discussed weeding tools. The best introduction to Hrabanus' compilation is J. Kreiner, *Legions of Pigs in the Early Medieval West* (New Haven, 2020), 178–80.

erudition, though the author's goal was far narrower than that. Known in the early Middle Ages as *De Rerum Naturis*, Hrabanus' compendium presented in twenty-two books the natures of all things. In classifying plants Hrabanus tended to defer to Isidore, but as he included only botanical data useful in biblical exegesis his deference had limits, and he omitted much Isidoran material.[15] In book 19, dedicated to agricultural things, he followed Isidore's botanical categories, with the weeds squeezed in among the trees (briers, brambles, etc.) or aromatic plants (nettles, for instance). Yet Hrabanus also integrated the information in the *Etymologies* with scriptural references to the plants in question, and allegorical interpretations of the resulting botanical–scriptural complex. The classification offered by *De Rerum Naturis* thus was a botanical concordance to the Bible, but a highly selective one that elided many of the holy book's citations of very bad plants and plenty of vegetation its exemplar had discussed.[16]

Hrabanus' work was a Carolingian classification in that it respected the past, while reinterpreting it for the purposes of the present. Dedicated to the emperor Louis the Pious, Hrabanus' huge book participated in the heroic Frankish effort to reform early medieval European societies and their knowledge systems, including classifications, according to more Christian standards. Hrabanus' unwillingness to single weeds out, to identify them as a type of plant, was part of Carolingian weed discourse. Categorically, bad plants did not exist, and anyway one should always expect phytosocial mobility. Weeds were that way temporarily, produced by the kind of people–plant relations that usually prevailed in the fallen world, and their intermittent goodness suggested how God originally intended them to be.

Like all classifiers, Hrabanus and other Carolingian authors were really just tidying up, which is an attempt to remake a better reality according to a cherished ideal.[17] As we have seen, that ideal was Christian: indeed, Carolingian taxonomies of plants built on late ancient and Dark Age erudite classifications precisely because they were impeccably Christian.[18] While peering with longing at the best landscape of all, the Edenic one described at the beginning of Genesis, where people and plants coexisted in harmony and perfect weedless order prevailed, Carolingian writers retraced the footsteps of their authorities. They did not adopt a consistent label for all weeds, and they eschewed the category as well. When they did (quite consistently) consider a few species of plant noxious and harmful, they followed various

---

[15] F. Paxton, "Curing Bodies, Curing Souls," *Journal of the History of Medicine* 50 (1995), 242, 247–8.

[16] B. Ribémont, *Les origines des encyclopédies médiévales* (Paris, 2001), 297–300, 310–13.

[17] Douglas, *Purity and Danger*, 2–3.   [18] Ribémont, *Les origines*, 273–5.

Church Fathers in these evaluations. In their selection of which plants to describe as impure, dangerous, or hideous, Carolingian intellectuals had to rely on what Mary Douglas called "a total structure of thought," an order of (botanical) things which alone permits the discernment of what is disordered.[19] The biblical, Christian structure they turned to was solid and convincing, and they relied on it because it satisfactorily explained the nature they saw around them.[20] It was the foundation of the "discourse community" that Carolingian power sustained in Europe for several generations.[21]

Though discussion and agreeing to disagree were integral to the Carolingian "discourse community," Carolingian weed classification tends toward univocality. Unusual within a generally debate-prone culture, this uniform Carolingian weedology is also odd among taxonomies.[22] For, as Harriet Ritvo revealed in her history of modern systems for classifying nature, the introduction and dissemination of new taxonomies is seldom uncontested. Usually, several competing systems for ordering the same type of thing coexist, each reflecting the interests of a different interest group, and even the scientific subdivisions of animals and plants into family, genus, and species that developed in the eighteenth and nineteenth centuries took into consideration how butchers, gardeners, shepherds, and farmers arranged nature. Moreover, the scientists who worked to impose their classifications and expertise on nineteenth-century British society disagreed vociferously among themselves on many classificatory matters.[23]

The near-unanimity of the textual tradition on weeds from the eighth and ninth centuries is therefore perhaps surprising, and certainly revealing. The fact that virtually no Carolingian thinker thought to divide plants into domesticates and weeds, or to sort bad plants from good ones, suggests how successful was the Carolingian courts' fostering of a shared "matrix of meaning," at least among the elite.[24] Though Notker might conceive of "useless plants" and "trashy" ones, when he generalized he had in mind a particular situation (a monastic garden) and particular people–plant engagements.[25] The vast majority of Carolingian writers did not need or seek such broad classifications. In virtually complete harmony, they accepted and divulged the idea that the relations established with

---

[19] Douglas, *Purity and Danger*, 41,
[20] H. Ritvo, *The Platypus and the Mermaid, and Other Figments of the Classifying Imagination* (Cambridge, MA, 1997), argued that new taxonomies of nature become culturally necessary when a society is in flux and the stability of social boundaries uncertain.
[21] R. Kramer, *Rethinking Authority in the Carolingian Empire* (Amsterdam, 2019), 43–9.
[22] A recent study stressing Carolingian openness to varying views: J. Timmermann, "An Authority among Authorities," *Early Medieval Europe* 28 (2020), 555–7.
[23] Ritvo, *The Platypus*, xi–xiii, 4–7, 29–50.   [24] Kramer, *Rethinking Authority*, 45.
[25] See the Introduction, above.

cultivators by certain plants like darnel or brambles tended to be harmful to human interests, but might occasionally become constructive and beneficial to those interests in certain circumstances.

And just as they shared an understanding of weeds' potential for status mobility, Carolingian men of letters classified as mostly bad the same plants, the ones with venerable literary traditions behind them. This agreement about what to look for in a plant and which plants one could expect to be harmful and noxious in most circumstances distinguishes the Carolingians' ordering of botanical reality. The lack of variety in Carolingian weed discourse, from the late eighth to the early tenth century, and the apparent absence of alternative categorizations, such as those peasants made, are important features of Carolingian literary weedology. Convinced they were members of a united community (the "ecclesia") conjured into being by Charlemagne's Christian imperial project, for more than a century ecclesiastical writers sustained a consensual, theologically inflected vision of the vegetable world and its organization.

The success of this classification suggests that Carolingian thinkers found in weeds a satisfying expression of their cosmologies: despite their phytosocial mobility, bad plants offered a stable and enduring reflection of fundamental truths about the natural world and the place of humans within it. While it would be nice to think that admiration for all weeds' irrepressible vitality, exuberant reproduction, stolid endurance of hardships, and ecological utility induced Carolingian people to perceive in these plants glimmers of their own aspirations for life on earth, Carolingian anthropomorphizing of vegetation was not that empirical. Instead, Carolingian authorities on nature and its structures tended to scrutinize plants in order to discern an order and coherence that reassured them about the ultimate purpose of creation, and its relation to the celestial perfections in which the faithful hoped to spend eternity.[26] Of course, anthropomorphizing and projection into the vegetable world (and particularly its margins) of constructions of social and moral order were not just an early medieval foible. The most basic assumptions of those who construct them appear in the plants people classify as (mostly) unproductive, hazardous, or ugly. The Carolingian version of this cultural habit rested on earlier classifications which accepted the goodness of creation, the potential for humans to find a legitimate place in it, and God's just administration of all things.

The Carolingian countryside was a lively place where humans and other organisms continuously co-evolved and co-adapted, while coping with local geologies and weather patterns. As we have seen, it was almost

---

[26] J. Palmer, "Climates of Crisis," *Viator* 48 (2017), 9–10.

certainly not permanently overrun with darnel and thistle, agents of evil or teachers of limits. But the men who left written records behind inhabited a Christian empire in which the most fearsome "bad herbs" had been the same old ones since humans were sent out to populate the earth. By accepting that noxious plants were sometimes helpful, even pleasant, these same Carolingians also recognized that the category "weed" was contingent. This flexible Carolingian weed discourse thus accurately reflected the botanical realities of Frankish Europe where plants, like nature, were dynamic and ever-changing relations arose between them and people. In this sense, however detached it might appear today from what transpired in real fields, Carolingian discussion of weeds and their place in the order of things was in the deepest sense empirical.

Select Bibliography

Primary Sources

Adalhard, "Brevis Quem ad Corbeiam Fieri Iussit," ed. J. Semmler, *Corpus Consuetudinum Monasticarum* 1 (Siegburg, 1961), 365–408.

"Additamenta ad Capitularia Regum Franciae Orientalis," ed. A. Boretius and V. Krause, *MGH Capitularia Regum Francorum* 2 (Hanover, 1897).

Agnellus Ravennatis, *Liber Pontificalis Ecclesiae Ravennatis*, ed. D. Deliyannis (Turnhout, 2006).

Alcuin, "Carmina," ed. E. Dümmler, *MGH Poetae* 1 (Berlin, 1881), 160–351.

"Epistolae," ed. E. Dümmler, *MGH Epistolae* 4 (Berlin, 1895), 1–481.

"Interrogationes et Responsiones in Genesin," ed. J. Migne, *PL* 100 (Paris, 1863), 515–66.

Aldhelm, "De Metribus et Enigmatibus ac Pedum Regulis," ed. R. Ehwald, *MGH Auctores Antiquissimi* 15 (Berlin, 1919),

Das altenglische Martyrologium, ed. G. Kotzor (Munich, 1981).

Die althochdeutschen Glossen 3, ed. E. Steinmeyer and E. Sievers (Berlin, 1895).

Ambrose, "Exameron," in *Sancti Ambrosii Opera* 1, ed. C. Schenkl (Vienna, 1896), 1–261.

Anastasius, "Epistolae sive Praefationes," ed. E. Caspar and G. Laehr, *MGH Epistolae* 7 (Berlin, 1928), 395–442.

Angelomus, "Commentarius in Genesin," ed. J. Migne, *PL* 115 (Paris, 1881), 107–243.

"Annales Mosellani," ed. V. Lappenberg, in *MGH Scriptores* 16 (Hanover, 1859), 491–99.

Augustine, *De Genesi contra Manichaeos*, ed. D. Weber (Vienna, 1998).

De Genesi ad Litteram, ed. J. Zycha (Vienna, 1894).

Basil of Caesarea, *Homélies sur l'Hexaéméron*, ed. S. Giet (Paris, 1949).

Bede, *De Temporibus Ratione*, ed. C. Jones (Turnhout, 1977), 263–544.

"In Lucae Evangelium Expositio," in *Bedae Venerabilis Opera* 2.3, ed. D. Hurst (Turnhout, 1960), 5–425.

"Libri Quatuor in Principium Genesis," in *Bedae Venerabilis Opera* 2.1, ed. C. Jones (Turnhout, 1960),

Boethius, *Philosophiae Consolationis*, ed. L. Bieler (Turnhout, 1957).

"Capitula Pistensis," ed. A. Boretius and V. Krause, *MGH Legum Sectio II* 2.2 (Hanover, 1893), 302–10.

"Capitulare de Villis," ed. A. Boretius, *MGH Capitularia Regum Francorum* 1 (Hanover, 1883).

Christian of Stavelot, *Expositio super Librum Generationis*, ed. C. Huygens (Turnhout, 2008).

Claudius of Turin, "Commentarii in Genesim," ed. J. Migne, *PL* 50 (Paris, 1859), 893–1048.

"Epistolae," ed. E. Dümmler, *MGH Epistolae* 4 (Berlin 1895), 586–613.

"Codicis Bernensis CCCLVIII Sylloga," ed. P. von Winterfeld, *MGH Poetae* 4.1 (Berlin, 1899), 242–60.

"Concilium Aquisgranense," ed. A. Werminghoff, *MGH Legum Sectio III* 2.1 (Hanover, 1906), 307–421.

"Concilium Cabillonense," ed. A. Werminghoff, *MGH Legum Sectio III* 2.1 (Hanover, 1906), 273–85.

"Concilium Parisiense," ed. A. Werminghoff, *MGH Legum Sectio III* 2.2 (Hanover, 1908), 473–551.

The Digest of Justinian, in *Corpus Iuris Civilis* 1, ed. T. Mommsen and P. Krueger (Berlin, 1954).

Dioscurides, *De Materia Medica*, ed. M. Wellman (Berlin, 1907).

Dungal, "Dungali Scotti Epistulae," ed. E Dümmler, *MGH Epistolae* 4 (Berlin, 1895).

Dynamidia, ed. A. Mai, *Classicorum Auctorum e Vaticanis Codicibus Editorum* 7 (Rome, 1835).

Einhard, "Passio Marcellini et Petri," ed. E. Dümmler, *MGH Poetae* 2 (Berlin, 1884), 126–35.

Ekkehard IV, "Casus S. Galli," ed. G. Pertz, *MGH Scriptores* 2 (Hanover 1829), XX.

Ermenrich of Ellwangen, "Ermenrici Elwangensis Epistola ad Grimaldum Abbatem," ed. E. Dümmler, *MGH Epistolae* 3 (Berlin, 1899), 534–79.

Eriugena, *Periphyseon*, ed. E. Jeauneau (Turnhout, 2000).

Eugenius of Toledo, "Carmina," ed. F. Vollmer, *MGH Auctores Antiquissimi* 14 (Berlin, 1905), 251–82.

Eusebius, *Die Kirchengeschichte*, ed. E. Schwartz and T. Mommsen 2.2 (Berlin, 1999).

Eustathius, *Ancienne version latine des neufs homélies sur l'hexaéméron de Basile de Césarée*, ed. E. Amand de Mendieta and S. Rudberg (Berlin, 1958).

"Exhortatio Poenitendi," ed. K. Strecker, *MGH Poetae* 4.2 (Berlin, 1914),

Félire Óengusso Céli Dé, ed. W. Stokes (London, 1905).

Flodoard of Reims, "De Triumphis Christi," ed. J. Migne, *PL* 135 (Paris, 1879).

Galen, "On the Powers of Foods," tr. M. Grant, in *Galen on Food and Diet* (London, 2000), 68–190.

Geoponika, tr. A. Dalby (Totnes, 2011).

Gregory of Tours, *De Virtutibus Beati Martini Episcopi*, ed. B. Krusch, in *MGH Scriptores Rerum Merovingicarum* 1.2 (Hanover, 1885), 585–661.

Historia Francorum, ed. W. Arndt, in *MGH Scriptores Rerum Merovingicarum* 1 (Hanover, 1885), 1–450.

Gregory the Great, *Gregorii Magni Dialogi*, ed. U. Moricca (Rome, 1924).

Moralia in Job, ed. M. Adriaen (Turnhout, 1979–85).

Haimo of Auxerre, "Commentarius in Genesim," ed. J. Migne, *PL* 131 (Paris, 1884), 51–134.

Hincmar of Reims, "De Divortio Lotharii Regis," ed. L. Böhringer, *MGH Concilia* 4.1 (Hanover, 1992), 107–261.

Historia Langobardorum Codicis Gothani, ed. G. Pertz, *MGH Scriptores Rerum Langobardicarum* (Hanover, 1878),

Hrabanus Maurus, "Allegoriae in Universam Sacram Scripturam," ed. J. Migne, *PL* 112 (Paris, 1878), 850–1088.

"Commentaria in Genesim," ed. J. Migne, *PL* 107 (Paris, 1864), 443–670.

"Commentariorum in Matthaeum Libri Octo," ed. J. Migne, *PL* 107 (Paris, 1864), 727–1156.

De Universo, ed. J. Migne, *PL* 111 (Paris, 1864), 9–613.

"Glossa Ordinaria, Evangelium Secundum Lucam," ed. J. Migne, *PL* 114 (Paris, 1879), 243–356.

"Homeliae," ed. J. Migne, *PL* 110 (Paris, 1864), 9–468.

Isidore of Seville, *Etymologiae*, ed. W. Lindsay (Oxford, 1911).

Itala. Das neue Testament in altlateinischer Überlieferung 1, ed. A. Jülicher (Berlin, 1938).

Der karolingische Reichskalender, ed. A. Borst, *MGH Libri Memoriales* 2.2 (Hanover, 2001).

Lex Salica, ed. K. Eckhardt, *MGH Leges Nationum Germanicarum* 4.2 (Hanover, 1969).

Liber Glossarum Digital, ed. A. Grondeux and F. Cinato (Paris, 2016), liber-glossarum.huma-num.fr/.

Nithard, "Historiarum Libri IIII," ed. E. Müller, *MGH Scriptores Rerum Germanicarum in Usum Scholarum* (Hanover, 1907).

Notker, *Gesta Karoli Magni*, ed. H. Haefele, *MGH Scriptores Rerum Germanicarum* n.s. 12 (Berlin, 1959).

The Old English Boethius, ed. S. Irvine and M. Godden (Cambridge, MA, 2012).

Opus Caroli Regis Contra Synodum (Libri Carolini), ed. A. Freeman, *MGH Concilia* 2.1 (Hanover, 1998).

Paschasius Radbertus, "Expositio in Mattheum," ed. J. Migne, *PL* 120 (Paris, 1879), 37–994.

Pedanius Dioscorides of Anazarbus, *De Materia Medica*, tr. L. Beck (Hildesheim, 2011).

Philargyrius, *Explanatio in Bucolica Vergilii*, in *Servii Grammatici qui Feruntur in Vergilii Carmina Commentarii* 3.2, ed. G. Thilo and H. Hagen (Leipzig, 1902).

Pliny, *Naturalis Historia*, ed. C. Mayhoff (Stuttgart, 1967).

Poeta Saxo, "Annales," ed. P. von Winterfeld, *MGH Poetae* 4.1 (Hanover, 1899).

Prudentius, *Aurelii Prudentii Clementis Carmina*, ed. M. Cunningham (Turnhout, 1966).

"Pseudoapulei Herbarius," ed. E. Howald and H. Sigerist, *Corpus Medicorum Latinorum* 4 (Leipzig, 1927),

The Reference Bible, ed. G. MacGinty (Turnhout, 2000).

Remigius, *Expositio super Genesim* 3.17, ed. B. Van Name Edwards (Turnhout, 1999).
Saeculi Noni Auctoris in Boetii Consolationem Philosophiae Commentarius, ed. E. Taite Silk (Rome, 1935).
Sedulius Scottus, "Carmina," ed. L. Traube, *MGH Poetae* 3 (Berlin, 1886), 151–240.
Serenus, *Liber Medicinalis*, ed. R. Pépin (Paris, 1950).
Smaragdus of St.-Mihiel, "Collectiones in Epistolas et Evangelia," ed. J. Migne, *PL* 102 (Paris, 1865), 15–552.
"Epistula de Processione Spiritus Sancti," ed. H. Willjung, in *MGH Concilia* 2, suppl. 2 (Hanover, 1998), 300–12.
Expositio in Regulam S. Benedicti, ed. A. Spannagel and P. Englebert (Siegburg, 1974).
Theodulf of Orléans, "Carmina," ed. E. Dümmler, *MGH Poetae* 1 (Berlin, 1881), 437–581.
Theophrastus, *Enquiry into Plants*, ed. A. Hort, 2 vols. (Cambridge, MA, 1916–26).
"Vita Dagoberti III Regis Francorum," ed. B. Krusch, *MGH Scriptores Rerum Merovingicarum* 2 (Hanover, 1888), 511–24.
"Vita Sancti Coemgeni," ed. C. Plummer, *Vitae Sanctorum Hiberniae* 1 (Oxford, 1910).
Walafrid Strabo, "Carmina," ed. E. Dümmler, *MGH Poetae* 2 (Berlin, 1884), 259–473.
"Glossa Ordinaria," ed. J. Migne, *PL* 114 (Paris, 1879), 63–178.
"Liber Psalmorum," ed. J. Migne, *PL* 113 (Paris, 1879), 842–1079.
Wandalbert of Prüm, "De mensium XII nominibus, signis, culturis," ed. E. Dümmler, *MGH Poetae* 2 (Berlin, 1884), 604–16.
Wettinus, "Vita Galli," ed. B. Krusch, *MGH Scriptores Rerum Merovingicarum* 4 (Hanover, 1902).
Wigbod, "Quaestiones in Octateuchum," ed. J. Migne, *PL* 96 (Paris, 1862), 1102–68.

Secondary Sources

Adams, J. *Bilingualism and the Latin Language* (Cambridge, 2003).
Alexandre, M. *Le commencement du livre de Genèse I–IV: la version grecque de la Septante et sa réception* (Paris, 1988).
Allen, H. *Mediterranean Ecogeography* (Harlow, 2001).
Alto Bauer, F. "Die Bau- und Stiftungspolitik der Päpste Hadrian I. (772–795) und Leo III. (795–816)," in *799: Kunst und Kultur der Karolingerreich*, ed. C. Stiegemann and M. Wemhoff (Mainz, 1999), 514–28.
Amar, Z. and E. Lev. *Arabian Drugs in Early Medieval Mediterranean Medicine* (Edinburgh, 2017).
Anderson, P. and F. Sigaut. "Reasons for Variability in Harvesting Techniques and Tools," in *Explaining and Exploring Diversity in Agricultural Technology*, ed. A. van Gijn et al. (Oxford, 2014), 85–92.
André, J. *Lexique des termes de botanique en Latin* (Paris, 1950).

"Notes de lexicographie botanique," *Archivium Latinitatis Medii Aevi* 23 (1953), 103–22.

Anker, P. *Imperial Ecologies* (Cambridge, MA, 2001).

Arthur, P., et al. "Roads to Recovery: An Investigation of Early Medieval Agricultural Strategies in Byzantine Italy in and around the Eighth Century," *Antiquity* 86 (2012), 444–55.

Bakels, C. "Archaeobotanical Investigations in the Aisne Valley, Northern France, from the Neolithic to the Early Middle Ages," *Vegetation History and Archaeobotany* 8 (1999), 71–7.

"Crops Produced in the Southern Netherlands and Northern France during the Early Medieval Period," *Vegetation History and Archaeobotany* 14 (2005), 394–99.

"The Early History of the Cornflower (*Centaurea cyanus*) in the Netherlands," *Acta Palaeobotanica* 52 (2012), 25–31.

The Western European Loess Belt (Dordrecht, 2009).

Baker, H. "The Evolution of Weeds," *Annual Review of Ecological Systems* 5 (1974), 1–24.

Beck, B. "Jardin monastique, jardin mystique," *Revue d'histoire de la pharmacie* 88 (2000), 377–91.

Beinart, W. and K. Middleton. "Plant Transfers in Historical Perspective." *Environment and History* 10 (2004), 3–29.

Belser, J. *Power, Ethics, and Ecology in Jewish Late Antiquity* (Cambridge, 2015).

Belting, H. "Die beiden Palastaulen Leos III. im Lateran und die Enstehung einer päpstliche Programmkunst," *Frühmittelalterliche Studien* 12 (1978), 55–83.

"Die Einhardsbogen," *Zeitschrift für Kunstgeschichte* 36 (1973), 93–121.

Bennett, B. "A Global History of Species Introduction and Invasion," *Environments of Empire*, ed. U. Kirchberger and B. Bennett (Chapel Hill, 2020), 224–45.

Bergmann, R. "Volkssprachige Wörter innerhalb lateinische Texte," *Die althoch-deutsche und altsächsische Glossographie* 1, ed. R. Bergmann and S. Stricker (Berlin, 2009), 938–44.

Bianchi, G. and S. Grassi. "Sistemi di stoccaggio nelle campagne italiane (sec. VII–XIII)," in *Horrea, Barns, and Silos: Storage and Incomes in Early Medieval Europe*, ed. A. Vigil-Escalera Guirado et al. (Bilbao, 2013), 77–102.

Birkhan, H. *Pflanzen im Mittelalter* (Vienna, 2012).

Bloor, D. "Durkheim and Mauss Revisited," *Studies in the History and Philosophy of Science* 13.4 (1982), 267–97.

Knowledge and Social Imagery (London, 1976).

Bogaard, A., et al. "An Index of Weed Size for Assessing the Soil Productivity of Ancient Crops," *Vegetation History and Archaeobotany* 7 (1998), 17–22.

Bolgia, C. "The Mosaics of Gregory IV at S. Marco, Rome," *Speculum* 81 (2006), 1–34.

Bonin, T. "Le site de Chessy et l'occupation du sol en Île-de-France (VIe–Xe siècles)," *Archéologie médiévale* 29 (2000), 1–68.

Borst, A. *Das Buch der Naturgeschichte: Plinius und seine Leser im Zeitalter des Pergaments* (Heidelberg, 1994).

Die karolingische Kalenderreform (Hanover, 1998).

Der Streit um den karolingischen Kalender (Hanover, 2004).

Botkin, D. *The Moon in the Nautilus Shell* (Oxford, 2012).

Bowker, G. and S. Star, *Sorting Things Out* (Cambridge, MA, 1999).

Brombacher, C., et al. "Bronzezeitliche und mittelalterliche Pflanzenfunde aus dem Kloster St. Johann in Müstair," in *Müstair, Kloster St. Johann* 4, ed. H. Sennhauser (Zurich, 2007), 75–98.

Brown, P. *Augustine of Hippo* (Berkeley, 2000).

Bruand, O. *Voyageurs et marchandises aux temps des Carolingiens* (Brussels, 2002).

Brun, C. "Biodiversity Changes in Highly Anthropogenic Environments (Cultivated and Ruderal) since the Neolithic in Eastern France," *The Holocene* 19.6 (2009), 861–71.

Buchet, L. "Apports de l'anthropologie en matière de démographie et de dynamique de l'occupation des sols dans l'occident des IVe–VIIIe sièces," *Antiquité tardive* 20 (2012), 75–85.

Buonincontri, M. "Farming in a Rural Settlement in Central Italy," *Vegetation History and Archaeobotany* 23 (2014), 775–88.

Buonincontri, M., et al. "Multiproxy Approach to the Study of Medieval Food Habits in Tuscany," *Archaeological and Anthropological Sciences* 9 (2017), 653–71.

Buonincontri, M., et al. "Shaping Mediterranean Landscapes," *The Holocene* 30 (2020), 1420–37.

Burbank, J. and F. Cooper. *Empires in World History* (Princeton, 2010).

Burrus, V. *Ancient Christian Ecopoetics* (Philadelphia, 2019).

Butzer, K. "The Classical Tradition of Agronomical Science," in *Science in Western and Eastern Civilization in Carolingian Times*, ed. P. Butzer and D. Lohrmann (Basel, 1993), 539–96.

Cabrol, F. and H. Leclercq. *Dictionnaire d'archéologie chrétienne et de liturgie*, 15 vols. (Paris, 1907–53).

Caillet, J. *L'art carolingien* (Paris, 2005).

Campbell, D. "The 'Capitulare de Villis,' the 'Brevium Exempla,' and the Carolingian Court at Aachen," *Early Medieval Europe* 18 (2010), 243–64.

Campkin, B. "Placing 'Matter Out of Place'," *Architectural Theory Review* 18 (2013), 46–61.

Camporesi, P. *Il pane selvaggio* (Bologna, 1983).

Cândido da Silva, M. "L'économie morale carolingienne," *Médiévales* 66 (2014), 159–78.

Carozzi, C. "La vie de saint Dagobert de Stenay," *Revue belge de philologie et d'histoire* 62 (1984), 225–58.

Castiglioni, E. and M. Rottoli. "Nogara, l'abitato di Molino di Sotto," *Nogara*, ed. F. Saggioro (Rome, 2011), 123–57.

Castiglioni, E., et al. "I resti archeobotanici," in *Archeologia a Monte Barro* 2, ed. G. P. Brogiolo and L. Castelletti (Lecco, 2001), 223–47.

Catizone, P. and G. Zanin. *Malerbologia* (Bologna, 2001).

Censier, D., et al., "Indices de productions au sein d'une communauté religieuse carolingienne," *Archéologie médiévale* 48 (2018), 101–28.

Chadwick, H. *Augustine of Hippo. A Life* (Oxford, 2009).

Chevalier, A., et al. "Factors and Issues in Plant Choice," in *Plants and People: Choices and Diversity through Time*, ed. A. Chevalier et al. (Oxford, 2014), 3–13.

Christie, N. "Charlemagne and the Renewal of Rome," in *Charlemagne, Empire, and Society*, ed. J. Story (Manchester, 2005), 167–82.

Clark, G. "Paradise for Pagans?" in *Paradise in Antiquity*, ed. M. Bockmuehl and G. Stroumsa (Cambridge, 2010), 166–78.

Clayton, M. "Weeds, People, and Contested Places," *Environment and History* 9 (2003), 301–31.

Coates, P. *American Perceptions of Immigrant and Invasive Species* (Berkeley, 2007).

Collins, M. *Medieval Herbals: The Illustrative Tradition* (London, 2000).

Comet, G. "Les céréales du bas-empire au Moyen Âge," in *The Making of Feudal Agricultures?*, ed. M. Barceló and F. Sigaut (Leiden, 2004), 120–76.

Le paysan et son outil (Rome, 1992).

Contreni, J. "The Patristic Legacy to c. 1000," in *The New Cambridge History of the Bible* 2, ed. R. Marsden and E. A. Matter (Cambridge, 2012), 505–35.

Corbin, A. *La fraîcheur de l'herbe* (Paris, 2018).

Costambeys, M., et al. *The Carolingian World* (Cambridge, 2011).

Cox Miller, P. "The Little Blue Flower is Red," *Journal of Early Christian Studies* 8 (2000), 213–36.

Crabtree, P. "Agricultural Innovation and Socio-economic Change in Early Medieval Europe," *World Archaeology* 42.1 (2010), 122–36.

P. Crabtree, P., et al., "Environmental Evidence from Early Medieval Antwerp," *Quaternary International* 460 (2017), 108–23.

Cronon, W. *Changes in the Land* (New Haven, 1983).

Crosby, A. *The Columbian Exchange* (Westport, CT, 1972).

"Ecological Imperialism," *Texas Quarterly* 21 (1978), 103–17.

Ecological Imperialism (Cambridge, 1986).

David, J. *L'outil* (Turnhout, 1997).

Davis, J. *Charlemagne's Practice of Empire* (Cambridge, 2015).

Davis, M., et al., "Don't Judge Species on their Origins," *Nature* 474 (June 9, 2011), 153–4.

de Jong, M. "Carolingian Political Discourse and the Biblical Past," in *The Resources of the Past in Early Medieval Europe*, ed. C. Gantner et al. (Cambridge, 2015), 87–102.

"The Empire as *Ecclesia*," in *The Uses of the Past in the Early Middle Ages*, ed. Y. Hen and M. Innes (Cambridge, 2009), 191–226.

The Penitential State (Cambridge, 2009).

Delatte, A. *Herbarius* (Brussels, 1961).

Deliyannis, D. *Ravenna in late Antiquity* (Cambridge, 2010).

Della Dora, V. *Landscape, Nature, and the Sacred in Byzantium* (Cambridge, 2016).

Delogu, P. "L'ambiente altomedievale come tema storiografico," in *Agricoltura e ambiente attraverso l'età romana e l'alto medioevo*, ed. P. Nanni (Florence, 2012), 67–108.

"The Popes and Their Town in the Age of Charlemagne," in *Encounters, Excavations and Argosies*, ed. J. Moreland et al. (Oxford, 2017), 106–15.

"Rome in the Ninth Century," in *Post-Roman Towns, Trade and Settlement in Europe and Byzantium* 1, ed. J. Henning (Berlin, 2007), 105–22.

Delumeau, J. "Que reste-t-il du paradis?," *Rivista di storia e letteratura religiosa* 48 (2012), 221–48.

Dendle, P. "Plants in the Early Medieval Cosmos," in *Health and Healing from the Medieval Garden*, ed. P. Dendle and A. Touwaide (Woodbridge, 2008), 47–60.

Depreux, P. "Ambitions et limites des réformes culturelles à l'époque carolingienne," *Revue historique* 623 (2002), 721–53.

Devroey, J. "La céréaliculture dans le monde franc," *Settimane del CISAM* 37 (Spoleto, 1990), 221–53.

Économie rurale et société dans l'Europe franque (VIe–IXe siècles) (Paris, 2003).

"Mise en valeur du sol et cycles de culture dans le système domanial (VIIIe–Xe siècle) entre Seine et Rhin," in *Cultures temporaires et féodalité*, ed. R. Viader and C. Rendu (Toulouse, 2014), 33–57.

La nature et le roi (Paris, 2019).

"La politique annonaire carolingienne comme question économique, religieuse, et morale," *Settimane del CISAM* 63 (Spoleto, 2016), 299–351.

Puissants et misérables (Brussels, 2006).

Devroey, J. and A. Nissen, "Early Middle Ages, 500–1000," in *Struggling with the Environment: Land Use and Productivity*, ed. E. Thoen and T. Soens (Turnhout, 2015), 11–68.

Dey, H. *The Afterlife of the Roman City* (Cambridge, 2015).

"Politics, Patronage and the Transmission of Construction Techniques in Early Medieval Rome, c. 650–750," *Papers of the British School at Rome* 87 (2019), 177–205.

Di Palma, V. *Wasteland: A History* (New Haven, 2014).

Di Pasquale, G., et al., "Human-Derived Landscape Changes on the Northern Etruria Coast (Western Italy) between Roman Times and the Late Middle Ages," *The Holocene* 24.11 (2014), 1491–1502.

Douglas, M. *Purity and Danger* (London, 1985).

Duby, G. *Rural Economy and Country Life in the Medieval West* (Columbia, SC, 1968).

Durand, A. "L'émergence d'outils empruntés aux sciences biologiques végétales en archéologie médiévale en France," in *Trente ans d'archéologie médiévale en France*, ed. J. Chapelot (Caen, 2010), 25–38.

Durkheim, É. and M. Mauss, "De quelques formes primitives de classification," *L'année sociologique* 6 (1903), 1–72.

Dutton, P. *Charlemagne's Mustache and Other Cultural Clusters of a Dark Age* (New York, 2004).

Egleston Robbins, F. *The Hexaemeral Literature* (Chicago, 1912).

Englisch, B. "Karolingische Reformkalender und die Fixierung des christlichen Zeitrechnung," in *Computus and its Cultural Context in the Latin West*, ed. I. Warntjens and D. Ó Cróinin (Turnhout, 2010), 238–58.

Espinosa, A. "A New Classification of the Fundamental Elements of the Tar-Baby Story on the Basis of Two Hundred and Sixty-Seven Versions," *Journal of American Folklore* 56 (1943), 31–7.

208 Select Bibliography

Etienne, D., et al. "Searching for Ancient Forests," *The Holocene* 23.5 (2013), 678–91.

Etienne, D., et al. "Two Thousand Year Reconstruction of Livestock Production Intensity in France," *The Holocene* 25.9 (2015), 1384–93.

Everett, N. *The Alphabet of Galen* (Toronto, 2012).

"The Manuscript Evidence for Pharmacy in the Early Middle Ages," in *Writing the Early Middle Ages*, ed. E. Screen and C. West (Cambridge, 2018), 115–30.

Ferdière, A., et al. *Histoire de l'agriculture en Gaule, 500 av. JC–1000 apr. JC* (Paris, 2006).

Ferrero, A., and P. Casini, "Mezzi meccanici," in *Malerbologia*, ed. P. Catizone and G. Zanin (Bologna, 2001), 251–62.

Fiege, M. "The Weedy West," *Western Historical Quarterly* 36 (2005), 23–47.

Firbank, L. "*Agrostemma Githago* L.," *Journal of Ecology* 76 (1988), 232–46.

Fleischer, J. "Living Rocks and *Locus Amoenus*: Architectural Representations of Paradise in Early Christianity," in *The Appearances of Medieval Rituals*, ed. N. Holger Petersen et al. (Turnhout, 2004), 149–71.

Flint, V. *The Rise of Magic in Early Medieval Europe* (Princeton, 1991).

Forni, G. "Innovazione e progresso nel mondo romano: il caso dell'agricoltura," in *Innovazione tecnica e progresso economico nel mondo romano*, ed. E. Lo Cascio (Bari, 2006), 145–79.

Fossier, R. *Polyptyques et censiers* (Turnhout, 1978).

Fourche, R. "Les nuisibles, symbole inamovible de l'utilitarianisme agricole?," *Sales bêtes! Mauvaises herbes!*, ed. R. Luglia (Rennes, 2017), 297–310.

Fox, M. "Alcuin the Exegete," in *The Study of the Bible in the Carolingian Era*, ed. C. Chazelle and B. Van Name Edwards (Turnhout, 2003), 39–51.

Foxhall, L., et al., "Human Ecology in the Classical Landscape," in *Classical Archaeology*, ed. S. Alcock and R. Osborne (Oxford, 2012), 91–121.

Frawley, J. and I. McCalman, "Invasion Ecologies: The Nature/Culture Challenge," in *Rethinking Invasion Ecologies from the Environmental Humanities*, ed. J. Frawley and I. McCalman (Abingdon, 2014), 3–14.

Fried, J. *Charlemagne* (Cambridge, MA, 2016).

"Karl der Grosse, Rom und Aachen," in *Von Kreuzburg nach München*, ed. M. Hartmann and C. Märtl (Cologne, 2013), 99–157.

Frühe, U. *Das Paradies ein Garten- der Garten ein Paradies* (Frankfurt, 2002).

Galil, B., et al. "Mare Nostrum, Mare Quod Invaditur: The History of Bioinvasion in the Mediterranean Sea," in *Histories of Bioinvasion in the Mediterranean*, ed. A. Queiroz and S. Pooley (Cham, 2018), 21–49.

Ganz, D. "Carolingian Bibles," in *The New Cambridge History of the Bible* 2, ed. R. Marsden and E. A. Matter (Cambridge, 2012), 325–37.

Garipzanov, I. *The Symbolic Language of Authority in the Carolingian World* (Leiden, 2008).

Garrison, M. "The Franks as the New Israel?" in *The Uses of the Past in the Early Middle Ages*, ed. Y. Hen and M. Innes (Cambridge, 2000), 114–61.

Gatto, A., et al. "Population Structure of *Cynara cardunculus* Complex and the Origin of the Conspecific Crops Artichoke and Cardoon," *Annals of Botany* 112 (2013), 855–65.

Gaulin, J. "Traditions et pratiques de la littérature agronomique pendant le haut Moyen Âge," *Settimane del CISAM* 37 (Spoleto, 1990), 103–35.

Geary, P. "Ethnic Identity as a Situational Construct in the Early Middle Ages," *Mitteilungen der anthropologischen Gesellschaft in Wien* 113 (1983), 15–26.

Géczi, J. *The Rose and its Symbols in Mediterranean Antiquity* (Veszprém, 2011).

Giertz, W. and S. Ristow, "Goldtessellae und Fensterglas," *Antike Welt* 44.5 (2013), 59–66.

Giunta, D. "I mosaici dell'arco absidale della basilica dei SS. Nereo e Achilleo e l'eresia Adozianista del secolo VIII," in *Roma e l'età carolingia* (Rome, 1976), 195–200.

Glacken, C. *Traces on the Rhodian Shore* (Berkeley, 1967).

Godinho, I. "Les definitions d'adventice et de mauvaise herbe," *Weed Research* 24 (1984), 121–25.

Goodson, C. *Cultivating the City in Early Medieval Italy* (Cambridge, 2021).

"Garden Cities in Early Medieval Italy," in *Italy and Medieval Europe*, ed. R. Balzaretti et al. (Oxford, 2018), 339–55.

"Material Memory: Rebuilding the Basilica of S. Cecilia in Trastevere, Rome," *Early Medieval Europe* 15 (2007), 2–34.

The Rome of Paschal I (Cambridge, 2010).

Gorman, M. "The Commentary on Genesis of Angelomus of Turin and Biblical Studies under Lothar," *Studi medievali* 40.2 (1999), 559–631.

"The Commentary on Genesis of Claudius of Turin and Biblical Studies under Louis the Pious," *Speculum* 72 (1997), 279–329.

Goullet, M. "L'imaginaire du jardin monastique," *Pris-Ma* 26 (2010), 43–73.

Grainge, C. "Assarting and the Dynamics of Rhineland Economies in the Ninth Century," *Agricultural History Review* 54 (2006), 1–23.

Gravel, M. *Distances, rencontres, communications: réaliser l'empire sous Charlemagne et Louis le Pieux* (Turnhout, 2012).

Greenblatt, S. *Renaissance Self-Fashioning* (Chicago, 1980).

The Rise and Fall of Adam and Eve (New York, 2017).

Grieco, A. "The Social Politics of Pre-Linnaean Botanical Classification," *I Tatti Studies* 4 (1991), 131–49.

Griffin-Kremer, C. "Humble Plants," in *Plants and People: Choices and Diversity through Time*, ed. A. Chevalier et al. (Oxford, 2014), 270–5.

Gronau, K. *Poseidonios und die jüdisch-christliche Genesisexegese* (Leipzig, 1914).

Guilbert, P. "Étude des pollens prélevées dans les couches archéologiques de Villiers-le-Sec," in *Un village au temps de Charlemagne* (Paris, 1988), 196–8.

Guizard-Duchamp, F. *Les terres du sauvage dans le monde franc (IVe–IX siècle)* (Rennes, 2009).

Gunderson, L., et al. "The Evolution of an Idea," in *Foundations of Ecological Resilience*, ed. L. Gunderson (Washington, DC, 2012), 423–44.

Gunther, R. *The Greek Herbal of Dioscurides* (Oxford, 1934).

Guthrie-Smith, H. *Tutira: The Story of a New Zealand Sheep Station* (Seattle, 1999).

Haas, J. *Die Umweltkrise der 3. Jahrhundert n. Chr. im nordwesten des Imperium Romanum* (Stuttgart, 2006).

210   Select Bibliography

Hall, M. "The Native, Naturalized, and Exotic," *Landscape Research* 28 (2003), 5–9.

Halstead, P. *Two Oxen Ahead* (Chichester, 2014).

Hammer, C. *Charlemagne's Months and Their Bavarian Labors* (Oxford, 1997).

Harlan, J. *Crops and Man* (Madison, 1992).

Hartmann, W. *Die Synoden der Karolingerzeit im Frankreich und Italien* (Paderborn, 1989).

Hartmann-Shenkman, A., et al. "Invading a New Niche," *Vegetation History and Archaeobotany* 24 (2015), 9–18.

Head, L. *Ingrained* (Farnham, 2012).

"Living in a Weedy Future," in *Rethinking Invasion Ecologies from the Environmental Humanities*, ed. J. Frawley and I. McCalman (London, 2014), 87–99.

Heber-Suffrin, F. "L'acanthe dans le décor architectural carolingien," in *L'acanthe dans la sculpture monumentale de l'antiquité à la Renaissance* (Paris, 1993), 189–210.

Henning, J. "Did the 'Agricultural Revolution' Go East with Carolingian Conquest?" in *The Baiuvarii and Thuringii*, ed. J. Fries-Knoblauch et al. (Woodbridge, 2014), 331–59.

"Germanisch-romanisch Agrarkontinuität und -diskontinuität in nordalpinen Kontinentaleuropa," in *Akkulturation*, ed. D. Hägermann et al. (Berlin, 2004), 396–435.

"Revolution or Relapse?" in *The Langobards before the Frankish Conquest*, ed. G. Ausenda et al. (San Marino, 2009), 149–64.

Südosteuropa zwischen Antike und Mittelalter (Berlin, 1987).

Henry, N. "The Lily and the Thorns: Augustine's Refutation of the Donatist Exegesis of the Song of Songs," *Revue des études augustiniennes* 42 (1996), 255–66.

Herbig, C. and F. Sirocko. "Palaeobotanical Evidence of Agricultural Activities in the Eifel Region during the Holocene," *Vegetation History and Archaeobotany* 22 (2013), 447–62.

Hillman, G. "Phytosociology and Ancient Weed Floras," in *Modeling Ecological Change*, ed. D. Harris and K. Thomas (London, 1991), 27–40.

Hodges, R. *Dark Age Economics* (London, 2012).

Hoffmann, R. *An Environmental History of Medieval Europe* (Cambridge, 2014).

Holt, J. "Weeds," in *Encyclopedia of Biological Invasions*, ed. D. Simberloff and M. Remánek (Berkeley, 2011), 692–8.

Holm, L. et al. *World Weeds: Natural Histories and Distribution* (New York, 1997).

Hondelmann, W. *Die Kulturpflanzen der griechisch-römischen Welt* (Berlin, 2002).

Horn, W. and E. Born. *The Plan of St. Gall* 2 (Berkeley, 1979).

Hulme, P. et al. "Evidence of Bias and Error in Understanding Plant Invasion Impact," *Trends in Ecology and Evolution* 28.4 (2013), 212–18.

Innes, M. "Memory, Orality and Literacy in Early Medieval Society," *Past and Present* 158 (1998), 3–35.

James, L. *Mosaics in the Medieval World* (Cambridge, 2017).

Jesset, S. "Les formes de l'exploitation rurale du IXe au IXe siècle," in *Lumières de l'an mil en Orléanais* (Turnhout, 2004), 89–93.

Jones, G. "Weed Ecology as a Method for the Archaeobotanical Recognition of Crop Husbandry Practices," *Acta Archaeobotanica* 42 (2002), 185–92.

Jones, G., et al. "Crops and Weeds," *Journal of Archaeological Science* 37 (2010), 70–7.

Jones, M. "Dormancy and the Plough," in *From Foragers to Farmers*, ed. A. Fairbairn and E. Weiss (Oxford, 2009), 58–63.

Jones, R. "Manure and the Medieval Social Order," in *Land and People*, ed. M. Allen et al. (Oxford, 2009), 215–25.

Jouffroy-Bapicot, I., et al. "7000 Years of Vegetation History and Landscape Changes in the Morvan Mountains (France)," *The Holocene* 23.12 (2013), 1888–1902.

Juster, A. *Saint Aldhelm's Riddles* (Toronto, 2015).

Kahn, S. "'Ego sum flos campi': Die Blume als theologisches Konzept im Bild des Mittelalters," *Marburger Jahrbuch für Kunstwissenschaft* 33 (2006), 29–57.

Karg, S. "Plant Diversity in the Late Medieval Cornfields of Northern Switzerland," *Vegetation History and Archaeobotany* 4 (1995), 41–50.

Kästner, H. "Pseudo-Dioscurides *De Herbis Femininis*," *Hermes* 3 (1896).

Kelly, F. *Early Irish Farming* (Dublin, 2000).

Keppels, J. *Karl der Grosse: Heilkunde, Heilkräuter, Hospitalitas* (Aachen, 2005).

Kershaw, P. *Peaceful Kings: Peace, Power and the Early Medieval Political Imagination* (Oxford, 2011).

Kessler, H. "'Hic Homo Formatur': The Genesis Frontispieces of the Carolingian Bibles," *Art Bulletin* 53 (1971), 143–60.

The Illustrated Bibles from Tours (Princeton, 1977).

King, L. "Some Early Forms of the Weed Concept," *Nature* 179 (June 29, 1957), 1366.

Weeds of the World (New York, 1966).

Kingsbury, N. *Hybrid* (Chicago, 2009).

Kjaergaard, T. "A Plant that Changed the World," *Landscape Research* 28 (2003), 41–9.

Knörzer, K. *Geschichte der synanthropen Flora im Niederrheingebiet* (Mainz, 2007).

Kramer, R. *Rethinking Authority in the Carolingian Empire* (Amsterdam, 2019).

Kreiner, J. *Legions of Pigs in the Early Medieval West* (New Haven, 2020).

Kreuz, A. "Frühgermanische Landwirtschaft und Ernährung," in *Germanen*, ed. G. Uelsberg and M. Wemhoff (Berlin, 2020), 118–45.

Krüssmann, G. *The Complete Book of Roses* (Portland, OR, 1981).

Lancel, S. *Saint Augustin* (Paris, 1999).

Landgraf, E. "Ein frühmittelalterlicher Botanicus," *Kyklos* 1 (1928), 114–46.

Lane Fox, R. *Augustine: Conversion to Confessions* (New York, 2015).

Lassère, J. *Africa, quasi Roma (256 av. J-C–711 ap. J-C)* (Paris, 2015).

Lauwers, M. "Le 'travail' sans la domination?" in *Penser la paysannerie médiévale, un défi impossible?*, ed. A. Dierkens et al. (Paris, 2017), 303–32.

Le Floc'h, E. "Invasive Plants of the Mediterranean Basin," in *Biogeography of Mediterranean Invasions*, ed. R. Groves and F. di Castro (Cambridge, 1991),

Leja, M. "The Sacred Art," *Viator* 47 (2016), 1–34.

Leonti, M. et al. "Wild Gathered Food Plants in the European Mediterranean," *Economic Botany* 60 (2006), 130–42.

Leopold, A. *A Sand County Almanac* (New York, 1949).

"What Is a Weed?" in *River of the Mother of God and Other Essays* (Madison, 1992), 306–9.

Leroy Ladurie, E. *Les paysans de Languedoc* (Paris, 1966).

Livarda, A. "Spicing up Life in Northwestern Europe," *Vegetation History and Archaeobotany* 20 (2011), 143–64.

Lodwick, L. "Arable Weed Seeds as Indicators of Cereal Provenance," *Vegetation History and Archaeobotany* 27 (2018), 801–15.

Lohrmann, D. "Alkuins Korrespondenz mit Karl dem Grossen über Kalender und Astronomie," in *Science in Western and Eastern Civilization in Carolingian Times*, ed. P. Butzer and D. Lohrmann (Basel, 1993), 79–114.

Longnon, A. *Polyptyque de l'abbaye de Saint-Germain des Prés rédigé aux temps de l'abbé Irminon* 1 (Paris, 1895).

Lovejoy, A. *The Great Chain of Being: A Study of the History of an Idea* (Cambridge, MA, 1957).

Loveluck, C. *Northwest Europe in the Early Middle Ages, c.* AD *600–1150* (Cambridge, 2013).

Luchterhandt, M. "Rinascita a Roma, nell'Italia carolingia e meridionale," *Storia dell'architettura italiana* 2, ed. S. de Blaauw (Milan, 2010), 322–73.

Mabey, R. *Weeds* (London, 2012).

McClendon, C. *The Origins of Medieval Architecture* (New Haven, 2005).

MacCormack, S. *The Shadows of Poetry* (Berkeley, 1998).

McCormick, M. *Origins of the European Economy: Communications and Commerce,* AD *300–900* (Cambridge, 2002).

McGrade, M. "O Rex Mundi Triumphator," *Early Music History* 17 (1998), 183–219.

McGregor, J. *Back to the Garden* (New Haven, 2015).

Mack, R. "The Commercial Seed Trade: An Early Dispenser of Weeds in the United States," *Economic Botany* 55 (2001), 257–73.

McKerracher, M. *Anglo-Saxon Crops and Weeds* (Oxford, 2019).

"Bread and Surpluses," *Environmental Archaeology* 21 (2016), 88–102.

Mackie, G. "Abstract and Vegetal Design in the San Zeno Chapel, Rome," *Papers of the British School at Rome* 63 (1995), 159–82.

McKitterick, R. "*Akkulturation* and the Writing of History in the Early Middle Ages," in *Akkulturation*, ed. D. Hägermann et al. (Berlin, 2004), 381–95.

Charlemagne (Cambridge, 2008).

McNeill, J. "Europe's Place in the Global History of Biological Exchange," *Landscape Research* 28 (2003), 33–9.

McNeill, J. and H. Gamer, *Medieval Handbooks of Penance* (New York, 1990).

MacQueen, H. "Canon Law, Custom, and Legislation: Law in the Reign of Alexander II," in *The Reign of Alexander II, 1214–49*, ed. R. Oram (Leiden, 2005), 221–51.

Maggiulli, G. and M. Buffa Giolito. *L'altro Apuleio* (Naples, 1996).

Maguire, H. *Nectar and Illusion: Nature in Byzantine Art and Culture* (Oxford, 2012).

Mane, P. *Le travail à la campagne au Moyen Âge: étude iconographique* (Paris, 2006).

Marder, M. *The Philosopher's Plant: An Intellectual Herbarium* (New York, 2014).

Marsh, G. *Man and Nature* (New York, 1865).

Meens, R. "Politics, Mirrors for Princes and the Bible," *Early Medieval Europe* 7 (1999), 345–57.

Mitterauer, M. *Why Europe? The Medieval Origins of Its Special Path* (Chicago, 2010).

Moe, D. and F. Fedele. "Alpe Borghetto," *Vegetation History and Archaeobotany* 28 (2019), 141–62.

Moesch, S. *Augustine and the Art of Ruling in the Carolingian Imperial Period* (London, 2020).

Montanari, M. *L'alimentazione contadina nell'alto medioevo* (Naples, 1979).

Mordek, H. "Karls des Grossen zweites Kapitular von Herstal und die Hungersnote der Jahre 778/779," *Deutsches Archiv für Erforschung des Mittelalters* 61 (2005), 1–52.

Moreland, J. "The Carolingian Empire," in *Empires*, ed. S. Alcock (Cambridge, 2002), 392–418.

Morimoto, Y. "L'assolement triennial au haut Moyen Âge," in *Économie rurale et économie urbaine au Moyen Âge*, ed. J. Devroey and Y. Morimoto (Ghent, 1994), 91–125.

"In ebdomada operatur, quicquid precipetur ei," in *Études sur l'économie rurale du haut Moyen Âge* (Brussels, 2008), 381–96.

Murray, O. "The Idea of the Shepherd King from Cyrus to Charlemagne," in *Latin Poetry and the Classical Tradition*, ed. P. Godman and O. Murray (Oxford, 1990), 1–15.

Musäus, I. *Der Pandoramythos bei Hesiod und seine Rezeption bis Erasmus von Rotterdam* (Göttingen, 2004).

Mütherich, F. "Die Erneurerung der Buchmalerei am Hof Karls des Grossen," in *799: Kunst und Kultur der Karolingerzeit*, ed. C. Stiegemann and M. Wernhoff (Mainz, 1999), 560–609.

Mütherich, F. and J. Gaehde. *Carolingian Painting* (New York, 1976).

Neson, J. "History-Writing," in *Historiograhie im frühen Mittelalter*, ed. A. Scharer and G. Scheibelreiter (Vienna, 1994), 435–42.

Nelson, J. "Charlemagne and Ravenna," in *Ravenna*, ed. J. Herrin and J. Nelson (London, 2016), 239–52.

"The Church and a Revaluation of Work in the Ninth Century?," in *The Use and Abuse of Time in Christian History*, ed. R. Swanson (Woodbridge, 2002), 35–43.

King and Emperor (Berkeley, 2019).

Newfield, T. "The Contours, Frequency, and Causation of Subsistence Crises in Carolingian Europe (750–950)," in *Crises alimentarias en la edad media*, ed. P. Benito I Monclús (Lleida, 2013), 117–72.

Niederer, M. *Der St. Galler "Botanicus": Ein frühmittlelaterliches Herbar* (Bern, 2005).

Nilgen, U. "Apsismosaik von SS. Nereo ed Achilleo," in *799: Kunst und Kultur der Karolingerreich*, ed. C. Stiegemann and M. Wemhoff (Mainz, 1999), 638–40.

"Die römischen Apsisprogramme der karolingischen Epoche," in *799: Kunst und Kultur der Karolingerreich*, ed. C. Stiegemann and M. Wemhoff (Mainz, 1999), 542–50.

Nitz, H. "The Church as Colonist," *Journal of Historical Geography* 9 (1983), 105–26.

Noble, T. *Images, Iconoclasm, and the Carolingians* (Philadelphia, 2009).

Oesterley, W. *The Gospel Parables in the Light of Their Jewish Background* (New York, 1936).

Olmstead, A. and P. Rhode. *Creating Abundance* (Cambridge, 2008).

Osborne, J. *Rome in the Eighth Century* (Cambridge, 2020).

Palmer, J. "Calculating Time and the End of Time in the Carolingian World," *English Historical Review* 126 (2011), 1307–31.

"Climates of Crisis," *Viator* 48 (2017), 1–20.

Pals, J. and B. van Geel. "Rye Cultivation and the Presence of Cornflower," *Berichten van de Rijkdienst voor het Oudheidkundig Bodemonderzoek* 26 (1976), 199–203.

Parolo, C. *Immagini del tempo degli uomini, immagini del tempo degli dei* (Oxford, 2017).

Paxton, F. "Curing Bodies, Curing Souls," *Journal of the History of Medicine* 50 (1995), 230–52.

Pearce, F. *The New Wild* (London, 2015).

Pérez-Díaz, S., et al. "A Palaeoenvironmental and Palaeoeconomic Approach to the Early Middle Age Record from the Village of Gasleiz," *Vegetation History and Archaeobotany* 24 (2015), 683–97.

Peytremann, E. *Archéologie de l'habitat rural dans le nord de la France du IVe au XIIe siècle* (Saint-Germain-en-Laye, 2003).

Peytremann, E. and S. Wiethold. "L'apport de la carpologie à l'étude du site du premier Moyen Âge (VIe–XIIe siècle) de Sermersheim (Bas-Rhin)," in *Des hommes aux champs*, ed. V. Carpentier and C. Marcigny (Rennes, 2012), 195–212.

Phillips, R. "Runcina," in *Brill's New Pauly* 12 (Leiden, 2008), 781.

Piron, S. "Ève au fuseau, Adam jardinier," in *Adam: la nature humaine avant et après*, ed. I. Rosier-Catach and G. Bruguglia (Paris, 2016), 283–323.

Pohle, F. *Die Erforschung der karolingischen Pfalz Aachen* (Darmstadt, 2015).

Poirier, N. "La dynamique du peuplement et des espaces agraires médiévaux en Berry," *Archéologie médiévale* 40 (2010), 15–32.

Pollard, E. "Pliny's 'Natural History' and the Flavian Templum Pacis," *Journal of World History* 20 (2009), 309–38.

Ponta-Zitterer, B. "Blüten in der karolingischen Flechsteinkunst in Karantanien," *Carinthia I* 207 (2017), 45–62.

Poque, S. *Le langage symbolique dans la prédication d'Augustin d'Hippone* 1 (Paris, 1984).

Postles, D. "Cleaning the Medieval Arable," *Agricultural History Review* 37 (1989), 130–43.

Potter, J. *The Rose* (London, 2010).

Preiss, S., et al. "Approche des pratiques agricoles durant le haut Moyen Âge en Hesbaye," in *Plantes, produits végéteaux et ravageurs*, ed. M. Dietsch-Sellami et al. (Bordeaux, 2016), 155–82.

Probst, R. *Wolladventivflora Mitteleuropas* (Solothurn, 1949).

Querrien, A., et al. "Évolution et exploitation du paysage végétale au Moyen Âge," in *Trente ans d'archéologie médiévale en France*, ed. J. Chapelot (Caen, 2010), 39–54.

Quirós Castillo, J. "Agrarian Archaeology in Early Medieval Europe," *Quaternary International* 346 (2014), 1–6.

Radosevich, S. et al. *Ecology of Weeds and Invasive Plants* (Hoboken, NJ, 2007).

Reigniez, P. "Histoire et techniques: l'outil agricole dans la periode du haut Moyen Âge," in *The Making of Feudal Agricultures?*, ed. M. Barceló and F. Sigaut (Leiden, 2004), 33–120.

Reveal, J. "What's in a Name? Identifying Plants in Pre-Linnaean Botanical Literature," in *Prospecting for Drugs in Ancient and Medieval European Texts*, ed. B. Holland (Amsterdam, 1996), 57–90.

Reynolds, S. "Empires: A Problem of Comparative History," *Historical Research* 79 (2006), 151–65.

Rhodes, J. and C. Davidson. "The Garden of Paradise," in *The Iconography of Paradise*, ed. C. Davidson (Kalamazoo, 1994), 69–109.

Ribémont, B. *Les origines des encyclopédies médiévales* (Paris, 2001).

Riddle, J. "Theory and Practice in Medieval Medicine," *Viator* 5 (1974), 157–84.

Rindos, D. *The Origins of Agriculture* (Orlando, FL, 1984).

Ristow, S. "Alte Grabungen, neue Erkenntnisse," in *814 Karl der Grosse 2014*, ed. E. Wamers (Regensburg, 2016), 23–45.

Ritvo, H. *The Platypus and the Mermaid, and Other Figments of the Classifying Imagination* (Cambridge, MA, 1997).

Roberts, E. "Boundary Clauses and the Use of the Vernacular in Eastern Frankish Charters, c. 750–c. 900," *Historical Research* 91 (2018), 580–604.

Rollason, D. *The Power of Place: Rulers and their Palaces, Landscapes, Cities and Holy Places* (Princeton, 2016).

Ros, J., et al. "Archaeobotanical Contribution to the History of Farming Practices in Medieval Northern Catalonia (8th–14th c.)," in *Archaeology and History of Peasantries* 1, ed. J. Quiros Castillo (Bilbao, 2020), 163–82.

Rösch, M. "Evidence for Rare Crop Weeds of the Caucalidion Group in Southwestern Germany since the Bronze Age," *Vegetation History and Archaeobotany* 27 (2018), 75–84.

"The History of Cereals in the Territory of the Former Duchy of Swabia (Herzogtum Schwaben) from the Roman to the Postmedieval Period," *Vegetation History and Archaeobotany* 1 (1991), 193–231.

"The History of Crops and Weeds in South-Western Germany from the Neolithic Period to Modern Times," *Vegetation History and Archaeobotany* 7 (1998), 109–25.

Rösch, M. and J. Lechterbeck. "Seven Millennia of Human Impact Reflected in a High Resolution Pollen Profile from the Profundal Sediments of Litzelsee, Lake Constance Region, Germany," *Vegetation History and Archaeobotany* 25 (2016), 339–58.

Rosenberg, S. "Forming the *Saeculum*: The Desacralization of Nature and the Ability to Understand it in Augustine's *Literal Commentary on Genesis*," *Studies in Church History* 46 (2010), 1–14.

Rothschild, N. "Sovereignty, Virtue, and Disaster Management," *Environmental History* 17 (2012), 783–812.

Rottoli, M. "Crop Diversity between Central Europe and the Mediterranean," in *Plants and People: Choices and Diversity through Time*, ed. A. Chevalier et al. (Oxford, 2014), 75–81.

"Reflections on Early Medieval Resources in North Italy," *Quaternary International* 346 (2014), 20–7.

Ruas, M. "Alimentation végétale, pratiques agricoles et environnement du VIIe au Xe siècle," in *Un village au temps de Charlemagne* (Paris, 1988), 201–11.

"Aspects of Early Medieval Farming from Sites in Mediterranean France," *Vegetation History and Archaeobotany* 14 (2005), 405–15.

"La parole des grains," in *Plantes exploitées, plantes cultivées*, ed. A. Durand (Aix, 2007), 149–70.

"Les plantes consommées au Moyen Âge en France méridionale d'après les semences archéologiques," *Archéologie du Midi médiévale* 15–16 (1998).

"Prés, prairies, pâtures: éclairages archéobotaniques," in *Prés et pâtures en Europe occidentale*, ed. F. Brumont (Toulouse, 2008), 13–44.

Ruas, M. and B. Pradat. "Les semences découvertes," in *Les habitats carolingiens de Montours et la Chapelle-Saint-Aubert*, ed. I. Catteddu (Paris, 2001), 65–79.

Ruas, M., et al. "Les avoines dans les productions agro-pastorales du nord-ouest de la France," in *Des hommes aux champs*, ed. V. Carpentier and C. Marcigny (Rennes, 2012), 327–65.

"Vestiges élucidés d'un parasite des céréales," in *Plantes, produits végétaux et ravageurs*, ed. M. Dietsch-Sellami et al. (Bordeaux, 2016), 43–64.

Russell, E. *Evolutionary History* (Cambridge, 2011).

Sadoks, J. *Crop Protection in Medieval Agriculture* (Leiden, 2013).

Sadori, L., et al. "Climate, Environment and Society in Southern Italy during the Last 2000 Years," *Quaternary Science Reviews* 136 (2016), 173–88.

Salisbury, E. *Weeds and Aliens* (London, 1961).

Sallares, R. *The Ecology of the Ancient Greek World* (London, 1991).

Salvadori, F. "The Transition from Late Antiquity to the Early Middle Ages in Italy," *Quaternary International* 499 (2019), 35–48.

Sattin, M. and F. Tei. "Malerbe componente dannosa degli agroecosistemi," in *Malerbologia*, ed. P. Catizone and G. Zanin (Bologna, 2001), 171–245.

Saulnier, M., et al. "A Study of Late Holocene Local Vegetation Dynamics and Responses to Land Use Changes in an Ancient Charcoal Making Woodland in the Central Pyrenees (Ariége, France), Using Pedoanthracology," *Vegetation History and Archaeobotany* 29 (2020), 249–58.

Scafi, A. "Epilogue: A Heaven on Earth," in *Paradise in Antiquity*, ed. M. Bockmuehl and G. Stroumsa (Cambridge, 2010), 210–20.

Mapping Paradise (Chicago, 2005).

Schönle, A. "Garden of the Empire: Catherine's Appropriation of the Crimea," *Slavic Review* 60 (2001), 1–23.

Scott, J. *Against the Grain* (New Haven, 2017).

Seaton, B. "Towards a Semiotics of Literary Flower Personification," *Poetics Today* 10 (1989), 679–701.

Secord, J. "Overcoming Environmental Determinism: Introduced Species, Hybrid Plants and Animals, and Transformed Landscapes in the Hellenistic and Roman Worlds," in *The Routledge Handbook of Identity and the Environment in the Classical and Medieval Worlds*, ed. R. Futo Kennedy and M. Jones-Lewis (London, 2016), 210–29.

Senda, T. and T. Tominaga. "Genetic Diversity of Darnel (*Lolium temulentum*) in Malo, Ethiopia," *Economic Botany* 58 (2004), 568–77.

B. Shaw, B. *Bringing in the Sheaves* (Toronto, 2013).

Shemesh, A. "'A Wheat May Change into a *Zunin* and a Male Hyena into a Bat,'" *Arquivio Maaravi* 11 (2017), 2–13.

Shimahara, S. "Charlemagne, premier souverain chrétien commenditaire d'exegèse biblique?" in *Charlemagne: les temps, les espaces, les hommes*, ed. R. Grosse and M. Sot (Turnhout, 2018), 101–17.

Haymon d'Auxerre, exégète carolingien (Turnhout, 2013).

Sigaut, F. *L'agriculture et le feu* (Paris, 1975).

"Crops and Agricultural Development in Western Europe," in *Plants and People: Choices and Diversity through Time*, ed. A. Chevalier et al. (Oxford, 2014), 107–12.

"L'evolution des techniques," in *The Making of Feudal Agricultures?*, ed. M. Barceló and F. Sigaut (Leiden, 2004), 1–31.

"Le labour, qu'est-ce que c'est?," in *Nous labourons* (Nantes, 2007), 21–8.

Sigerist, H. "Zum Herbarius Pseudo-Apulei," *Sudhoffs Archiv für Geschichte der Medizin* 23 (1930), 197–209.

Sillasoo, Ü. "Medieval Plant Depictions as a Source for Archaeobotanical Research," *Vegetation History and Archaeobotany* 16 (2005), 61–70.

Simberloff, D. *Invasive Species: What Everyone Needs to Know* (Oxford, 2013).

Smith, B. *The Parables of the Synoptic Gospels* (Cambridge, 1937).

Sonnante, G., et al. "The Domestication of Artichoke and Cardoon," *Annals of Botany* 100 (2007), 1095–1100.

Springsfeld, K. "Karl der Grosse, Alkuin, und die Zeitrechnung," *Berichte zur Wissenschaftsgeschichte* 27 (2004), 53–66.

Squatriti, P. "Barbarizing the *Belpaese*," in *A Companion to Ostrogothic Italy*, ed. J. Arnold et al. (Leiden, 2016), 390–421.

"Good and Bad Plants in Merovingian Francia," in *The Oxford Companion to the Merovingian World*, ed. B. Effros and I. Moreira (Oxford, 2019), 717–38.

"Of Seeds, Seasons, and Seas," *Journal of Economic History* 74 (2014), 1205–20.

"The Vegetative Mediterranean," in *A Companion to Mediterranean History*, ed. P. Horden and S. Kinoshita (Chichester, 2014), 26–42.

Stancliffe, C. "Red, White, and Blue Martyrdom," in *Ireland and Early Medieval Europe*, ed. D. Whitelock et al. (Cambridge, 1982), 21–46.

Starostine, D. "'In die festivitatis,'" *Early Medieval Europe* 14 (2006), 465–86.

Steen Henriksen, P. "Rye Cultivation in the Danish Iron Age," *Vegetation History and Archaeobotany* 12 (2003), 177–85.

Stone, R. "Kings Are Different," in *Le prince au miroir de la littérature politique de l'Antiquité aux Lumières*, ed. F. Lachaud and L. Scordia (Mont-Saint-Aignan, 2007), 69–86.

Sullivan, R. "The Carolingian Age," *Speculum* 64 (1989), 267–306.

Thomas, G., et al. "Technology, Ritual, and Anglo-Saxon Agriculture," *Antiquity* 90 (2016), 742–58.

Thomas, H., et al. "Evolution, Physiology, and Phytochemistry of the Psychotoxic Arable Mimic Weed Darnel (*Lolium temulentum L.*)," *Progress in Botany* 72 (2011), 73–104.

"Remembering Darnel," *Journal of Ethnobiology* 36 (2016), 29–44.

Thunø, E. *The Apse Mosaic in Early Medieval Rome* (Cambridge, 2015).

Timmermann, J. "An Authority among Authorities," *Early Medieval Europe* 28 (2020), 532–59.

Tobin, B. *Colonizing Nature* (Philadelphia, 2005).

Totelin, L. "Botanizing Rulers and their Herbal Subjects," *Phoenix* 66 (2012), 122–44.

Toulemonde, F., et al. "A Brief History of Plants in North-Eastern France," *Vegetation History and Archaeobotany* 30 (2021), 1–15.

Trumper, J. and M. Vigolo. "Il perché della 'malerbologia,'" in *Malerbologia*, ed. P. Catizone and G. Zanin (Bologna, 2001), 11–18.

Tsing, A. L. *The Mushroom at the End of the World* (Princeton, 2017).

Utro, U. "Una 'falsa testimonianza,'" in *Atti del IX colloquio dell'Associazione italiana per lo studio e la conservazione del mosaico* (Ravenna, 2004), 507–18.

Vaccaro, E. *Sites and Pots: Settlement and Economy in Southern Tuscany* (Oxford, 2011).

van der Veen, M. "Archaeobotany, the Archaeology of Human–Plant Interactions," in *The Science of Roman History*, ed. W. Scheidel (Princeton, 2018), 53–92.

"The Materiality of Plants," *World Archaeology* 46 (2014), 799–812.

van der Veen, M., et al. "New Food Plants in Roman Britain," *Environmental Archaeology* 13 (2008), 11–36.

van Liere, F. *An Introduction to the Medieval Bible* (Cambridge, 2014).

van Zeist, W., et al. "Plant Husbandry and Vegetation of Early Medieval Douai," *Vegetation History and Archaeobotany* 3 (1994), 191–218.

Verhulst, A. "The 'Agricultural Revolution' of the Middle Ages Reconsidered," in *Law, Custom, and the Social Fabric in Medieval Europe*, ed. B. S. Bachrach and D. Nicholas (Kalamazoo, 1990), 17–28.

The Carolingian Economy (Cambridge, 2002).

"Karolingische Agrarpolitik: Das *Capitulare de Villis* und die Hungersnote von 792–3 und 805–6," *Zeitschrift für Agrargeschichte und Agrarsoziologie* 13 (1965), 175–89.

Vieyra-Odilon, L. and H. Vibrans. "Weeds as Crops: The Value of Maize Field Weeds in the Valley of Toluca, Mexico," *Economic Botany* 55 (2001), 426–43.

Walker, W. *All the Plants of the Bible* (New York, 1957).

Watson, A. *Agricultural Innovation in the Early Islamic World* (Cambridge, 2008).

Weber, E. *Invasive Plant Species of the World* (Wallingford, 2017).

Wehling, U. *Die Mosaiken im Aachener Münster und ihre Vorstufen* (Cologne, 1995).

Wickham, C. *The Inheritance of Rome* (London, 2009).

Willerding, U. *Zur Geschichte der Unkräuter Mitteleuropas* (Neumünster, 1986).

Wisskirchen, R. "Leo III und die Mosaikprogramme von S. Apollinare in Classe in Ravenna und SS. Nereo ed Achilleo in Rom," *Jahrbuch für Antike und Christentum* 34 (1991), 139–51.

Wolff, A., et al. "In the Ruins," *Weed Science* 70.2 (2022), 1–28.

Wozniak, T. *Naturereignisse im frühen Mittelalter* (Berlin, 2020).

Yi-Fu, H., et al. "Identification of Oxalic Acid and Tartaric Acid as Major Persistent Pain-inducing Toxins in the Stinging Hairs of the Nettle *Urtica thumbergiana*," *Annals of Botany* 98 (2006), 57–66.

Zadoks, J. *Crop Protection in Medieval Agriculture* (Leiden, 2013).

Zanin, G., et al. "Definizione e classificazione delle malerbe," in *Malerbologia*, ed. P. Catizone and G. Zanin (Bologna, 2001), 23–52.

Zimdahl, R. *Fundamentals of Weed Science* (Amsterdam, 2013).

Ziska, L. and J. Dukes. *Weed Biology and Climate Change* (Ames, IA, 2011).

Zohary, D. *Plants of the Bible* (Cambridge, 1982).

Zug Tucci, H. "Le derrate agricole," *Settimane del CISAM* 37 (1990), 884–902.

Index

For EU product safety concerns, contact us at Calle de José Abascal, 56–1°,
28003 Madrid, Spain or eugpsr@cambridge.org.

www.ingramcontent.com/pod-product-compliance
Ingram Content Group UK Ltd.
Pitfield, Milton Keynes, MK11 3LW, UK
UKHW020309140625
459647UK00015B/1805